DINING AT
Walt Disney World

The Definitive Guide

RICHARD KILLINGSWORTH
AND PAULA BROWN

The Definitive Guide to Disney Dining

INTRODUCTION AND DEDICATION

This publication is dedicated to our families, friends, and everyone who has encouraged us to dream big. Especially, Walt Disney himself. We have learned from Walt Disney that we should never underestimate our ability to change the world.

Walt was a man from humble beginnings, but his vision and creativity changed movies, entertainment, theme parks, and Central Florida forever.

His vision for Disneyland was for a magical place where parents and their children could have fun together and escape reality for a little while.

Mr. Disney didn't live long enough to see his dream completed in Central Florida. He died of lung cancer on December 15, 1966. In his 65 years, he made a mark that will still be felt decades from now. His dreams changed us all.

On October 1, 1971, Walt Disney World opened. The original name was supposed to be just "Disney World", but Roy Disney insisted that it be called "Walt Disney World" to honor his brother.

Since 1971 Walt Disney World has grown and expanded. There are now four theme parks, two water parks, an entertainment and shopping district, thousands of hotel rooms, and hundreds of dining options.

It is our hope that you'll be able to use the information within these pages to make your visit to Walt Disney World your best vacation ever.

"I hope we never lose sight of one thing -
that it was all started by a mouse."
- Walt Disney

Contents

SECTION ONE:

TIPS, SUGGESTIONS, AND GENERAL INFORMATION

In this section we aim to help you make every minute and every dollar of your Disney World Vacation count! We offer great tips on saving time and money, making reservations, the Disney Dining Plan, character dining, and other extensive information and advice you need to know to enrich your Walt Disney World Dining experience.

One

WALT DISNEY WORLD DINING BASICS

Dining at Walt Disney World may seem overwhelming, but it doesn't have to be. Here are a few basics and tips that you should know before you leave home.

Reservations

At Walt Disney World, most of the table service restaurants accept reservations. These can be made up to 180 days in advance. You can make reservations online on the Walt Disney World website, on the My Disney Experience phone app, or by calling 407-WDW-DINE (407-939-3463). Many of the more popular restaurants will fill up early, so make your reservation as soon as you can. You can later change or cancel your reservation if your plans change. A credit card is required to hold your spot, and you will be charged a flat fee per person if you don't show up and didn't cancel. You should receive an email that will remind you of the reservation a couple of days in advance, but don't rely on that. Keep track of your reservations.

Check Hours and Prices

Be aware that restaurant hours can change. Some places are seasonal, and a select few seem to have very random hours. Prices and menu items change often as well. Check the restaurant hours for the day that you plan to be there to avoid disappointment. If you arrive at a restaurant and the item that you had your heart set on is no longer on the menu, ask. Sometimes they will still make it for you.

Disney Dining Plan

The Disney Dining Plan is only available to guests staying at a Disney owned resort hotel. It's a way to prepay for your meals and snacks. There are restrictions and requirements that must be met in order to be eligible for the plan.

Resort Restaurants

One common misconception is that you need to be staying at a particular resort in order to eat there. With the exception of Shades of Green Resort (which is owned by the United States Department of Defense, not Disney) that is not the case at all. If you're driving to a resort for a meal, you'll need to stop at a security booth. Show the guard your ID and tell him where you'll be eating. He'll then let you know where to park. The Disney-owned hotels all have free self parking, and valet parking is available for a fee. Valet parking is complimentary if you dine at Victoria & Albert's.

Character Dining

A meal with the characters is not just for children. Disney brings out the kid in anyone, so a character meal can be a lot of fun at any age. The more popular character meals fill up quickly and can get quite loud, so if you're looking for a more relaxed pace you might want to consider something outside of the parks.

Dinner and Fireworks

The Magic Kingdom Resort Area hotels offer great views of Wishes each night. Make your dinner reservation before or after the scheduled fireworks time, and then enjoy the show away from the crowds. Cast members will let you know where the best viewing areas are.

You can also catch parts of IllumiNations from Epcot if you're in the Epcot Resort Area. Enjoy your meal, then head to one of the two bridges on Crescent Lake to see the show.

Alcohol

The drinking age in the state of Florida is 21. Have your ID ready, because you will likely be carded no matter how old you are. You can not bring alcohol with you into the parks. You also can't buy a drink and leave a park with it, you must finish it or throw it out before you exit.

Two

MAKING THE HARD TO GET RESERVATIONS

While it is always a good idea to make a reservation at any Walt Disney World table service restaurant, there are some eateries where reservations are essential. The problem is, these restaurants are so popular that reserving a spot can be hard to do. Here are a few suggestions that *might* help you score that difficult reservation, and ideas on what to do instead if you don't.

Reserve as Soon as Possible

Walt Disney World allows you to make dining reservations 180 days in advance. Know what that date is and start trying immediately. Some of the more popular restaurants will fill up that early, so you will want to try the moment reservations are open.

Call Instead of Booking Online

These days it is easier and more convenient to go online than to make contact with a live human being. However, if you're trying to make a difficult-to-obtain reservation, it makes more sense to call 407-WDW-DINE (407-939-3463) than to see what's available online. The operator will have more information available than you can find online and will do her best to get a spot for you.

Be Flexible

Don't have only one time or even one meal in mind when you start trying to get a reservation. If breakfast isn't available at Cinderella's Royal Table, try to book lunch instead. If you were hoping for an 8:00 dinner at Le Cellier and the only opening is at 5:30, take it. If you're not flexible, there will be less of a chance that you will get a spot at the restaurant in question.

Keep Checking Back

If you can't make a reservation at the desired restaurant, keep checking back. Six months is a long time, and people's plans change. When someone else cancels their trip, the reservations will need to be canceled as well. A spot will open up, and you just might be able to grab it. Remember as well if you have reservations that you aren't going to use, cancel them so that someone can have the spot. Disney now requires a credit or debit card to hold restaurant reservations. If you don't cancel, you will be charged.

Look for Alternatives

It never hurts to have a backup plan. If you want a princess meal and can't get a reservation at Cinderella's Royal Table, try Akershus Royal Banquet Hall at Epcot instead. FastPass+ for lunch at Be Our Guest Restaurant is available to guests who are staying at a Disney Resort Hotel, which is a good alternative to the hard to get dinner reservation. Want to watch Wishes but couldn't get a reservation at California Grill? Try Kona Cafe at Disney's Polynesian Village Resort and then watch the fireworks from the beach. If it's a meal with Mickey that you want, try booking Tusker House Restaurant or The Garden Grill instead of Chef Mickey's. He usually makes an appearance at those character meals as well. Some restaurants have lounges where you can order from the full menu, and a reservation isn't needed.

Download the App `BEST TIP`

If you arrive at Walt Disney World and you still haven't made the reservation that you really want, make sure that you download the My Disney Experience app. You'll then be able to put your time in line to good use by checking throughout the day to see if there are any openings.

Try the Day Before

Walt Disney World requires a credit card to hold a dining reservation. An email will be sent to remind the party of the reservation, giving them time to cancel. If the reservation is not canceled the day before and the party does not show, the card will be charged. Because of this, people are canceling their unwanted reservations. Trying the day before might snag a spot that someone else just gave up.

Ask at the Check-In Desk

It's a long shot, but sometimes it's possible to walk up to a restaurant and get a table. Ask at the check-in desk if there are any openings. If there aren't, see if there is a standby list and how long you'll have to wait if there is.

THREE

DINING DISCOUNTS AND MEAL DEALS

Dining while on a Walt Disney World vacation can be expensive. You can leave the property and find dining deals, but that will also cost you time from your vacation. There really aren't all that many discounts available for dining on property, but there are a few that some people are eligible for.

Free Quick Service Dining Plan

From time to time the Quick Service version of the Disney Dining Plan will be offered for free. That will include two counter service meals and one snack a day for each member of your party. It cannot be combined with other discounts, and restrictions apply. There is no set time that the free plan is offered, and it could be discontinued at any time.

Disney Vacation Club

If you love to travel, you might want to look into the Disney Vacation Club. One of the benefits is that you'll be eligible for dining discounts in some Walt Disney World Restaurants. The discount is usually 10% and it is available only at select restaurants.

Annual Passholders

If you plan to head to Central Florida at least twice a year, you might want to consider buying annual passes for your family. They could save you money, and you'll have perks like free parking. One of the advantages to having an annual pass is that some of the restaurants offer discounts. Quick service restaurants and snack kiosks usually don't, but you can save 10% at many of the table service restaurants. The list of participating restaurants changes from time to time, so you'll want to ask if there is a discount when you order.

Tables in Wonderland

Sometimes you have to spend money in order to save money. That is what Tables in Wonderland is all about. Disney Vacation Club Members, Annual or Seasonal Passholders, and Florida residents are eligible. For an annual membership fee, you will receive a Tables in Wonderland membership card, which will allow you to save 20% on food and beverages including alcohol at over 100 Walt Disney World restaurants. Restrictions may apply, and there may be blackout dates. The prices are currently $100.00 for an Annual/Seasonal Passholder, $50.00 for a second card, and for a Florida Resident who is not an Annual/Seasonal Passholder, the cost is $125.00.

Earl of Sandwich

One of the best sandwich bargains at Walt Disney World is Earl of Sandwich. Located in the Marketplace area of Downtown Disney, this popular eatery has reasonably priced sandwiches for all three meals. If you'll be in Central Florida near your birthday, visit earlofsandwichusa. com a few weeks before you leave home and sign up for "Club Sandwich". You'll receive a coupon for a free brownie, just for signing up. You'll also receive a coupon for a free birthday sandwich! The coupon will arrive by email a few days before your birthday and it will be good for 30 days. Note, it does not need to be used on your exact birthday.

Frequent Dining Program

If you're a fan of the restaurants at the Walt Disney World Swan and Dolphin, sign up for the Frequent Dining Program. It's free to join. As you dine, you'll earn loyalty points. Save them for gift certificates, special experiences, and more.

Landry's Select Club

If you like T-REX, Rainforest Cafe, and Yak & Yeti, you might want to join the Landry's Select Club at landrysselect.com. There is a small fee which reverts to a credit once you register your card. After spending $250.00 on the card you'll receive a $25.00 credit. The card does not need to be used in Orlando, you can use it at any Landry's restaurant.

Four

THE DISNEY DINING PLAN

The Disney Dining Plan is a way to include the price of your meals in your vacation. It is only available to guests staying at a Walt Disney World owned resort hotel. If you stay off property you are not eligible for the Disney Dining Plan. Guests of Shades of Green Resort, Disney's Dolphin Resort, and Disney's Swan Resort are not eligible for the dining plan, since those hotels are not owned by Disney. The restaurants at those hotels are also not on the plan.

Your entire party needs to be on the same plan; you can't have some members on the plan and others not on it. Your entire party will also need to have theme park tickets, since the plan is part of a Magic Your Way Package. If you want to try a lot of the restaurants while on your vacation, it might be a good deal for you.

Children under the age of three do not need to be on any dining plan. The children's plan is for kids ages 3-9. If your child is on the kid's plan, he or she must order from the children's menu when one is available. Anyone older than nine will be included on the adult plan.

The plan is simple to use. When you stop by a restaurant or participating snack stand, your MagicBand or Key to the World Card will be swiped. On your receipt, you will see how many credits you have left on your plan. How you use your credits is up to you, although they do expire at 11:59pm on the day that you checkout of your hotel. Your plan is based on the number of nights that you stay.

Not all restaurants participate in the Disney Dining Plan. At some restaurants, the more expensive entrees might not be included. While the meals include drinks, alcoholic beverages are never included in the Disney Dining Plan; they will cost extra.

Snacks on the plan vary. If you are ordering from a kiosk, the snacks that you can use the plan for will have a DDP symbol in purple and white next to it. Some of the common snacks that you can enjoy on the plan are pretzels, popcorn, ice cream bars, whole fresh fruit, chips, fountain drinks, coffee, bottled soda, and bottled water. Plenty of other snacks are also available; they vary by location.

If you have purchased the Disney Dining Plan, each member of your party will also receive a Refillable Mug. You can keep filling it up for free with fountain drinks or hot beverages for the length of your stay. You can refill the mug only at the resorts. If you go to a different resort, you can also refill your mug there.

They can not be used at the theme parks or the water parks. (The Disney Water Parks have their own refillable mug program.)

You will need to book the Disney Dining Plan when you make your reservation; you can't just add the plan once you arrive on property. If you didn't initially add it, call 407-939-7675 at least 48 hours before your reservation and ask to add the Disney Dining Plan.

There are several choices when it comes to the Disney Dining Plan:

Quick Service Dining Plan

This plan allows each member of your party to have two quick ser-vice meal credits and one snack credit for each day. If you're using a meal credit for breakfast you will receive one entree or one combo, and one non-alcoholic beverage. If you use your meal credit for lunch or dinner, you will receive an entree or a combo, a dessert, and a beverage. You will also receive a snack for each day of your vacation. If you want to dine at a full service restaurant, you will need to pay out of pocket for it. Disney will sometimes offer the Quick Service Dining Plan for free during the slower times of the year. Restrictions apply, and there are no set annual dates for free dining.

Basic/Plus Dining Plan

This plan will allow you to have one table service credit, one quick service credit, and one snack credit each day. A table service meal includes one entree, one dessert (for lunch or dinner), and one beverage. Buffets are also included as table service. For the quick service meal you'll receive one entree or combo, one beverage, and a dessert if it's lunch or dinner. You will also get a snack. Be careful with the table service credits, because some restaurants require two credits instead of one.

Deluxe Dining Plan

If you're looking for the most dining flexibility while on your vacation, you might want to consider adding the Deluxe Dining Plan. You'll receive three meals for each day of your plan, and two snacks a day as well. The meals can be either quick service or table service. Quick service meals include an entree or combo, a beverage, and a dessert if it's lunch or dinner. The table service meals on the Deluxe Dining Plan include an entree, a beverage, and for lunch or dinner you will also receive an appetizer and a dessert. Buffets are also included.

Premium and Platinum Plans

As far as dining is concerned, the Premium and Platinum Magic Your Way Packages are similar to the Deluxe Plan. You'll receive three meals and two snacks for each day of your vacation. The main difference is that the restaurants that require two table service credits will only require one on either of these plans. There are other benefits of these plans that are not dining related.

The signature restaurants are more expensive. Therefore, they will cost you more than one table service credit on the Disney Dining Plan. The restaurants that currently require two table service credits are Artist Point, California Grill, Cinderella's Royal Table, Citricos, The Dining Room at Wolfgang Puck Grand Cafe, Flying Fish Cafe, Fulton's Crab House, The Hollywood Brown Derby, Jiko - The Cooking Place, Le Cellier Steakhouse, Monsieur Paul, Narcoossee's, and Yachtsman Steakhouse. Sometimes special event dining, such as Star Wars character meals, are also included on the Disney Dining Plan for two credits. The list does change from time to time without notice, so if you have a reservation at a more expensive restaurant, check before your trip.

Is the Disney Dining Plan Worth it? That's up to you to decide. Opinions vary greatly with strong sentiments on both sides of the debate. Look at the menus and prices before you book your vacation and see if the cost makes sense for you. When thinking about the price, remember that your refillable mug is included. The Disney Dining Plan is convenient, and you'll have a chance to try restaurants that you might have skipped otherwise. Remember that the gratuity is not included, so please tip generously for good service.

FIVE

DISNEY DINING PLAN FREQUENTLY ASKED QUESTIONS

Here are a few frequently asked questions about the Disney Dining Plan:

Who is eligible for the plan? Only guests staying at a Walt Disney World owned resort hotel.

Can I add a friend to the plan who isn't staying with me? No. If your friend is staying at a Disney owned hotel, he or she may sign up, but not on your plan.

I'm meeting a friend for lunch. Can she use one of my credits? No, credits are not transferable. Tell your server that you will need separate tickets.

Part of my party wants the Disney Dining Plan, but part doesn't. Is it possible to break it up? No, everyone staying in your room has to be included, and you can't have two different types of plans in the same room.

Can we order the Disney Dining Plan for just part of our vacation? No, you must sign up for your entire stay.

What does Disney consider a day? As far as the Disney Dining Plan is concerned, the number of days is really the number of nights that you'll be staying.

I didn't use all my credits. Can I save some for my next vacation? No, your credits expire at 11:59pm on the day that you checkout.

Do I have to use a certain amount of credits per day? No, the plan is flexible. You can skip one day and double up the next. Use the credits in the combination that will work best for you and your family.

Can I order the Disney Dining Plan for my toddler? Children under the age of three are not eligible to participate in the plan.

How will my two-year-old eat without the plan? At a full or quick service restaurant, your little one will share your meal, or you can order something separately for the child and pay out of pocket. Kids under three can have their own plates from a buffet for no additional charge.

My kids don't want to eat off of the children's menu. Can they order an adult meal? When there is one available, children ages 3-9 must eat off of the children's menu if they are on the Disney Dining Plan. If they want an adult entree, you'll pay full price.

What does my child eat if there's no children's menu? If there is no children's menu, your child will order from the adult menu.

How do I keep track of my credits? The amount that you have left will be printed on each receipt.

What if I run out of credits? You'll need to pay for your meals out of pocket.

Can I add the Disney Dining Plan when I check in? No, it needs to be added to your reservation at least 48 hours in advance.

Does beer or wine count as a beverage? No, alcohol is never part of the Disney Dining Plan. You'll pay separately for it.

Is a milkshake considered a beverage on the Disney Dining Plan? It depends on the restaurant. Ask your server when you order.

Is a turkey leg a snack? No, a turkey leg is considered a quick service meal. The same goes for hot dogs and corn dogs.

What about special dietary requests? If you follow a special diet of some type, you are still eligible for the Disney Dining Plan. The credits will work the same way, even if your meal is specially prepared for you.

Does the Disney Dining Plan work at the Epcot Food & Wine Festival? Yes. You can't buy alcohol, but most of the special food items cost one snack credit.

How do I know what restaurants are included on the plan? You can look the restaurants up on the Walt Disney World website. There you will find whether or not a restaurant is on the Disney Dining Plan, which plans are accepted, and how many credits are required. You will also receive a complete list of available dining options when you check into your resort.

Will I have to buy a Refillable Mug? No, each member of your party will receive a mug as part of the plan. You can refill it only at the resort hotels for your entire stay.

Are character meals included? If you are on a dining plan that has table service credits, character meals are included. The exception is Garden Grove at the Walt Disney World Swan Hotel, which does not accept the dining plan. Most character meals only require one credit, making them a good deal. Cinderella's Royal Table, Mickey's Backyard BBQ, and special event character meals usually require two credits.

Why are some hotel restaurants not included? Not all hotels on Walt Disney World property are owned and operated by Disney. Those hotels do not offer the Disney Dining Plan to their guests, and the restaurants at them are not included either. Shades of Green, Walt Disney World Swan and Dolphin, and several other places aren't run directly by Disney (though they are located on Disney property).

My hotel offers in-room pizza delivery. Can I use my credits for that? Yes, except on the Quick Service Plan. Pizza delivery consists of one pizza, two beverages, and two desserts, and two adult table service credits can be used to pay for it. Children's credits won't work.

My hotel offers room service. Can I use my credits for it? Yes, except for the Quick Service Plan. You can order one beverage, one appetizer, one entree, and one dessert from room service for two table service credits.

Can I order the most expensive item from a menu? For the most part, yes. Your server will tell you if any items are not included.

Why do some restaurants cost two table service credits? Because those restaurants are more expensive than others. Most of the signature restaurants will require two table service credits.

I've heard great things about Victoria & Albert's. Do they participate in the Disney Dining Plan? No, you'll need to pay full price.

When is the quick service plan offered for free? There are no set annual dates, but often it will take place during the value season.

Can I combine the free Quick Service Dining Plan with other discounts? No, you'll pay full price for everything else including your room. Other things such as a PhotoPass package might also be required in the package in order to be eligible for free dining.

Will the Disney Dining Plan save me money? You're the only one who can figure out the answer to that question. Look over the menus and the prices, and see if you will pay less if you use the plan.

SIX

RAPID REFILL MUGS

If you spend a day or two at Walt Disney World, you're sure to see plenty of Rapid Refill Mugs. They're easy to spot. The mugs have a picture of Mickey and the gang with brightly colored tops and handles. While they may be everywhere, many people are confused about what they really are.

Rapid Refill Mugs are for use at the Walt Disney World resort hotels. If you purchase the Disney Dining Plan, a mug will be included in the price for each member of your party. If you're not on the Dining Plan you can still purchase the mugs; you don't even have to be staying at a Disney hotel to buy one. You pick the number of days that the mug is good for. Then you can refill the mug as often as you want after the first use. The mugs are for fountain beverages, coffee, tea, and hot chocolate. They cannot be used for alcoholic choices or for specialty coffee creations.

The mugs are useless at the parks, and you can't fill them at the water parks. The water parks have their own refillable mug program. You can fill the mug during your usage window at any Disney owned resort even if you are not staying there.

The clock on your Rapid Refill Mug will start the first time that you use it. You can't break up the days. For instance, you're not allowed to buy the mug for two days and use it only Monday and Thursday. Each day is a calendar day, not a period of 24 hours. The day for the mug starts at midnight. If you fill up your mug for the first time at 11:59pm, that will count as your first day.

If you're not sure how many days you have left on your mug, you'll learn when you fill it up. There is a screen at the drink machine that will give you the information that you need.

Not everyone in your room needs to buy a mug. You also do not need to have all the mugs in your party be for the same length of time. If one person wants a mug for only one day and someone else wants it for the whole vacation, that's possible. It's a flexible program. You also don't need to reserve your mugs when you make your room reservation. You can purchase them once you arrive, or at any time during your vacation.

Refill stations are located throughout the resorts. Look for a food court or another quick service option. If you can't find the nearest refill station, ask a cast member.

Here are a few common questions and answers about Rapid Refill Mugs:

Can I refill my mug in the parks? No, not at this time. This is not expected to change in the future.

How do the mugs work? There is an RFID (radio-frequency identification) code on the bottom of each mug. The refill station will scan the code. If your code is no longer valid, the drink won't dispense.

I bought the mug for only one day, but I love it. Can I add days? Yes, just tell a cast member at a quick service restaurant.

A friend is coming for the day who isn't staying at a Disney hotel. Can he get a mug? Yes, anyone can buy a Rapid Refill Mug.

I'm staying at Disney's Swan. Can I buy a mug there? No, mugs are not available at Disney's Swan, Dolphin, Shades of Green, or any other resorts that are not owned by Disney. You can purchase a mug at a Disney owned resort, but you won't be able to use it at your hotel.

What are my choices for how long I can use the mug? You can purchase a mug for one day, two days, three days, or the entire length of your stay.

If I can't use the mug in the parks, what is the point? The mugs can be used for your morning coffee and for a cold drink at the end of the day. Also, many families plan an off-day when they will spend the day enjoying the hotel pool. You can then fill up the mug as many times as you would like at a Disney resort.

What do I do with my mug when I return home? Do I have to turn it in? The mug is yours to keep. They make great souvenirs.

How do I keep the mug clean? There are sinks where you can wash your mug near the filling stations.

Can I fill up my mug and then bring it into a park? Yes, you're allowed to do that. Keep in mind, though, that the mugs don't hold all that much, and your drink won't stay cold for very long. You'll then need to carry the mug with you for the rest of the day.

How much does each mug hold? While Disney has not said the exact amount that each mug holds, somewhere between 12 and 16 ounces is a pretty good guess.

How do I use the mug? Place the mug on the tray. (It won't work otherwise.) Then press the button. You can fill it partially, or wait until the "fill complete" message appears. You will also learn the ending date of your program when you fill it.

Do I have to drink the same thing each time? No, you can pick and choose what you want. If you want soda one refill and lemonade the next, that's up to you.

I like to mix different types of soda. Can I still do that? Yes. Just keep mixing until the "fill complete" message appears.

Do the mugs work for hot beverages? Yes, they work well for both hot and cold drinks.

I reheat coffee all the time at home. Are the mugs microwaveable? Yes, you can safely use the mug to reheat coffee or another hot item in the microwave.

How do I wash the mug at home? Rapid Refill Mugs are dishwasher safe.

Seven

BUDGETING FOR FOOD

It is easy to overspend while at Walt Disney World. Food is going to take up a large part of your vacation budget. To avoid credit card shock once you return home, those on a tight budget need to make a plan and stick to it.

Consider the Disney Dining Plan

If you're staying at a Walt Disney World resort hotel, you might be eligible for the Disney Dining Plan. Look over the options and see if one will work for you and your family. If you do decide to sign up for the plan, a large amount of your food budget will be taken care of. Remember that the DDP does not include gratuities.

Research Prices Ahead of Time

Before you leave home, research the various Walt Disney World restaurants. It is not difficult to get a general idea of how much each one will cost you. If you know what you're getting into, setting a budget will be easier.

Set an Amount and Stick With It

Once you know how much the restaurants are going to cost you, set your budget. Make sure your entire party knows the plan. Include in your budget must try items like Mickey Ice Cream Bars. Know how much you can afford to spend on food each day, and do not go over that amount.

Buy a Gift Card

Once you know how much you can afford to spend on food each day, buy some Disney gift cards. Purchase one for each day of your trip. Use one gift card a day while on your vacation for your food purchases. If there is anything left on the card at the end of the day, you'll have a little extra for the next day.

Plan on a Splurge

Include at least one meal splurge during your Walt Disney World vacation. Find a restaurant that you really want to try, and make a reservation. Check the menu before you leave home so you'll know how much the splurge will cost and so you'll have an idea of what to order. Stick to your budget, but have fun at the same time.

EIGHT

TIME SAVING TIPS

When you and your family are spending a day in the magic, you're going to have to take time to eat. The trick is to not take too much time out of your day for a meal while still appreciating the uniqueness of each restaurant. These tips are meant to help you maximize your time, so that you can enjoy Disney restaurants without feeling like you're missing out on the fun.

Bring Your Own Snacks and Drinks

Since Walt Disney World allows you to bring food and drinks into the parks, do it. If you have a bag of animal crackers or a few granola bars with you, your family will have something quick to eat when it's not mealtime. You can save even more time by bringing in your own water bottle or container and filling it up at a water fountain. You won't have to wait in line when hunger or thirst strike.

Eat Early

Most of the quick service restaurants are least crowded when they first open. Plan to eat earlier than the rest of the lunch or dinner crowd. You'll spend less time in line, and it will be easier to get a table.

Eat Late

If you can wait a little while for your meal, the lines will be shorter and you'll save time. If there is a quick service restaurant that you really want to try, stop by 45 minutes before it's set to close. Most of the other park guests will have already eaten, so the lines should be manageable. Near the end of the day you will most likely be tired, so you'll welcome the chance to sit down and relax.

Skip the Parade

The parades at Walt Disney World are incredible. That said, the lines for the restaurants are shorter when the time for a parade grows near. If seeing the parade isn't near the top of your Disney to-do list, it can be a great time to dine.

Arrive Early

Even though you have a reservation, it is still a good idea to arrive at a table service restaurant a few minutes early. Your name will not be the only one on the list for your particular time. You'll want to be seated ahead of other parties who also have reserved a table in the same time slot. As soon as you arrive, your name gets moved up. Just because you have a reservation does not mean that you will be seated immediately; you'll be seated when there is an available table. Arriving a few minutes early might help you to be seated faster.

Make Lunch Your Big Meal

Lunch reservations can be easier to nab than dinner reservations. For some reason, many park guests will plan a quick service lunch and a table service dinner. Plan to make lunch your big meal of the day. You can enjoy an air conditioned break from the heat, and you'll have saved some time. Don't forget to make a reservation because the table service restaurants can still get crowded at lunchtime.

Save Some of Your Meal for Later

If your combo comes with a side of chips or something else that can be put into a backpack without being ruined, save it for later. You won't be as stuffed after your meal, and you'll have a snack for when hunger hits again. You won't have to wait in line to buy a snack at a kiosk.

Check Your FastPass+ Times

FastPass+ is designed to save you time. Check your ride times before you get in line for a meal. You don't want to miss your reservation. If you realize that time is tight, use the My Disney Experience app on your phone, or send one member of your party to a FastPass+ kiosk to try to change the time in question.

Read Menus Ahead of Time

One great way to save a little bit of time is to know what you want to order. Read the menus and decide what you want. You can do that on your phone while you're standing in line for a ride. You'll be ready to order when you arrive at the restaurant, which will make everything go faster.

Stay in the Park

You might be able to save a few dollars by leaving Walt Disney World and grabbing a meal at a nearby fast food restaurant, but think about all the time that it will cost you. It is easy to lose a couple of hours if you decide to leave the park and see what cheap meal you can find in the area. If you're planning on leaving the park for a few hours for a nap or a swim anyway, that's one thing, but leaving specifically to eat will cut a big chunk of time out of your day.

Leave the Park, but Stay on Disney Property

There are some great restaurants that are still on Disney property but aren't in any of the parks. If you're spending the day at the Magic Kingdom, consider a meal at Disney's Grand Floridian, or Disney's Polynesian Village. Both are just a quick monorail ride away. You can make it even faster to Disney's Contemporary because there is a walking trail. The Epcot Resort Area has some great choices that you can walk to from either Epcot or Disney's Hollywood Studios. (There is also a boat, but that takes more time.) You can leave the park for a meal, but you won't have to worry about moving your car. The pace at the resort restaurants is more relaxed, so you'll be able to take a break from the park for a little while, but you won't waste a lot of time.

NINE

MONEY SAVING TIPS

If your vacation budget is tight, there are ways to cut back on the costs of food. You'll still be able to enjoy great meals in unique restaurants, but you won't have to worry about maxing out your credit card. Here are a few suggestions that might help you to save on meals while in Central Florida. These tips all assume that you're not using the Disney Dining Plan. However, if you are on the plan, you might still find them helpful.

Pay With Cash

It's easier to overspend if you pay with a credit card. There are automated teller machines in all four parks. Take out the amount that you will need when you arrive each day, and then put your card away. Even if you have to pay a surcharge, you'll end up spending less in the long run because you'll have a set amount of money in hand. This works for souvenirs as well as food. If you aren't comfortable carrying cash, head into a store and buy a gift card. Use that for your food purchases for the day.

Bring in Snacks

Walt Disney World does not frown upon you bringing food into the parks. Make sure that your snacks can hold up well in a backpack under the hot Florida sun. Stay away from chocolate, but many packaged snacks should be fine. Make sandwiches so that you can skip a meal. Apples and bananas will help to hold back hunger, and they won't weigh you down too much. If you have an insulated lunch bag, use that for bottled water or soda (glass bottles are not allowed). Remember that everything you bring in will need to be carried until you eat it, so don't plan on anything that is too heavy.

Skip the Character Meals

If your food budget is extremely tight, you might want to skip the character meals. While they are a lot of fun, they are also expensive. There are other places to meet characters in the parks for free, and there are also cheaper places to eat.

Order Without the Sides

Many of the quick service restaurants have burgers, individual pizzas, and sandwiches that come with French fries or a salad. The menu does not state that ordering the entree without a side is possible, but it is. Unless you really want those French fries, order your entree without them.

Have Your Kids Split an Adult Meal

If you have young children who don't usually clean their plates, ordering from the Kids' Menu may not always be the cheapest choice. Instead of ordering two kids' meals, get one adult meal for them and have them split it. Some of the meals on the Kids' Menu are small, so there's a good chance that your children will end up better satisfied if they share an adult meal.

Drink Ice Water

You can ask for a cup of ice water at any quick or table service restaurant. It will still be cold and refreshing, but it won't cost you anything.

Use the Water Fountains

There are plenty of water fountains at Walt Disney World. When you're thirsty, find one and quench your thirst. You'll save a lot since you won't be buying bottled drinks. You can also use the water fountain to refill an empty bottle so that you won't have to stop as often. Look for a water fountain that is in the shade, and let it run for a few seconds. You'll be surprised by how cold and refreshing the water is.

Make Lunch Your Big Meal

Some of the table service restaurants have different menus for lunch and dinner. The lunch items will often cost less. You'll still enjoy great food and atmosphere, but it will cost you less.

Dine on Appetizers

It's easy to think that the table service restaurants are out of reach because of the price. It is possible to enjoy the food, the ambiance, and save some money at the same time. When you receive your menu, find an appetizer that looks delicious and filling, and make your meal out of that. If you're not sure if the dish will fill you up, ask your server how big it is.

Share

One of the simplest ways to save money on your meals is to share. The entrees at most Walt Disney World restaurants are huge, if you eat the whole thing you'll walk away stuffed. Share with your child and then you won't have to pay for a kids' meal. Split an appetizer so that everyone can have a taste. Share dessert. By sharing, you won't miss out on anything, and you'll still pay less.

Skip Dessert

The desserts at Walt Disney World are tempting, especially at the table service restaurants. They are also expensive. Skip the dessert and save both money and calories. If the dessert is too tempting and you can't say no, order one and split it. Paying $4.00 for one piece of cake will allow everyone to satisfy that sweet tooth, and it will be a lot easier on your wallet than paying $4.00 for each member of your family.

Ten

SPECIAL DIETARY NEEDS

Dining while on vacation can be difficult if you follow a restricted or special diet. Fortunately, Walt Disney World makes it easy to enjoy delicious food even if there are things that you can't or won't eat.

If you have a dietary need that the restaurants cannot accommodate, bring your meals into the park with you. Walt Disney World allows guests to bring in snacks, and small coolers are also permitted. Just tell the security guard at bag check that you have a special dietary need.

Food Allergies

Walt Disney World chefs are well-trained to accommodate those with food allergies, and they will make sure that you don't consume anything that will make you ill. Many food allergies are listed online when you make a table service reservation; all that you'll need to do is to check a box. If your need is not listed, email Special.Diets@DisneyWorld.com at least 14 days before your reservation to make sure that the restaurant will be able to accommodate your request. If you make your reservation by calling 407-WDW-DINE (407-939-3463), mention your needs to the operator to have them noted. Also, mention the allergy to your server as well, just to be on the safe side.

Gluten-Free

If gluten is not part of your diet, you'll still be able to enjoy meals at most Walt Disney World restaurants. With advance notice, you can feast on gluten-free waffles, breads, pasta, and other great dishes. Splitsville at Downtown Disney has GF options listed right on the menu. Look for BabyCakes NYC products in the bakeries, they are made without gluten as well. At a full service restaurant, remind the server that you follow a gluten-free diet. If you're at a quick service option, talk to a cast member. Many places will modify a dish, replace a bun, or offer suggestions so that you'll be able to have a filling and satisfying meal.

Lactose-Free

Another option when you make your dining reservation is dairy-free. Full service restaurants will then have products like Tofutti on hand so that you can enjoy a creamy dessert at the end of your meal. Talk to your server about your individual needs, since everyone is different. At a quick service restaurant, ask to see the book that lists ingredients, or tell your needs to a cast member. Many choices can be prepared without dairy, but it might take a few extra minutes.

Kosher

Most table service restaurants will happily prepare a kosher meal for you, but they need to have at least 48 hours advance notice in order to have the proper ingredients on hand. You might not have as many choices, so if there is something special at the restaurant that you'd like, discuss it with the operator when you call. The quick service kosher options are a lot more limited, but there are choices. Each park has one quick service restaurant that serves kosher meals. At the Magic Kingdom, head to Cosmic Ray's Starlight Cafe. At Epcot, you'll want to try Liberty Inn. Disney's Hollywood Studios has kosher meals at ABC Commissary. At Disney's Animal Kingdom, you'll need to go to

Pizzafari. Once you arrive at the restaurant, talk to a cast member about your options. BabyCakes NYC products, sold in many WDW bakeries, are kosher as well.

Vegetarian

Vegetarian dining is so easy at Walt Disney World that it's not even listed under special dietary requests when you make your reservation. Most full and quick service restaurants have at least one meatless choice on the menu. The word "vegetarian" is being included in more and more meal descriptions. When you arrive at a full service restaurant, let your server know immediately that you are a vegetarian. He or she will then let you know which menu items you can eat or what can be made without meat. Some sauces are made with animal stock, so it is always a good idea to ask. Vegetarian options seem to change often at full service restaurants. At quick service restaurants, you'll often find veggie burgers or vegetable wraps. The vegetarian snacks are clearly marked at the Epcot International Flower & Garden Festival and the Epcot International Food & Wine Festival. At the latter, everything at the Terra booth is vegetarian, which features Gardein meatless products.

Vegan

Vegan dining is more complicated at Walt Disney World than vegetarian, but it can still easily be done. Most full service restaurants can prepare a vegan meal. It's a good idea to call 48 hours in advance of your reservation so that the restaurant will be prepared. You'll also want to tell your server immediately that you're vegan. Sometimes the chef will come to your table to discuss your options. If you're dining at a buffet, have a cast member point out the vegan choices. Vegan meals are possible at most quick service eateries, but they will often take longer, so you might want to plan your meals when the restaurants aren't as busy. There are also a few vegan snacks that you can enjoy. Most of the pretzels are vegan, as is the kiosk popcorn. (Ask, just to be on the safe side.)

If you're at the Magic Kingdom, Plaza Ice Cream Parlor serves Tofutti. Another cool vegan treat is any fruit flavor of Dole Whip. BabyCakes NYC items, sold in some of the bakeries, are also vegan.

Other Requests

If you follow a low sugar or sodium diet, send an email or call 407-WDW-DINE (407-939-3463) so that you can make arrangements for your meals. The same holds true for alternative diets, like macrobiotic. The Walt Disney World chefs will do whatever they can to create meals that you'll enjoy as well as fit your needs. Not all restaurants will be able to accommodate every request. There will be more options with full service restaurants than with quick service. Since full service meals are prepared individually, the most important thing that you can do is to make arrangements early.

Special mention needs to be made of Gardens Kiosk at Disney's Animal Kingdom. Gluten-free and vegan snacks are sold there, but that is not the only reason to stop by. They have information on the park's restaurants to share with guests. If you have a food allergy or follow a special diet, you can learn ahead of time what dishes you will be able to eat at any restaurant in the park.

ELEVEN

TIPS FOR EATING HEALTHY AT WALT DISNEY WORLD

While on vacation it is all too easy to take a vacation from healthy eating habits. Temptations are around every corner. Fortunately, there are plenty of healthier choices at Walt Disney World that are also delicious. You can eat foods that won't pack on the pounds and still enjoy some of the best meals in Central Florida. Here are a few tips for eating healthy while on your vacation.

Snacks

All four parks sell fresh fruit, which is not only good for you, but it is refreshing on a hot day. Hummus with veggies for dipping is also popping up in the theme parks, giving you another healthy snack choice. You can even splurge on a sweet snack from time to time without blowing your recommended calorie intake. A Mickey's Premium Ice Cream Bar has 330 calories, which is far less than many other snacks. Mickey's Premium Ice Cream Sandwich has 280 calories. Frozen fruit treats sold at the same kiosks may have even less. You can even enjoy Dole Whip if you're watching your figure. A half cup has only 80 calories. Of course a serving is larger than half a cup, and that number is for regular Dole Whip, not the float. But you don't have to look far in a park to find a filling snack that you can eat without the guilt.

Breakfast

Don't skip breakfast. Instead, look for the healthiest options. Breakfast meats are high in fat and will weigh you down. Instead, order an omelet made with egg whites, filled with fresh veggies. If you want a Mickey Waffle go ahead and try one. Ask for the syrup and butter on the side and then add it sparingly yourself. Yogurt with fruit and granola is another breakfast option at many locations. Be careful with the pastries and other sweet goodies that are sold for breakfast. They won't fill you up for as long, and they are often high in fat, sugar, and calories.

Extras

One easy way to add extra fat and calories to your meal is to order a full combo, especially at a counter service restaurant. What is not commonly known is that you can order your entree without the fries. You'll not only save fat and calories, you'll save money as well. If you decide that you do want a side, ask if apple slices or grapes can be exchanged for the fries.

Entree Choices

Sometimes all that you'll need to do to find the healthier options is scan the menu. There are plenty of wraps sold at quick service restaurants. Look for foods that contain fresh ingredients, especially veggies. Stay away from fried foods and instead order entrees that are sautéed, broiled, or baked. You'll save calories and won't feel as stuffed.

Ask Questions BEST TIP

If you're at a counter service restaurant and you can't tell which are the healthiest choices, ask a cast member if you can see a copy of the restaurant's nutritional information. You'll be able to learn everything that you need to know. At a full service restaurant or buffet, ask your server what the healthiest choices are. If there is something that you want to try that seems too heavy, see if it can be served with the sauce on the side, or if any other alterations can be made to cut down on the fat, sugar, and calories. You might end up with the most delicious meal of your vacation.

TWELVE

HEALTHY EATING FOR KIDS

Walt Disney World makes it simple to find healthier dishes for your children. The food will taste so delicious that your kids won't realize it's good for them.

Kids can get carrot sticks, apple slices, or grapes to start off their meals or as sides at many restaurants. Lowfat milk, juice, and water are better beverage choices than soda. Look at the children's menu ahead of time and decide what to order before you arrive at a restaurant. That way you can steer your kids towards the healthier options.

Disney has made it easier than ever for your kids to enjoy healthy meals that taste great. Mickey Check Meals are nutritionally balanced. They are also low in fat, sugar, and sodium. Each Mickey Check Meal comes with an entree, a side, a healthy dessert, and either lowfat milk or water. The choices differ, depending on the location. Fish, turkey, chicken, and pasta are often among the entrees. You can also expect to find whole grains and fresh fruits or vegetables. Mickey Check Meals are easy to spot, just look for the black Mickey shape with the white check mark going through it. The number of choices are growing, with new meals available and more restaurants joining the program all the time.

Even if a child is old enough to order from the adult menu, you can still encourage healthy food choices. Look for baked, broiled, or sautéed dishes instead of fried.

THIRTEEN

DINNER WITHOUT THE CHILDREN

While Walt Disney World may be one of the top family destinations on the planet, but that doesn't mean every moment needs to be spent with the kids in tow. You can make arrangements for children ages 3-12 to spend an evening in one of several Children's Activity Centers. Your kids will have a great time, and you'll have a chance for a little bit of adult alone time. Call 407-WDW-DINE (407)-939-3463 for more information or to make a reservation. If your kids aren't old enough, or if you'd prefer that they stay in the room, Walt Disney World recommends the babysitting service Kid's Nite Out. Call (407) 828-0920 to learn more.

You might wonder where to go once you know that the kids are safe for the evening. Here are a few suggestions on where you can dine without the kids. None of these selections are located in the parks.

Artist Point
Disney's Wilderness Lodge

Celebrate the Pacific Northwest at this rustic eatery. The murals alone are worth the trip. Considered by many to be a hidden gem, you'll dine on game, steak, or seafood. The menu changes seasonally. There is an award winning wine list, featuring choices from wineries in the Pacific Northwest. Artist Point may be a little out of the way for some Disney guests, but it's worth the trip.

California Grill
Disney's Contemporary Resort

Refurbished in 2013, California Grill is still a classic. You'll both enjoy the chic atmosphere. Fresh describes the food and the menu. Items change seasonally, with selections like sushi, seafood, beef, and chicken. There is an incredible wine selection, with over 300 choices available. One of the the best things about California Grill is the view. The restaurant is located on the 15th floor (you'll have to board a private elevator to get there, how romantic is that?) and there are two outdoor decks. The view of the Magic Kingdom is spectacular, especially once it's time for Wishes. The soundtrack is played, and you'll get caught up in the magic. If you didn't time your reservation right for Wishes, don't worry. Just bring your receipt to the check-in desk and you'll be able to enjoy the show.

The Dining Room at Wolfgang Puck Grand Cafe
Downtown Disney West Side

Wolfgang Puck is one of the best known chefs in the world. It is easy to find his creations at Downtown Disney, because there are four different choices. The Dining Room at Wolfgang Puck Grand Cafe is intimate and elegant. Enjoy the low lighting as you dine on a three or four course meal that features some of the chef's famous creations. Ask for a table by the window and you will have a spectacular view of Village Lake. The food is influenced by Asian and Californian cuisine.

There's an extensive wine list. Ask about pairings if you're not sure what to order.

Flying Fish Cafe
Disney's BoardWalk

While Flying Fish Cafe has a whimsical theme, the food is taken very seriously. You'll enjoy what could be the best seafood on Walt Disney World property. For something extra special, make a reservation for the Chef's Wine Tasting Dinner. After your meal, spend some time together and enjoy all that is taking place on Disney's BoardWalk. The area comes alive at night.

Jellyrolls and Atlantic Dance Hall
Disney's BoardWalk

You won't be able to order a meal at either of these nightclubs, they only serve beverages. Both places are strictly for the 21 and up crowd. Jellyrolls is a dueling piano bar. Atlantic Dance Hall features music of the 80's, 90's, and current hits. Both have cover charges. Please remember to drink responsibly.

Jiko - The Cooking Place
Disney's Animal Kingdom Lodge

African cuisine and wines, an open kitchen, and low lighting will transport you to the heart of Africa; Jiko offers an ideal setting for an adult meal. Seafood, beef, pork, and chicken dishes with an African flair are featured. The restaurant is also a favorite of both vegetarians and vegans, but no matter what your eating habits, you're sure to find something delicious. Once your meal is over, stroll the grounds and watch the animals for a little while.

Narcoossee's
Disney's Grand Floridian Resort & Spa

Casual and elegant at the same time, this restaurant features mostly seafood and steaks. There are great views of the Magic Kingdom, so try to make your reservation near Wishes and the Electrical Water Pageant for a view that you won't soon forget. Don't mention that part to your children, just tell them that you enjoyed a sophisticated meal. They don't need to find out that you saw a dancing sea monster and then enjoyed one of the most famous fireworks displays in the world!

Victoria & Albert's
Disney's Grand Floridian Resort & Spa

The best adult dining experience at Walt Disney World can be found at Victoria & Albert's. Children under the age of ten are not even allowed at the restaurant. It is the only AAA Five Diamond Award winning restaurant on Disney property, and it is an award that it has proudly earned each year since 2000. The restaurant has won many other awards as well. There are three different dining experiences available at Victoria & Albert's: the main dining room, Queen Victoria's Room, and the Chef's Table. Depending on which experience you book, you'll enjoy seven to ten courses. There are over 700 wine selections, including some rare vintages. The dress code is more strict as well. Men should wear dinner jackets and slacks or dress pants. Ties are optional. Women should wear dresses, dress suits, pant suits, or skirts and blouses. Proper footwear for all is also required. Jeans, shorts, capris, flip flops, sandals, and tennis shoes are not allowed. Give yourself plenty of time. Dinner at Victoria & Albert's is not just a meal, it is the ultimate adult Disney dining experience.

Fourteen

TIPPING AT FULL SERVICE RESTAURANTS

In the United States a restaurant is allowed to pay its servers less than the normal minimum wage. The rest of the servers' income is expected to be made through tips. This system is supposed to keep the costs of eating out down, and it inspires the wait staff to try harder, hoping that a good dining experience will lead to a better tip.

The full service Walt Disney World restaurants are no exception to this. The servers rely on your tips. While tipping is not mandatory in most cases, it is a way to reward your server for taking good care of you. It is not an easy job and servers are often under appreciated, so leaving a good tip will thank your server for his or her hard work.

If you are at a snack stand or a quick service restaurant, you do not need to leave a tip. You should leave one at a full service restaurant or at a buffet. The amount that you leave is up to you. The standard is to leave a tip amount of between 15 and 20 percent of your bill before taxes. Tip a little extra if the service was exceptional. If you're not sure how to figure out the amount, Disney has you covered. On your bill the amounts for 18% and 20% are printed so that you will not have to do the math. There are also tip calculator applications for smart phones if you want to give a different amount.

Sometimes Walt Disney World will add the tip for you. If you have a party of six or more, a gratuity of 18% will be added automatically. The number of people in your party is based solely on the number seated at your table including infants. A gratuity of 18% is also added at dinner shows and at Cinderella's Royal Table. You can add to the 18% if you'd like.

Tips are not included in your credits if you are using the Disney Dining Plan. There will still be a space on your receipt where you can leave a tip, or you might prefer to leave cash on the table. Either way, include tipping your server as part of your budget, even when using the Disney Dining Plan. If you can't afford to leave a tip, please don't dine in a full service restaurant. The server is counting on you to make ends meet, so please be generous.

FIFTEEN

SPECIAL DINING EVENTS

Disney wants to make every meal special. There are times, though, when a little bit of extra magic is added to the mix. Sometimes it is a special meal, other times it is an event that will take place throughout an entire park. Here is some information on a few of the special dining events that are available at Walt Disney World. New experiences are added on occasion, sometimes without much notice, and Disney does make changes to old favorites. It is all in an effort to give guests the best vacation possible.

Epcot International Food & Wine Festival
Park-wide, Epcot

Each year in mid-to-late September, World Showcase changes. Approximately thirty special booths are set up, and they represent countries and regions that are not usually part of World Showcase. You'll be able to buy snack sized favorite dishes from around the world, and most of them count as a snack credit on the Disney Dining Plan. For those 21 and older, there are also adult beverages for sale that are not usually found in any of the parks. The festival is about more than just sampling food and drink. There are cooking classes taught by celebrity chefs, seminars, autograph signings, special meals, merchandise, and more. Theme park admission is required to attend, and there is an additional charge for some of the extras. The festival ends each evening with the Eat to the Beat Concert Series, which is a free concert by a well known artist. The Epcot International Food & Wine Festival usually runs through mid-November.

Epcot International Flower & Garden Festival
Park-wide, Epcot

Although this springtime festival is not quite as food-focused as its sibling in the fall, you'll still find plenty of special dining choices. The event features "outdoor kitchens", which are special kiosks that are set up to allow you to order things that aren't normally served in the park. You can try items such as Florida Kumquat Pie or Ghost Pepper-dusted Tilapia. Adult specialties are served, including the popular pineapple soft serve with rum (think Dole Whip without the "Dole" name attached.) The Epcot International Flower & Garden Festival also features special guests from HGTV, topiaries of popular Disney characters, and the Flower Power Concert Series. Park admission is required, and there is an additional charge for some special activities. The Epcot International Flower & Garden Festival starts in March and wraps up in May.

Star Wars Weekends
Park-wide, Disney's Hollywood Studios

Each May and June the Force is stronger than usual at Disney's Hollywood Studios. Star Wars Weekends are held Fridays, Saturdays, and Sundays, beginning in mid-May and wrapping up in mid-June. While the event is not about dining, Disney always creates some special options to keep *Star Wars* fans happy and full. Darth Vader and Yoda cupcakes are always a hit. Past items include drink containers shaped like stormtroopers and Darth Vader souvenir popcorn buckets. Guests 21 and older can purchase Light Side and Dark Side adult beverages, and non-alcoholic versions are available as well. In 2014 two *Star Wars* themed character dining experiences were introduced: breakfast at Sci-Fi Dine-In Theater Restaurant and Dinner at Hollywood & Vine. Also introduced in 2014 was the Feel the Force Premium Package, which features special viewing areas and a dessert party at the end of the night. Star Wars Weekends include special shows, celebrities from the movies and animated TV shows, extra character experiences, a *Star Wars* themed parade, collectable event merchandise, a fireworks display, and more. Park admission is required.

Tomorrowland Terrace Fireworks Dessert Party
Tomorrowland, Magic Kingdom

Everyone knows that watching Wishes is one of the best ways to end a day at the Magic Kingdom. Walt Disney World has come up with a way to make the end of the day even better. Held on select nights, Tomorrowland Terrace Fireworks Dessert Party features a buffet of desserts and non-alcoholic beverages. You can enjoy chocolate dipped strawberries, cheesecake, tarts, cookies, fresh fruit, and plenty of other delicious treats. After you've had your fill, you and the other guests will have a perfect view of the fireworks. Reservations are strongly recommended for the Tomorrowland Terrace Fireworks Dessert Party.

IllumiNations Sparkling Dessert Party
World Showcase Plaza, Epcot

Held on select nights, the IllumiNations Sparkling Dessert Party is the sister to the Tomorrowland Terrace Fireworks Dessert Party at the Magic Kingdom. You can enjoy some of your favorite desserts from the countries represented in World Showcase: baklava, churros, tiramisu, shortbread cookies, and other goodies. Wine and champagne are included in the price for those 21 and older. Other beverages include coffee, tea, iced tea, and lemonade. Once you have finished eating, you can enjoy a spectacular view of IllumiNations. Reservations for the IllumiNations Sparkling Dessert Party are recommended.

Afternoon Tea at the Garden View Tea Room
Garden View Tea Room, Disney Grand Floridian Resort & Spa

Too much time is spent rushing around from one place to another on a Walt Disney World vacation. Fortunately, there is a dining experience that will allow you to sit back and relax for a little while. Tea is served each afternoon, starting at 2:00pm. You'll enjoy finger sandwiches, scones, pastries, and tarts on fine china. There are several types of tea for you to enjoy. The hotel is a quick monorail ride from the Magic Kingdom, but you'll feel like you've traveled across the ocean. Reservations are strongly recommended.

Fantasmic! Dinner Package
Various locations, Disney's Hollywood Studios

The best way to end the day at Disney's Hollywood Studios is by seeing Fantasmic!. The show features live action, animation, fireworks, water screens, and special effects that have to be seen to be believed. The problem is the limited seating for Fantasmic!. That is where the Fantasmic! Dinner Packages come into play. The idea is simple. You book the package for lunch or dinner at Hollywood Brown Derby, Hollywood & Vine, or Mama Melrose's Ristorante Italiano. Your meal will include an entree, a dessert, and a non-alcoholic beverage, except at Hollywood & Vine, which has a buffet. When you're finished with your meal, you'll receive a voucher so that you and your party can enjoy special seating for Fantasmic!. You then won't have to show up hours early in order to get a seat, you'll just head to the VIP viewing area. When you make your reservation, make sure that it's for the Fantasmic! Dinner Package. A meal at the restaurant without reserving the package will not get you a voucher.

Candlelight Processional Dinner Package
Various locations, Epcot

The Candlelight Processional is one of the highlights of the Christmas season at Epcot. A celebrity narrator will tell the biblical story of the birth of Jesus, backed by a choir and a 50 piece live orchestra. Seating is limited, and even though there are three shows nightly people are still turned away. The Candlelight Processional Dinner Package works the same way as the Fantasmic! Dinner Package. You will reserve lunch or dinner at a participating restaurant, and when your meal is over you will receive a seating voucher for your party. Make sure that you arrive at the correct time, since there are three shows each evening. You need to book the Candlelight Processional Dinner Package when you make your reservation; you can't just eat at a participating restaurant and receive a voucher.

Dining with an Imagineer
Flying Fish Cafe, Disney's BoardWalk
Hollywood Brown Derby, Disney's Hollywood Studios

Ever wonder how Disney magic is really made? You can find out and enjoy a delicious meal at the same time. Dining with an Imagineer will allow you and up to nine other people a chance to meet an Imagineer and ask anything that you are curious about. Lunch is served at Hollywood Brown Derby and dinner takes place at Flying Fish Cafe. At the end of your meal, the Imagineer will personalize a plate for you. It's a great way to learn more about Walt Disney World and the Walt Disney Company in general. Reservations are required.

Jiko Wine Tasting
Jiko - The Cooking Place, Disney's Animal Kingdom Lodge

This special dining event takes place each Wednesday afternoon at 3:00. Three different African wines will be sampled. They are paired with artisanal cheese and fruit. Guests must be 21 or older in order to sample wine. Reservations are strongly recommended. There is a dress code.

Flying Fish Cafe - Chef's Tasting Wine Dinner
Flying Fish Cafe, Disney's BoardWalk

Sit at the chef's counter and watch as he prepares some of his specialties. You'll enjoy a five course meal that features the perfect wine pairings. The dinner is held twice nightly, Sunday through Thursday. All guests must be ten or older, and non-alcoholic beverages are available for those under 21 or who prefer not to drink. The price includes the food and the wine. Only six spots are available at each seating, so make your reservation early. There is a dress code at Flying Fish Cafe.

SIXTEEN

CHARACTER DINING

Character dining can be a lot of fun. You'll have a chance to spend more than just a moment with some of your favorite characters, and enjoy a delicious meal at the same time. If you have shy little ones you might want to schedule a character meal, because it's a great way to introduce them to the larger than life figures. That's not to say that character meals are just for children. People of all ages will have a great time and make memories that will last forever. Character meals can be expensive, but for some people they are the best part of their vacations.

There are a couple of things to remember when booking your character meal. First, just because a restaurant has one character meal does not mean that all meals will feature characters. It could be that breakfast has characters but lunch and dinner don't, or some other combination. Second, the characters may change from time to time. The characters listed here are the ones that usually appear at that meal, but that does not guarantee they will be there when you dine.

If you're on the Disney Dining Plan, most of the character meals require one table service credit. Cinderella's Royal Table and Mickey's Backyard BBQ each require two credits. Garden Grove does not accept the Disney Dining Plan.

One nice thing about character meals is they can give you a "Disney feel", even if you are taking a day off from the parks. Some families like to have a character dinner the evening that they fly into Orlando. That way they can start their vacation in a fun way without using a day from their theme park tickets. Remember, if you reserve a character meal inside a park, you will need a theme park ticket in order to get to your restaurant. Reservations are strongly recommended for all character meals, especially if the desired meal is within a theme park.

The character dining experiences at Walt Disney World and the expected characters are as follows:

1900 Park Fare
Disney's Grand Floridian Resort & Spa

There are three very different character experiences available here. The day begins with the Supercalifragilistic Breakfast. Food is served buffet style. The characters present may include Mary Poppins, Alice, and Mad Hatter.

Wonderland Tea Party takes place in the afternoon. It is not a full meal. Kids ages 4-12 can play games, sing songs, decorate cupcakes, and enjoy "tea" that tastes strangely like apple juice. Adults are not allowed, this is an event for kids only. Alice and Mad Hatter may attend.

Cinderella's Happily Ever After Dinner is the third character experience at the restaurant. Food is served buffet style. This dinner offers a rare chance to see Prince Charming. Cinderella also will be there. Other characters might include Lady Tremaine, Anastasia, and Drisella.

Akershus Royal Banquet Hall
Norway Pavilion, Epcot

If you or a member of your party wants to meet princesses, this is a great place to do it. It's considered by many to be a great alternative to Cinderella's Royal Table, but that doesn't mean that you should try it only if you can't get a reservation at the Magic Kingdom. Food is served all-you-can-eat family style. Norwegian and American favorites are available. Plenty of princesses will attend. Characters might include Snow White, Ariel, Aurora, Belle, Cinderella, and Mary Poppins. A keepsake photo is included in the price.

Cape May Cafe
Disney's Beach Club Resort

Only breakfast is a character meal at Cape May Cafe. An all-you-can-eat buffet is featured. Characters included could be Minnie, Goofy, and Donald. They're all ready to hit the beach. If you're looking for classic characters and a fairly easy to get reservation, you might want to consider breakfast here. The International Gateway entrance to Epcot is a short walk or boat ride away.

Chef Mickey's
Disney's Contemporary Resort

Chef Mickey's is extremely popular. It's an all-you-can-eat buffet for breakfast and dinner, and characters appear at both meals. You can arrive at Disney's Contemporary from the Magic Kingdom by monorail, boat, or a walking path. The characters are dressed up as chefs. You might find Mickey, Minnie, Donald, Goofy, and Pluto. Chef Mickey's is a fantastic place to meet classic characters and take a break from the crowds in the Magic Kingdom.

Cinderella's Royal Table
Fantasyland, Magic Kingdom

Cinderella Castle is the icon that most people picture when they think of Walt Disney World. Cinderella's Royal Table allows guests a chance to dine inside of it. This is one of the hardest to obtain reservations at Walt Disney World, so start trying as early as you can. Breakfast, lunch, and dinner are all served. When you arrive, you'll have a photo taken with Cinderella. You might also meet Aurora, Belle, Snow White, and the Fairy Godmother. If you're using the Disney Dining Plan, remember that the meal will cost you two table service credits. The keepsake photo with Cinderella is included for each party. Note: Cinderella's Royal Table will be closed for refurbishment for part of 2015, starting in January.

The Crystal Palace
Main Street, U.S.A., Magic Kingdom

Characters from the Hundred Acre Wood come indoors for this fun experience. Breakfast, lunch, and dinner are all character meals. Food is served buffet style, and there is a separate buffet for the little ones. Pooh, Eeyore, Piglet, and Tigger usually make an appearance. If you're dining near Easter you might meet Rabbit as well.

The Garden Grill
Future World, Epcot

Only dinner at The Garden Grill is a character meal. The restaurant is unique because it revolves. The movement is slow so you won't have to worry about motion sickness. You'll see different scenes as you dine, such as a farmhouse and a thunderstorm. The meal is served family style and is hosted by Chip 'n' Dale. Mickey and Pluto might make an appearance as well.

Garden Grove
Walt Disney World Swan Hotel

Character dining is kind of tricky at Garden Grove. Dinner is a character meal, and breakfast also has characters on Saturdays and Sundays only. If you're not sure if there will be characters when you'll be there, call 407-WDW-DINE (407-939-3463), just to make sure. You can enjoy the buffet, or order a la carte. The characters at Garden Grove change often. There will be at least two characters appearing. In the past Pluto, Goofy, Timon, and Rafiki have all made appearances. If you're on the Disney Dining Plan remember it is not accepted here. You'll need to pay out of pocket.

Garden View Tea Room
Disney's Grand Floridian Resort & Spa

The character experience here is known as My Disney Girl's Perfectly Princess Tea Party. While the celebration was designed with princess-obsessed girls in mind, boys are also welcome to attend. Finger sandwiches and apple juice (masquerading as tea) are served. It is hosted by Rose Petal, who will lead the children in games and songs. Princess Aurora should also make an appearance. There are gifts for the children. The party is held at 10:30am on select days. For reservations or more information, call 407-WDW-MYTEA (407-939-6983).

Hollywood & Vine
Echo Lake, Disney's Hollywood Studios

This character meal was designed with the littlest ones in mind. Breakfast and lunch are both character meals. Known as Disney Junior Play 'n Dine, you and your kids can sing and dance, and then enjoy the buffet. Characters are based on what is hot on Playhouse Disney. You might see Doc McStuffins, Handy Manny, Jake and the Never Land Pirates, and Sofia the First. Remember that dinner is not a character meal at Hollywood & Vine.

Mickey's Backyard BBQ
The Campsites at Disney's Fort Wilderness Resort

There's a difference between Mickey's Backyard BBQ and the other character meals that you can reserve. Here you'll not only get dinner, but also a show. The food is served as an all-you-can-eat buffet. Characters most likely will include Mickey, Minnie, Goofy, and Chip 'n' Dale. The experience requires two table service credits on the Disney Dining Plan. Mickey's Backyard BBQ takes place on select nights, and may be canceled due to inclement weather.

'Ohana
Disney's Polynesian Village Resort

While 'Ohana serves both breakfast and dinner, characters are present only at breakfast. This is a popular experience because after the meal you can easily catch the monorail to the Magic Kingdom. It's also a lot of fun. The food is served family style, and other parties might be seated with you at the same table. Lilo and Stitch are your hosts. This is called the Best Friends Breakfast. Mickey and Pluto might make an appearance as well.

Tusker House Restaurant
Africa, Disney's Animal Kingdom

There are characters present at both breakfast and lunch here. Donald's Dining Safari is hosted by everyone's favorite duck. Other characters could include Daisy, Mickey, and Goofy. The characters are ready to head out on safari, and are dressed in the appropriate attire. Food is served buffet style. There are no characters at dinner.

Special Events

Sometimes Disney will have special event character dining. For example, in 2014 two character experiences were added to celebrate Star Wars Weekends. Usually these special experiences will be announced several weeks in advance. The price is often higher than a regular character meal, and most likely the meal will cost two table service credits on the Disney Dining Plan.

Seventeen

BEST WALT DISNEY WORLD BREAKFASTS

It is important to start your day at Disney with a good breakfast. You'll be on your feet for hours before it's time for lunch, and the Florida heat and humidity can quickly take a toll. Here are a few suggestions on delicious ways to begin your day.

Grab 'n' Go Items, Hotel Food Courts
Various Walt Disney World Resorts

If you're staying at a Walt Disney World resort hotel, stop by the food court before getting in line for the bus. The food courts are designed to get you in and out in a hurry, and grab 'n' go items will save you even more time. The exact items available will depend on which resort you are staying at, but you'll usually find muffins, pastries, bagels with cream cheese, breakfast sandwiches, and other delicious choices. Since the food is already prepared you can just grab it, pay, and then be on your way.

Eggs Benedict, Grand Floridian Cafe
Grand Floridian Resort & Spa

If you're looking to start your day in relaxed elegance, make a reservation at Grand Floridian Cafe. The Eggs Benedict is arguably the best at Walt Disney World. It's served with Broiled Tomato Au Gratin and asparagus. Add a croissant on the side, and enjoy a frozen cappuccino as well. Once you're finished, the Magic Kingdom is a short monorail ride away.

Chocolate Croissant, Starring Rolls Cafe
Sunset Boulevard, Disney's Hollywood Studios

While a chocolate croissant might not be the healthiest breakfast that you'll ever have, it will be one of the most delicious. The buttery goodness is drizzled with chocolate icing for a treat that is unforgettable. Starring Rolls Cafe has other yummy pastries, and you can also order your morning coffee. There's limited outdoor seating, or you can enjoy your food while you head towards Tower of Terror or Rock 'n' Roller Coaster.

Warm Cinnamon Roll, Gaston's Tavern
New Fantasyland, Magic Kingdom

When Main Street Bakery was converted to a Starbucks, many people feared that the delicious cinnamon rolls would be a thing of the past. They are still available; you just need to know where to find them. The rolls are now sold at Gaston's Tavern in the Enchanted Forest section of New Fantasyland. They're just as large and delicious as ever. They are also just as filling, so they can qualify as a breakfast.

Breakfast Panini, Sunshine Seasons
Future World, Epcot

The Land pavilion at Epcot is one of the first places that many guests head when the park opens so that they can get in line for Soarin'. After the ride, make your next stop Sunshine Seasons for breakfast. The Breakfast Panini contains bacon, eggs, pork, and cheese. It's served with potatoes on the side. You can get your morning coffee there as well. After having spent all that time hang gliding, you'll need to refuel.

Nutella and Fresh Fruit Waffle Sandwich, Sleepy Hollow
Liberty Square, Magic Kingdom

Sleepy Hollow is easy to miss as you're rushing to Splash Mountain. It's worth a stop, especially if you haven't yet had breakfast. The Nutella and Fresh Fruit Waffle Sandwich will give you the energy that you need to make it until lunch. A large waffle is smothered with Nutella. A generous amount of fresh fruit (usually bananas and berries) will then top the creation. While at Sleepy Hollow, you can also get your morning coffee.

Tonga Toast, Kona Cafe
Disney's Polynesian Village Resort   FAN PICK

Tonga Toast is considered a Walt Disney World breakfast classic. Sourdough French toast is stuffed with bananas and then deep fried. It's then topped with cinnamon-sugar. A generous amount of Strawberry Compote is served on the side, and it comes with your choice of bacon, ham, or sausage. Add a French Press Pot of Kona Coffee and you just might think it's the best breakfast ever. Once you're finished, you can take the monorail to the Magic Kingdom.

EIGHTEEN

TEN SPECIAL SANDWICHES

Sandwiches are a large part of the American diet. Most likely you will have at least one or two while you are at Walt Disney World. Here are ten sandwiches that you might want to consider if you're looking for something tasty and filling. Burgers are not included. This list offers a variety of locations, so that you'll be able to find a delicious sandwich no matter where you are on Disney property.

Sweet and Spicy Chicken Waffle Sandwich, Sleepy Hollow
Liberty Square, Magic Kingdom

The idea is simple. You take a large waffle, add some toppings, and fold it over to make a sandwich. In this case the waffle is topped with fried chicken breast, coleslaw, and arugula. The Asian dressing is slightly spicy, so it's a good thing that Sleepy Hollow also serves ice cream so that you can cool off your mouth after you've finished your sandwich.

Pork Sandwich, Flame Tree Barbecue
Discovery Island, Disney's Animal Kingdom

Flame Tree Barbecue serves what many people claim is the best barbecue on Walt Disney World property. If you love barbecue, you won't go wrong with anything on the menu. The Pork Sandwich comes with a generous helping of meat on a soft bun. It is served with coleslaw on the side. It's a simple sandwich, but you'll soon realize why Flame Tree Barbecue is so popular.

Open-faced Chicken Sandwich, Akershus Royal Banquet Hall
Norway, Epcot

If you're looking for a quick bite to eat, this is not the spot for you. If you're interested in dining with Disney princesses and enjoying a great meal, make your reservation. One of the entree choices is the Open-faced Chicken Sandwich. You'll enjoy chicken, tomatoes, bacon, arugula, and Jarlsberg Cheese, all served on sourdough bread. The sandwich comes with your choice of soup.

Smoked Turkey Sandwich, Sci-Fi Dine-In Theater Restaurant
Commissary Lane, Disney's Hollywood Studios

Sometimes the simpleness of a dish makes it a classic. The Smoked Turkey Sandwich is simply comprised of turkey, bacon, lettuce, and tomato. It's served on multigrain bread and topped with avocado mayo. A cucumber salad is served on the side. You'll have a chance to enjoy a delicious meal while dining in one of the most uniquely themed Disney restaurants.

Chicken Pita, The Mara
Disney's Animal Kingdom Lodge

While a Chicken Pita may sound like a fairly ordinary sandwich, there is nothing ordinary about the one served at The Mara. The pita is filled with chicken, cucumbers, mixed greens, and tomatoes. It is the combination of tomato hummus and mint yogurt sauce that make this sandwich exceptional. It comes with your choice of fries or couscous. A meatless version is also sold; the chicken is replaced with falafel.

Bacon Wrapped Meatloaf, Wolfgang Puck Grand Cafe West Side, Downtown Disney

Don't think of this as your mother's meatloaf. Chef Wolfgang Puck is famous for his unique creations, and this sandwich aims to take comfort food to the next level. Juicy meatloaf is wrapped with bacon, then topped with mozzarella, garlic aioli, and crispy onion strings. It's served with potato chips that were made in-house. A slightly different version of the sandwich can also be found at Wolfgang Puck Express at Downtown Disney Marketplace.

Grilled Chicken Panini, Fresh Mediterranean Market Walt Disney World Dolphin Hotel

Fresh Mediterranean Market is a nice place for lunch because you can easily leave the craziness of Epcot and not have to go too far. It is also under the radar for many people, so getting a reservation should not be too difficult. The Grilled Chicken Panini is worth the trip. It's a relatively simple sandwich; chicken, pesto, and vinegar peppers are grilled together to perfection. Fries are served on the side. Fresh Mediterranean Market also has a dessert bar. The all-you-can-eat desserts are included in the price if you order an entree.

Moroccan Kefta Sandwich, Tangierine Cafe Morocco, Epcot

For something a little bit different than the norm, head to Tangierine Cafe at Epcot. You'll find many Moroccan treats that most likely aren't available back home. The Moroccan Kefta Sandwich is seasoned ground beef (a.k.a. kefta) on a grilled bun. Fries and fresh salsa are served on the side.

Lighthouse Sandwich, Columbia Harbour House
Liberty Square, Magic Kingdom

You don't have to be a vegetarian to enjoy this meatless meal. Hummus, broccoli slaw, and tomatoes are served on toasted multigrain bread. It's a lighter alternative to the many heavy dishes that are sold in the park, but it's just as filling. The sandwich comes with chips on the side.

The Original 1762, Earl of Sandwich
Downtown Disney Marketplace

If it's a sandwich that you're looking for, you can't go wrong at Earl of Sandwich. A tribute to John Montagu, the fourth Earl of Sandwich, the restaurant features over a dozen hot creations. The Original 1762 is a throwback to the first sandwich, which legend says was invented by Montagu so that he could eat while playing cards. The sandwich features roast beef, cheddar cheese, and horseradish sauce. Sandwiches are made to order. The restaurant tends to get crowded, especially at traditional meal times, so plan accordingly.

Nineteen

SNACKS OF THE WORLD

Snacking is a part of any Walt Disney World vacation. A snack can tide you over until your next meal, or it might even help you to save money by totally replacing a meal. You can bring snacks into the parks with you, but if you don't, there are plenty of delicious options. Here are a few that you might want to keep an eye out for. Not everything listed here counts as a snack credit on the Disney Dining Plan. If you have a question, ask a cast member.

Popcorn

You can get popcorn in all four theme parks, and at several other locations as well. Although it tastes buttery, the popcorn sold in the parks is vegan. You can often purchase it in a souvenir bucket that will celebrate a holiday or a special event. If you want something more than plain popcorn, many of the stores carry packages of flavored popcorn. You can get cheese, chocolate drizzle, confetti, and other flavors.

Churros

A theme park favorite is the churro. If you've never seen one it is a long, thin, Spanish doughnut. Churros can be eaten plain, or you might find them with either chocolate or caramel dipping sauce.

Funnel Cake

This theme park classic is sold in all four parks and at several other snack stands as well. Dough is forced through a funnel and then fried, hence the name. Funnel cake is usually served with powdered sugar on top. Depending on the location, your funnel cake can be topped with ice cream, whipped cream, fruit, or chocolate syrup.

Cupcakes

If you have a sweet tooth you'll be thrilled with the variety of cupcakes that are found at Walt Disney World. Just head to the nearest bakery and marvel at all the choices. You'll find traditional cupcakes, but there are also creations such as the Butterfinger Cupcake, the White Chocolate Elephant Cupcake, and the Oreo Bon Bon Cupcake. There are so many choices that you might have to order more than one and share.

Mickey Ice Cream Bars

One must-try treat on any Disney vacation is the Mickey Ice Cream Bar. It's simple: vanilla ice cream on a stick covered with chocolate. What makes it special, of course, is the fact that it's shaped like Mickey. The bars are sold all over the place; you can find them at some quick service restaurants, at portable kiosks, at snack stands, and even in many stores. The best part of all is that the bars are refreshing and delicious. They're also lower in calories than most snacks. One bar has 330 calories, which is definitely lower than the Butterfinger Cupcake. If you want to enjoy a cool Mickey treat and save a few more calories, the Mickey Ice Cream Sandwich has 280. It's as delicious as the bar and is just as cute.

Other Ice Cream and Frozen Treats

You can't go far at Walt Disney World without encountering some type of frozen treat. They seem to be everywhere! You can order soft serve ice cream, hand scooped ice cream, fruit bars, dairy-free frozen treats, sundaes, sandwiches, gelato, snow caps, Kakigori, and other frozen creations. If you're not sure what type of ice cream you want, try the Kitchen Sink at Beaches & Cream Soda Shop. It will definitely satisfy your ice cream craving.

Smoked Turkey Legs

For some people a smoked turkey leg is a snack; others will enjoy it as a meal. Available in all four parks and the water parks, smoked turkey legs are large and filling. There is no truth to the rumor that the legs are made out of emu meat; they really are turkey. Each leg weighs in at approximately 1.5 pounds. If you're watching your sodium, these might not be the snack for you. Smoked Turkey Legs are so popular that the gift shops sell car air fresheners with their scent, and you can also find them on a T-shirt.

Fresh Fruit

If you're looking for a healthier snack option, try fresh fruit. You can find whole fruit such as apples, oranges, and bananas at many quick service restaurants. Cold sliced fruit such as watermelon and pineapple is also sold in the parks. Whole fruit is also available. One nice thing about fresh fruit is that it not only curbs your hunger, it satisfies your thirst as well.

Pretzels

There are some great pretzel choices at Walt Disney World. The most common pretzels are shaped like Mickey. They are another vegan snack that taste great. You can often order Mickey Pretzels with cheese, chocolate, or caramel sauce for dipping. For a different pretzel treat try a filled cream cheese or jalapeno pretzel. For more variety, stop by Wetzel's Pretzels at Downtown Disney. Another pretzel treat which will leave a smile on your face is sold at Epcot's Kringla Bakeri Og Kafe. They sell sweet raisin pretzels topped with either chocolate or almonds. They're simply delicious.

Dole Whip

Dole Whip is the ultimate classic Walt Disney World snack. Available at Aloha Isle at the Magic Kingdom, you can order pine-apple, orange, or vanilla. The fruit flavors are vegan, and all choices are gluten-free. Can't decide which flavor you want? Order two of them in a twist. You can have your Dole Whip in a cup, or you might instead want to order it as a float. Dole Whip has started popping up elsewhere on Walt Disney World property, but Aloha Isle will always be the iconic place to buy it.

TWENTY

I SCREAM, YOU SCREAM...

There is a very good chance that ice cream will be a part of your Walt Disney World vacation. It seems to be everywhere! It comes in many different shapes, sizes, and flavors. While it would be next to impossible to include every place where ice cream is available, here is a quick guide so that you can know what is close by when the craving hits. Ice cream is either the focus or one of the main things served at the following places. Just because a restaurant or stand is not mentioned does not mean that there's no ice cream available. Also, snack bars and funnel cake stands aren't mentioned here. Chances are that they sell Mickey Bars or another type of ice cream.

Magic Kingdom:

On busy days Disney will set mobile carts near popular attractions so that you can enjoy a Mickey Bar or another frosty confection. There are also a few places to check out that sell frozen treats.

Aloha Isle (**Adventureland**) sells Dole Whip. It's not quite ice cream, but it's just as refreshing. It comes in pineapple, orange, vanilla, or swirl, and you can order a cup or a float.

Auntie Gravity's (**Tomorrowland**) is a great place for soft serve. Chocolate, vanilla, and swirl are available. You can order your ice cream in a cup, a cone, as a sundae, or in a float. Smoothies are also sold.

Plaza Ice Cream Parlor (Main Street, U.S.A.) resembles an old fashioned ice cream parlor. The sweet smell alone will draw you in. All the popular flavors of hand-scooped ice cream are available. Cups, cones, and some great sundae choices are sold. You can also find frozen treats for people with special dietary needs.

Storybook Treats (Fantasyland) is another soft serve location. Chocolate, vanilla, and swirl are sold. You might want to order a cone, a cup, or try one of their sundaes. Floats and milkshakes are served as well.

Sunshine Tree Terrace (**Adventureland**) isn't just for ice cream. If you're looking for a slush or another frozen beverage, this is the place. Soft serve ice cream is available in chocolate, vanilla, or swirl. You might want to try the Citrus Swirl; it's orange and vanilla soft serve mixed together.

Epcot:

What is nice about ice cream in Epcot is that you'll have a chance to try something a little bit different. You can still enjoy your favorites, or you can instead savor an international take on ice cream.

Gelati (**Italy, World Showcase**) serves gelato, which is Italian ice cream. It's softer than American hand-scooped, and lower in butterfat. It's still loaded with taste. Enjoy two scoops in a cup or a cone. Or try the gelato sandwich, which is your pick of flavors between two fresh chocolate chip cookies. Special sundae creations are sold as well, including one designed with coffee lovers in mind.

Kabuki Cafe (**Japan, World Showcase**) sells Kakigori, which is Japanese shaved ice. Several traditional flavors are available including rainbow. Caramel Ginger Ice Cream, Strawberry Azuki Ice Cream, and Green Tea Ice Cream are also served. Kabuki Cafe allows you to try flavors that you won't find in most ice cream shops.

L'Artisan des Glaces (**France, World Showcase**) features 16 flavors of French hand-scooped ice cream and sorbet. The ice cream is slightly softer than American hand-scooped. It's sold in cups and cones. L'Artisan des Glaces is also where adults can try an Ice Cream Martini.

Refreshment Cool Post (**Outpost, World Showcase**) offers a different "twist" on soft serve. Instead of the traditional flavors, you can try pineapple, coconut, or swirl frozen yogurt. Slushes are also sold.

Refreshment Port (**Showcase Plaza**) has traditional soft serve ice cream. Chocolate, vanilla, and twist are available in a waffle cone.

Disney's Hollywood Studios:

Disney's Hollywood Studios is the smallest of the four theme parks, but there are some great ice cream choices here.

Dinosaur Gertie's Ice Cream of Extinction (**Echo Lake**) is hard to miss. Just look for the giant seaweed-eating dinosaur in Echo Lake. Open seasonally, Dinosaur Gertie's sells chocolate, vanilla, and swirl soft serve in a waffle cone or a cup. Ice cream bars are also available.

Hollywood Scoops (**Sunset Boulevard**) is part of Sunset Ranch Market Snacks. They feature hand-scooped ice cream in all your favorite flavors. Cups, cones, and sundaes are sold, as well as ice cream sandwiches on fresh baked cookies, and apple crisp a la mode.

KRNR Station (**Sunset Boulevard**) is right next to the Rock 'n' Roller Coaster exit. The kiosk features chocolate, vanilla, and swirl soft serve in a cup or a waffle cone. Floats, smoothies, and frozen lemonade are available as well.

Peevy's Polar Pipeline (**Echo Lake**) doesn't sell ice cream per say, but they do carry frozen drinks. You can cool off with frozen lemonade, wild cherry, coke, or other flavors.

Disney's Animal Kingdom:

You can satisfy your ice cream craving at the following locations:

Anandapur Ice Cream Truck (**Asia**) sells soft serve ice cream in waffle cones. You can choose from chocolate, vanilla, or twist. You can also have your ice cream as part of a soda float.

Dino-Bite Snacks (**DinoLand U.S.A.**) is where you should go for hand scooped ice cream. Chocolate, vanilla, strawberry, and chocolate chip are sold. You can order your ice cream in a waffle cone, or made into a sandwich. You can pick between fresh baked chocolate chip, sugar, and oatmeal raisin cookies. Hot fudge sundaes are sold as well.

Discovery Island Ice Cream (**Discovery Island**) sells hand-scooped Haagen-Dazs. You can get chocolate, vanilla, strawberry, or cookies and cream. Edy's No Sugar Added Butter Pecan is also available. You can order your ice cream in a waffle cone, or you might want it between two fresh chocolate chip cookies. Discovery Island Ice Cream also has the Bugs Sundae for sale. It's topped with gummy worms and crumbled cookies that look like dirt.

Disney Water Parks:

It's not hard to find ice cream at either of the Walt Disney World Water Parks. Of special note is the Sand Pail Sundae. It's made of chocolate and vanilla soft serve and topped with waffle cone pieces, chocolate and caramel sauces, whipped cream, and a cherry. It's served in a pail and your spoon is a shovel. It's big enough to share.

Arctic Dots (**Typhoon Lagoon**) sells cups of tiny dot ice cream. It's the kind that is flash frozen using liquid nitrogen, leaving behind little balls of ice cream. Several flavors are available.

Happy Landings Ice Cream (**Typhoon Lagoon**) features soft serve ice cream in chocolate, vanilla, and swirl. Try it in a waffle cone, or maybe you'd prefer a sundae. Happy Landings is one of the places where you can buy the Sand Pail. Floats, Mickey Bars and similar treats are sold as well.

I.C. Expeditions (**Blizzard Beach**) has chocolate, vanilla, and swirl soft serve. Waffle cones and sundaes are sold. The Sand Pail is available here too. You can also order floats, Mickey Bars and other ice cream bars, and frozen drinks.

Lottawatta Lodge (**Blizzard Beach**) sells full meals, but it's also a great place to get your ice cream fix. You can find chocolate, vanilla, and swirl soft serve here. Sundaes, including the Sand Pail, are also sold, as are frozen bars.

Snack Shack (**Typhoon Lagoon**) sells full meals as well as ice cream. They also carry the Sand Pail sundae. Other sundaes, and soft serve waffle cones are available as well. You can also get Mickey Bars and similar treats here.

Snow Balls (**Blizzard Beach**) sells snow. Enjoy shaved ice, topped with your favorite fruit flavor. Mickey bars and similar treats are available as well.

Warming Hut (**Blizzard Beach**) is a great place to stop for lunch, but don't forget to order dessert. Soft serve chocolate, vanilla, and twist are sold in cups or waffle cones. Mickey Bars and other frozen treats are also available.

Downtown Disney:

Downtown Disney is slowly transforming into Disney Springs. It's still a great place to find frozen treats, even during the construction.

Downtown Snow Company (**Marketplace**) doesn't have ice cream, but they do sell a refreshing frozen treat. The "snow" is shaved ice, and you can get it in a variety of flavors. "Snow Caps" of marshmallow cream or sweetened condensed milk are also available.

Ghirardelli Ice Cream & Chocolate Shop (**Marketplace**) is a chocolate and ice cream lover's dream come true. You can get decadent ice cream in a homemade waffle cone, sugar cone, or a cup; or you might want to try one of their sundae creations. With choices like Cookie Bottom Sundae and Mint Bliss, you might want to stop by more than once on your vacation. Shakes and floats are sold as well.

Haagen-Dazs Kiosk (**West Side**) features over a dozen flavors. You can order a cone, a cup, or a sundae. Coffee frappes are available, as well as shakes with or without toppings.

Resorts:

You're going to find lots of ice cream at the resorts. It's sold in the food courts, at the snack stands, at some pool bars, and even in the occasional store. Those places aren't listed here. Listed instead are restaurants where ice cream is a large part of what they are all about.

Beaches & Cream Soda Shop (**Disney's Beach Club Resort**) is home to the ultimate Walt Disney World ice cream treat. It's called the Kitchen Sink and it serves four. The sundae contains eight scoops of ice cream. Other items in the creation include brownies, cookies, cake, banana, whipped cream, and, according to Disney, "every topping we have". The colossal sundae is served in, you guessed it, a kitchen sink. Beaches & Cream also has other sundaes, and hand scooped ice cream by the cone or cup. Shakes, floats, and ice cream sodas are served as well.

Seashore Sweets' (**Disney's BoardWalk**) is a candy store with an ice cream counter. Edy's ice cream is served. You can order hand-scooped ice cream in a cup or a waffle cone. Sundaes are created as well, just tell the cast member what you want on it. Mickey and other frozen bars are also served. There's outdoor seating, or stroll around the BoardWalk and take in the sights.

The Fountain (**Walt Disney World Dolphin**) is designed to look like an upscale diner. If you're in the mood for ice cream, it's the dessert counter that you'll want to check out. Homemade hand-scooped ice cream is sold, as well as soft serve. You can create your own sundae or try one of the restaurant's creations. If you don't want a whole sundae, order a cup or a cone. Waffle, sugar, and cake cones are available. There are also creative shakes (like PB&J), floats, and malts served. Those 21 and older can order an ice cream beverage with a kick.

Twenty-One

CRAVING CANDY?

If you're craving candy while at Walt Disney World, you will not have to go far to get your fix. It is sold in many of the gift shops, even if the store does not exclusively sell food. Just look near the register and see what is available. Even though there are places that sell candy all over Walt Disney World property, there are also some unique stores that specialize in candy. Those are listed here.

Big Top Souvenirs (**New Fantasyland, Magic Kingdom**) is located in the Storybook Circus section of the park. You can't miss it. Just look for a circus tent. While it is not just a candy store, there are many tasty treats that you can buy while you are there. Look in the center where you'll find caramel apples with personality, crispy rice treats, caramel popcorn, cotton candy, fudge, chocolate-dipped fruit skewers, and other sweet offerings. The caramel corn is house-made and you can watch as the caramel apples are created. Goofy's Glaciers are also sold at Big Top Souvenirs.

Disney's Candy Cauldron (**West Side, Downtown Disney**) is a lot of fun. You'll enter the Wicked Queen's dungeon as a "villager". The cast members speak in Old English and might ask you to pay with "pebbles and stones" instead of dollars and cents. There's a good assortment of candy here, with everything from lollipops to boxed chocolates to

Disney-themed Pez. The highlight, though, is the made-to-order specialty apples. You pick the coating and the topping, and yours will be made while you wait. If you don't want to wait, there are also apples that have already been made.

Ghirardelli Ice Cream & Chocolate Shop **(Marketplace, Downtown Disney)** smells so sweet that it will draw you in. As you might guess, the shop features Ghirardelli chocolate. Pick up a free chocolate square as you enter. The store features mostly gift packs of Ghirardelli chocolate in various sizes. The flavor that you were given upon entering is often for sale in the center of the small store.

Goofy's Candy Company (Marketplace, Downtown Disney) just might be the most unique candy shop you'll ever visit. What else would you expect from Goofy? You'll find bagged candy with Goofy's name and picture on it (it's also available in plenty of Walt Disney World stores) but that's not the reason that people stop by. It's the chance to make your own treat that makes the store so popular. You'll pick a base (for example, a crispy rice treat or pretzel rods), a coating, a topping, and a drizzle. It is then created right before your eyes. The treats are so popular that birthday parties are held on the premises. Goofy's Glaciers are also sold here.

Karamell-Kuche **(Germany, World Showcase, Epcot)** is a caramel lover's dream come true. The store can get crowded. You'll find caramel popcorn, caramel apples, caramel covered strawberries, and more. Packaged treats are also sold.

Main Street Confectionery **(Main Street, U.S.A., Magic Kingdom)** sells candy, cookies, and other delicious treats. You can watch as confectioners create the items in the back of the store. In addition to lollipops and cotton candy, the store also makes and sells peanut brittle.

Seashore Sweets' **(Disney's BoardWalk)** is a small candy and ice cream store. You can find jelly beans, chocolate covered pretzels, sugar tubes that you fill yourself, fudge, and other delicious items.

Sweet Spells **(Sunset Boulevard, Disney's Hollywood Studios)** is easy to rush by on your way to Tower of Terror or Rock 'n' Roller coaster. After your ride, reward yourself for your bravery. Dipped apples, crispy rice treats, fudge, bagged candy, and other delicious items are sold.

TWENTY-TWO

CUPCAKE CREATIONS

Cupcakes have become an important part of Disney dining. There seems to be some sort of competition between the pastry chefs as to who can come up with the most decadent creation. New varieties are being added all the time, and cupcakes that aren't selling as well may no longer be available. Not all cupcakes named here will be available on a daily basis. Disney chefs also seem to take pride in seasonal creations. The purpose of this list is to get you started on your search...and to make you hungry for a cupcake.

Magic Kingdom

Be Our Guest Restaurant (**New Fantasyland**): Lemon Meringue Cupcake, The Master's Cupcake, Strawberry Cream Cheese Cupcake, Triple Chocolate Cupcake.

Big Top Souvenirs (**New Fantasyland**): Dumbo Cupcake, Popcorn Cupcake.

Main Street Bakery (**Main Street, U.S.A.**): Peanut Butter and Chocolate Cupcake, Red Velvet Cupcake, seasonal cupcakes.

Epcot

Karamell Kuche **(Germany, World Showcase):** Caramel Corn Cupcake, Chocolate Caramel Cupcake, Vanilla Caramel Cupcake.

Sunshine Seasons **(Future World West):** Carrot Cupcake, Chocolate Raspberry Cupcake, Guava Cream Cheese Cupcake.

Disney's Hollywood Studios

Mama Melrose's Ristorante Italiano **(Streets of America):** Spaghetti and Meatball Cupcake.

Pizza Planet Arcade **(Streets of America):** Cappuccino Cupcake, specialty cupcakes.

Sweet Spells **(Sunset Boulevard):** Chocolate Mickey Cupcake, Vanilla Mickey Cupcake, Vanilla Princess Cupcake.

Starring Rolls Cafe **(Sunset Boulevard):** Butterfinger Cupcake, Carrot Cupcake, Jack Sparrow Cupcake, Lemon Meringue Cupcake, Marble Cupcake, Peanut Butter and Chocolate Cupcake, Sorcerer Hat Cupcake, Strawberry and Cream Cupcake, seasonal cupcakes.

The Writer's Stop **(Streets of America):** Bright Blue Cupcake, Bright Pink Cupcake.

Disney's Animal Kingdom

Gardens Kiosk **(Discovery Island):** vegan, gluten-free, Kosher and allergy-friendly BabyCakes NYC Mini-Cupcakes.

Kusafiri Coffee Shop & Bakery **(Africa):** Cotton Top Tamarin Cupcake, White Chocolate Elephant Cupcake, Zebra Cupcake.

Downtown Disney

Cookes of Dublin **(Pleasure Island):** daily selection of cupcakes.

Earl of Sandwich (**Marketplace**): Cupcake Coronets in various flavors.

FoodQuest (**inside DisneyQuest, West Side**): assorted cupcakes.

Goofy's Candy Company (**Marketplace**): Colorful Cupcake, assorted cupcakes.

Resorts

Beach Club Marketplace (**Disney's Beach Club Resort**): BabyCakes NYC Mini-Cupcakes, German Chocolate Cupcake, Peanut Butter and Chocolate Cupcake, Red Velvet Cupcake, Vanilla Cupcake, seasonal cupcakes.

BoardWalk Bakery (**Disney's BoardWalk**): BabyCakes NYC Mini Cupcakes, Cappuccino Cupcake, Coffee Mocha Cupcake, Orange Cream Cupcake, Oreo Bonbon Cupcake, Peanut Butter Cupcake, Peanut Butter and Chocolate Cupcake, S'mores Cupcake, Strawberry Shortcake Cupcake, seasonal cupcakes.

Captain Cook's (**Disney's Polynesian Village Resort**): Chocolate Beer Cupcake, Chocolate Macadamia Cupcake, Lemon Ginger Cupcake, Mango Passion Fruit Cupcake, Mickey Chocolate Mousse Cupcake, Minnie Chocolate Mousse Cupcake, Peanut Butter and Jelly Cupcake, Pina Colada Cupcake, Red Velvet Cupcake, seasonal cupcakes.

Contempo Cafe (**Disney's Contemporary Resort**): Black Forest Cupcake, Chocolate Coconut Cupcake, Dos Leches Cupcake, Lemon Cupcake, Mickey Birthday Cupcake, Minnie Birthday Cupcake, Peanut Butter and Chocolate Cupcake, Pineapple Rum Cream Cheese Cupcake, Red Velvet Cupcake, Spices Apple Cupcake, Strawberry Lemonade Cupcake, Worms and Dirt Cupcake, seasonal cupcakes.

Everything POP (**Disney's Pop Century Resort**): BabyCakes NYC Mini-Cupcakes, The King Cupcake.

Gasparilla Grill and Games (**Disney's Grand Floridian Resort & Spa**): Cherry-Berry Cupcake, Florida Orange Cupcake, German Chocolate Cupcake, Pina Colada Cupcake, S'mores Cupcake, seasonal cupcakes.

Landscape of Flavors (**Disney's Art of Animation**): BabyCakes NYC Mini-Cupcakes, Macaroon Cupcake, Mickey Oreo Cupcake.

The Mara (**Disney's Animal Kingdom Lodge**): BabyCakes NYC Mini-Cupcakes, Chocolate Butterfinger Cupcake, Giraffe Cupcake, Orange Marmalade Cupcake, Vanilla Cupcake, Zebra Cupcake.

Old Port Royale Food Court (**Disney's Caribbean Beach Resort**): Chocolate Cupcake, Peanut Butter Monkey Cupcake, Vanilla Cupcake.

Roaring Fork (**Disney's Wilderness Lodge**): Carrot Cupcake, Chocolate Caramel Cupcake, S'mores Cupcake.

Section Two

RESTAURANT DESCRIPTIONS

In this section you'll find descriptions of the Walt Disney World restaurants. Theme park restaurants are listed in each chapter by category, and then alphabetically.

The resort descriptions are listed in order of dining experience. They are as follows: fine dining, full service, character dining, quick service, pool bar, lounge, nightclub. In each of those categories, the restaurants are listed alphabetically.

Remember that prices, restaurant hours, and menu items can change without notice.

The price key is based on adult meals and is as follows:

$ - $14.99 or less
$$ - $15-$29.99
$$$ - $30-$59.99
$$$$ - $60 or more

TWENTY-THREE

TYPES OF DINING OPTIONS

When you're trying to understand all of the choices for dining at Walt Disney World, you should find out about the different types of dining options. Learning a little bit about each type of restaurant will enable you to better make the right selections. Here are the categories that are used on the Walt Disney World website.

Fine/Signature Dining

Signature dining and fine dining are the same thing. In fact, the two terms are listed together on the WDW website. Signature experiences are the best that you will find on Walt Disney World property. World class chefs have come up with the menus, and the food is fresh and creative. Signature restaurants are also going to be expensive. Starting at around $30.00 per entree, most are much more. (Dinner at Victoria & Albert's, for example, will end up costing hundreds of dollars.) Some of the signature restaurants have dress codes and might even limit the ages of those who can dine there. If the signature restaurant is located within a park, it will most likely be open for lunch and dinner. The signature restaurants in the resorts are usually open for dinner only. You will want to make a reservation at a signature restaurant.

Casual Dining

Casual dining at Walt Disney World is a fairly vague term. Most of the time it means a full service, sit down restaurant. The theme parks have plenty of casual dining options. You'll also find them at Downtown Disney, and the more expensive resorts. It is a good idea to make a reservation, especially if there is a casual restaurant that you really want to try.

Unique/Themed Dining

These restaurants are similar to casual in that they are full service, sit down eateries. The difference is the atmosphere. There is a theme that will set each unique restaurant apart from the others. Often there is some type of story, and the cast members will play along. Themed restaurants still pride themselves on the food, but the staff will want your meal to be an experience that you won't soon forget. Some of the themed restaurants are quite popular and you should make a reservation as soon as possible. In the restaurant descriptions in this publication, themed restaurants and casual restaurants are both listed under "full service".

Character Dining

One thing that will enhance your Disney vacation is a character dining experience. They are not just for children. Character meals will usually feature at least three different characters, who will make their rounds and greet all of the guests. If you have a shy little one, you might want to book a character meal to get him or her used to the larger than life figures. Most character meals are all-you-can-eat, either buffet or family style. All four theme parks offer character dining, and there are also character meals held at some of the resorts. Just because a restaurant has characters at one meal does not mean that they will be there for all three. Make sure that it is a character meal that you book when you make your reservation. Characters do change from time to time, so don't promise your little ones that they will definitely meet Donald at a meal. You can tell them that there will be characters there, but let them be surprised by who shows up.

Dinner Shows

If you like to be entertained while you dine, you might want to book a dinner show. There are currently three unique options at Walt Disney World. Mickey's Backyard BBQ features a hoedown with Mickey and his friends. Disney's Spirit of Aloha Dinner Show is a luau with dancers and performers. Hoop-Dee-Doo Musical Review brings the spirit of the Old West to life. All three shows are all-you-can-eat and include beer and either wine or sangria for those 21 and older. Give yourself plenty of time, and make your reservation well in advance.

Buffet/Family Style

If you want to fill up, you might want to consider a buffet or a family style meal. Reservations are strongly suggested. A buffet is a meal where you will head to an area and fill up your plate with whatever is available. With a family style option, you will stay at your table and the food will be brought on plates. You and your party will then serve yourselves from the food that is placed in front of you. Both buffets and family style restaurants are all-you-can-eat. Dessert and non-alcoholic beverages are usually included as well.

Quick Service

There are three quick categories for grabbing a meal in a hurry. You'll find Quick Service, Fast Casual, and Quick & Casual options.

All three are pretty much the same. You'll stand in line and order your food at a counter. You'll then pick up what you ordered. Some of the quick options sell full meals, others are more for snacks. A quick service restaurant might have indoor seating, there could be an outdoor place to sit, and some have a combination of both. There are also plenty of quick restaurants that do not have seating nearby, so keep that in mind when you order.

Food Courts

If you are staying at a Disney resort, the food courts will give you a chance to grab something in a hurry. They are fast options that are made to get you in and out quickly, or you can take your time if you would like. The food court will reflect the general theme of the resort. You do not have to be staying at a particular hotel in order to eat at its food court, they are open to the public. They open early for breakfast and stay open late so that you can have a snack before bed. They usually have grab and go items, as well as food that is prepared after you order it. In this publication, food courts are listed as quick service restaurants.

Snacks

Snacks are sold all over Walt Disney World. You'll find everything from traditional theme park snacks like funnel cake to more creative items such as egg rolls. Snacks are available for those with special dietary needs as well. Disney will set up movable kiosks on popular days so that the snacks will be even closer. Most snack stands also sell drinks so that you can stay hydrated.

Pool Bar

Most of the larger Disney resort hotels have bars at their pools. Those of age can order a drink, and there are plenty of non-alcoholic specialties as well. A pool bar may or may not serve snacks. Some also offer complete meals. The rule of thumb is usually the more expensive the hotel, the fancier the pool bar, and the more extensive the food menu.

Lounges

A lounge sells alcohol to those who are old enough, in fact you can sit right at the bar, but it will still be family friendly. There are no age restrictions for sitting in the lounges. You can usually order appetizers, and if there is a restaurant associated with the lounge you might be able to order a meal from the restaurant's menu.

Nightclubs

A nightclub is strictly for those 21 and older. They serve alcohol but little if any food. There may be a cover charge. In general, they open at 9:00pm and remain open until 2:00am. There aren't currently too many nightclubs at Walt Disney World, but it is rumored that more will open with the transformation of Downtown Disney to Disney Springs.

TWENTY-FOUR

A BRIEF INTRODUCTION TO THE MAGIC KINGDOM

The Magic Kingdom is where the magic in Central Florida all began. The park opened on October 1, 1971. It is the most attended theme park on the planet. Cinderella's Castle is not only the park's icon, it symbolizes Walt Disney World as a whole. There have been many changes in the years since it opened, but the park maintains the same charm that it had on opening day.

There are six themed lands at the Magic Kingdom. Cinderella Castle is the central hub, and a trip around it will lead you to the other lands. The Magic Kingdom has something for everyone. There are quiet rides that the whole family can enjoy, as well as thrill rides for those seeking adventure. The Magic Kingdom is known for its triple mountain threat: Space Mountain, Splash Mountain, and Big Thunder Mountain Railroad. The newest thrill is Seven Dwarfs Mine Train, a roller coaster designed with families in mind. This is also the park with classic rides like Dumbo, It's a Small World, and Pirates of the Caribbean.

In 2011, Mickey's Toon Town Fair permanently closed. The space was then used for the largest expansion in Magic Kingdom history. The area is known as New Fantasyland. That is broken up further into two sections; Storybook Circus and Enchanted Forest. New Fantasyland opened in stages, starting in 2012. The expansion was completed with the addition of Seven Dwarfs Mine Train in 2014.

There are plenty of great places to meet characters at the Magic Kingdom. Most days there are two parades. Check your map and Times Guide for more information. Make sure you stay for Wishes Nighttime Spectacular. There are good viewing spots for the nightly fireworks show all over the park.

The Magic Kingdom has many delicious dining choices, some with movie tie-ins. Two of the most popular Walt Disney World character meals, Cinderella's Royal Table (inside Cinderella Castle) and The Crystal Palace, are located in the park. Alcohol is not served in the Magic Kingdom, except at Be Our Guest Restaurant, which sells beer and wine.

There are three special events that are held annually at the Magic Kingdom. Night of Joy takes place on two consecutive evenings each September and features the hottest acts in contemporary Christian music. Mickey's Not-So-Scary Halloween Party is held on select nights starting in September and ending in early November. Soon after, Mickey's Very Merry Christmas Party begins on select nights. It runs through the middle of December. All three special events require separate park admission.

TWENTY-FIVE

FULL SERVICE AND CHARACTER DINING AT THE MAGIC KINGDOM

Full Service Dining

Be Our Guest Restaurant
Fantasyland - $, $$

FAN PICK

Dinner at Be Our Guest Restaurant is one of the hardest to make reservations at Walt Disney World. The restaurant is unique in that lunch is quick service and dinner is full service. You will dine inside Beast's Castle. Three different rooms from the movie have been recreated: The West Wing, the Rose Gallery, and the Ballroom. Each has its own charm.

The food at Be Our Guest Restaurant is French. You might want to start with a bowl of French Onion Soup or Assorted Meats and Sausages. The entrees include choices such as Chicken Breast Provencal, Sauteed Shrimp and Scallops, and Layered Ratatouille. For dessert you'll finally have the opportunity to try The "Grey Stuff", or if you're not quite that adventurous you might want a Strawberry Cream Cheese Cupcake or a Chocolate Cream Puff instead. Be Our Guest Restaurant is the only place in the Magic Kingdom where you can purchase alcohol. There is a nice selection of wines, and several types of beer are also available. No liquors are served. Non-alcoholic choices include fruit punch, lemonade, fountain drinks, and hot beverages. Be

Our Guest Restaurant is open daily for a quick service lunch, and as a full service option for dinner.

Liberty Tree Tavern
Liberty Square – $, $$

Take a step back in time at Liberty Tree Tavern. Colonial New England is the theme. You'll feel like Paul Revere should be arriving at any moment to join you for dinner. There are six different themed rooms, each commemorating one of the country's founders.

Lunch at Liberty Square is served a la carte. You can start with a hot bowl of Clam Chowder, then move on to an entree such as New England Pot Roast, Freedom Pasta, or The Liberty Boys BLT. The Ooey Gooey Toffee Cake is a great option for dessert, or maybe you'd prefer Martha Washington's Cake instead.

Things are a little bit different for dinner. A traditional Thanksgiving dinner with all the trimmings is served. The food arrives family style, and it is all-you-can-eat. You'll feast on turkey, beef, pork, stuffing, mashed potatoes, and other sides. Johnny Appleseed's Cake is served for dessert. Liberty Tree Tavern is open daily for lunch and dinner.

The Plaza Restaurant
Main Street, U.S.A. - $

Charming is the perfect word to describe The Plaza Restaurant. It has an early 1900's feel to it. There are two dining areas that might remind you of an old-fashioned ice cream parlor. If you forgot to make a reservation for a meal at the Magic Kingdom, try The Plaza Restaurant. It is probably the easiest-to-obtain reservation in the park. It is also one of the more affordable full service restaurants.

Sandwiches are the star at The Plaza Restaurant. You will find grilled chicken, cheese steak, burgers, turkey, tuna, vegetarian, and other options. Sandwiches come with fries, homemade chips, or broccoli slaw. A meatloaf meal is also available. You will want to stay for dessert.

The menu features incredible ice cream creations. If you're not in the mood for ice cream, try the cheesecake. Milkshakes, floats, and other hot and cold beverages are available. The Plaza Restaurant is open daily for lunch and dinner.

Tony's Town Square Restaurant
Main Street, U.S.A. - $$

Who could forget the scene from *Lady and the Tramp* where the young dogs share a plate of spaghetti outside of a restaurant? If you've wondered what that eatery looks like on the inside, make a reservation at Tony's Town Square Restaurant. It is located at the front of the park, next to the Town Square Theater. If you're a fan of the famous canine couple, you'll love the fountain that features their likeness. The main dining room is filled with references to the film. There is also a sun room and patio dining.

The food at Tony's Town Square Restaurant is what you would expect to find in an Italian restaurant. Appetizers include Tomato and Mozzarella Salad, and Zucchini Fries. Seafood, steak, pork, and pasta are among the entrees. Of course Spaghetti and Meatballs made it onto the menu. There are some delicious dessert options, including Tiramisu and the Chef's Signature Cheesecake. Hot and cold beverages are available. Tony's Town Square Restaurant is open daily for lunch and dinner.

Character Dining

Cinderella's Royal Table
Fantasyland - $$$

Note: Cinderella's Royal Table will be closed for refurbishment for part of 2015, starting in January.

This is one of the most coveted meals at all of Walt Disney World. If you plan to go, make sure that you reserve your spot as soon as you know the date because reservations fill up quickly. Who wouldn't want a chance to dine inside Cinderella Castle? Upon your arrival, you will meet Cinderella and you and your group will have a complimentary picture taken with her. From there you'll be escorted to the Grand Hall, where you'll enjoy your meal. Other princesses will make the rounds. Those attending could include Aurora, Snow White, Jasmine, and Ariel. The whole event is hosted by the Fairy Godmother.

The meals at Cinderella's Royal Table arc served family style. For breakfast you'll have choices like Caramel Apple Stuffed French Toast and Lobster and Crab Crepes. More traditional breakfast items are also available. Lunch starts with the Chef's Tasting Plate and then moves on to entrees such as Pan-seared Chicken Breast, Chef's Fish of the Day, and Rice with Roasted Vegetables. End your meal with the chocolate dish The Clock Strikes Twelve. Appetizers at dinner include Crawfish and Shrimp with Grits and A Royal Tasting of Cheese. From there, you'll be able to choose from such royal entrees as Gnocchi with Roasted Vegetables, Beef Tenderloin, and Slow-roasted Bone-In Pork. The Chef's Dessert Trio is the perfect ending to a magical meal. Cinderella's Royal Table is not just a restaurant, it is an experience. It requires two credits on the Disney Dining Plan. Cinderella's Royal Table is open daily for breakfast, lunch, and dinner.

The Crystal Palace
Main Street, U.S.A. - $$, $$$ FAN PICK

The Crystal Palace is strikingly gorgeous. It has a Victorian greenhouse theme that will take you back in time. There are plenty of windows, many of which have great views of Cinderella Castle. The Crystal Palace is a popular character experience, featuring Winnie the Pooh and friends as they celebrate Friendship Day. Tigger, Piglet, and Eeyore usually appear with Pooh. Rabbit is sometimes there as well. The characters will interact with guests and might even encourage children to join them in a parade around the restaurant.

Food at the Crystal Palace is served buffet style. For breakfast you can have an omelet created for you. All of the other typical breakfast selections are also available, including potatoes, breakfast meats,

Mickey Waffles, cereal, fresh fruit, and pastries. You might want to try the Breakfast Lasagna, it's a favorite. The lunch buffet includes salads, carved meats, fish, pasta, and other items. Added to the buffet for dinner are more beef, chicken, and vegetable creations, as well as shrimp. There are plenty of dessert selections for both lunch and dinner. Choices may include cheesecake, cookies, and create your own sundaes (the ice cream is house-made). There is a separate buffet at all three meals for the kids. The Crystal Palace is open daily for breakfast, lunch, and dinner.

TWENTY-SIX

QUICK SERVICE DINING AT THE MAGIC KINGDOM

Be Our Guest Restaurant
Fantasyland - $, $$

Lunch does not require a reservation, it is a quick service meal. Be warned that the line can grow long quickly. You will order your meal from a keypad and then take a seat in one of the three dining areas. Dining inside of Beast's Castle is like stepping into the movie. The three dining rooms are the West Wing, the Rose Gallery, and the Ballroom. The food has a French flair, with dishes like French Onion Soup, Tuna Nicoise Salad, Vegetable Quiche, and Carved Turkey Sandwich on Millet Bread. There are different types of cream puffs and cupcakes on the dessert menu. Be Our Guest has French wines and beer available to adults. Other hot and cold beverages are also sold. Be Our Guest Restaurant is open daily as a quick service option for lunch, and as a table service restaurant for dinner.

Casey's Corner
Main Street, U.S.A. – $

You might want to reread the poem *Casey at the Bat* before you hit this popular baseball themed eatery. Located on the end of Main Street, U.S.A., Casey's Corner gets crowded at traditional meal times. There is indoor seating with a ballpark feel, and a few tables outdoors as well. A pianist named Jim might be on hand outdoors to entertain you as you eat. Ballpark food is featured, with different hot dog creations, nachos, chicken nuggets, and Polish sausage. For dessert you can get cotton candy and, of course, Cracker Jack. Casey's Corner is open daily for lunch and dinner.

Columbia Harbour House
Liberty Square - $

At Columbia Harbour House you'll step back into Colonial New England. The nautical theme is evident in even the small details. There is plenty of indoor seating (upstairs tends to be quieter) and there are some tables outdoors as well. The menu also has a Coastal New England theme, with choices such as the Anchors Away Sandwich, the Lighthouse Sandwich, and the Lobster Roll. Grilled salmon, fried fish, and chicken nuggets are also sold. Don't forget a side of New England Clam Chowder! The Seasonal Cobbler is the perfect way to wrap up your meal. Lemon Slush and other hot and cold beverages are available. Columbia Harbour House is open daily for lunch and dinner.

Cosmic Ray's Starlight Cafe
Tomorrowland - $

Cosmic Ray's Starlight Cafe is one of the most popular quick service restaurants at the Magic Kingdom. It has the feel of a campy science fiction movie. Sonny Eclipse is an audio-animatronic alien who is also a lounge singer. While there is plenty of seating at Cosmic Ray's, it can still be hard to find a table at traditional meal times. The main dining area is often packed, so you might want to check the other seating areas, away from Sonny. There are also tables outdoors. At Cosmic Ray's there are three "bays" from which you can order. You can't mix and match, you can order only what is offered at the bay in front of you. Bay 1 features chicken. Bay 2 is for burgers. At Bay 3 you'll find soups and sandwiches. There is a toppings bar that features condiments, mushrooms, sauteed onions, lettuce, tomatoes, and other items. French fries and strawberry yogurt are available at all three bays. Desserts at all bays include Triple-Chocolate Cake, Carrot Cake, and gelato. Kosher meals are available. Cosmic Ray's Starlight Cafe is open daily for lunch and dinner.

The Diamond Horseshoe
Liberty Square - $

Step back into the Not-So-Wild West at The Diamond Horseshoe. This saloon-style restaurant has two floors of indoor seating. The menu features sandwiches that probably were not found in the Wild West, with choices like Tuna Salad with Croissant, Hand-carved Pork Brisket Sandwich, and Portobello Sandwich. Sandwiches are served with your choice of potato chips or apple slices. Salads are also available. Mixed fruit or cake are sold for dessert. For your beverage you can order lemonade, a Frozen Root Beer Slush, or another hot or cold drink. The Diamond Horseshoe is open seasonally for lunch.

The Friar's Nook
Fantasyland - $

The Friar's Nook is located near The Many Adventures of Winnie the Pooh and on your way to New Fantasyland. Everything is located outdoors and you will be scrambling to find a seat. They serve hot dogs, bacon cheeseburgers with mac & cheese, and hummus with vegetables and chips. One thing that makes The Friar's Nook stand out is the fact that they make their own potato chips. The Lemon Slush tastes great on a hot Florida afternoon. Other hot and cold beverages are also available. The Friar's Nook is open seasonally for lunch.

Golden Oak Outpost
Frontierland - $

This small stand is designed to resemble a brick building from the Old West. There is outdoor seating to the side. The menu is simple and features a spicy chicken sandwich or chicken nuggets. French fries, cake, and cookies are also available. The location also sells hot and cold beverages. Golden Oak Outpost is open seasonally for lunch and dinner.

The Lunching Pad
Tomorrowland - $

If you're looking for a quick meal you might want to try The Lunching Pad. You can grab a hot dog with or without chili and onions. They're served with chips or apple slices. Mickey pretzels and sweet cream cheese pretzels are also sold. They carry several carbonated frozen beverages, as well as fountain drinks and hot choices. There is outdoor seating. The Lunching Pad is open daily for lunch and dinner.

Pecos Bill Tall Tale Inn and Cafe
Frontierland - $

Pecos Bill's is a restaurant that is designed to resemble a saloon from the Old West. The eatery is quite popular and can get busy during traditional meal hours. There is both indoor and outdoor seating available. You can use the automated system to order (it's simple), or you can place your order with a cast member. The menu features Angus burgers, a veggie burger, and a taco salad. Burgers come with your choice of corn on the cob, fries, sweet potato fries, or apple slices. There is a toppings bar with sauteed mushrooms, lettuce, pickles, tomatoes, melted cheese, salsa, condiments, and other items. Cake or strawberry yogurt are sold for dessert. Fountain drinks and hot beverages are also available. Pecos Bill Tall Tale Inn and Cafe is open daily for lunch and dinner.

Pinocchio Village Haus
Fantasyland - $

One thing that is nice about several of the Magic Kingdom restaurants is that they make you feel as if you are truly stepping into a story. Fans of the puppet who wanted to become a real boy will not be disappointed at Pinocchio Village Haus. The restaurant has a childlike charm to it. While you'll feel like you're eating in the Swiss Alps, the food served has an Italian flair. Flatbread pizzas, and a meatball or an Italian sub are available. Soups and salads are also on the menu. Dessert features cake or gelato. There is indoor seating, some of which overlooks It's a Small World, and there are outdoor tables as well. Pinocchio Village Haus is open daily for lunch and dinner.

Sleepy Hollow
Liberty Square - $

At first glance you might think that Sleepy Hollow is just another funnel cake and snack stand. You will change your mind once you realize that this is where you can find waffle sandwiches! They're available with Sweet and Spicy Chicken; Ham, Prosciutto, and Swiss; and Nutella and Fresh Fruit. You can also get waffles topped with other treats, and funnel cakes. There is a large variety of beverages, including cappuccino and other hot options, juice, milk, and fountain drinks. Sleepy Hollow is open daily for breakfast, lunch, dinner, and snacks.

Tomorrowland Terrace Restaurant
Tomorrowland - $

The view is reason alone to enjoy a meal at Tomorrowland Terrace Restaurant. The covered outdoor seating area offers spectacular views of Cinderella Castle. There are plenty of tables. Menu items change occasionally. They might include pasta, shrimp, chicken, and a Lobster Roll. There are also salads. Cake or yogurt can end your meal. You can also order fountain drinks and other beverages. Tomorrowland Terrace Restaurant is open seasonally for lunch and dinner.

Tomorrowland Terrace Restaurant is also the home of the Tomorrowland Terrace Fireworks Dessert Party. Reservations are strongly recommended for the event.

Tortuga Tavern
Adventureland - $

This restaurant is perfect for people who love anything that has to do with pirates. Formerly called El Pirata Y El Perico, Americanized Mexican food is featured. Entrees include beef, chicken, or vegetarian burritos, taco salads, and beef nachos. After you get your food, head over to the toppings bar, and add lettuce, tomatoes, cheese, salsa, and some heat if you'd like. Chocolate cake and gelato are on the dessert menu. You might want to try the Tropical Fruit Slush to quench your thirst. Other hot and cold beverages are also sold. There is indoor and covered outdoor seating. Tortuga Tavern is open seasonally for lunch.

TWENTY-SEVEN

SNACKS AND BEVERAGES AT THE MAGIC KINGDOM

Snacks

Aloha Isle
Adventureland - $

There are two words that make this snack counter popular: Dole Whip. It's a soft frozen pineapple treat that is lactose and gluten-free, and is also vegan. It is lower in calories than most snacks that you'll find at Walt Disney World, and it is perfect for a hot day. Aloha Isle always has Dole Whip on the regular menu. The refreshing treat is available in pineapple, orange, vanilla, or twist. (Only the fruit flavors are lactose free and vegan.) You can also get it as a float. Coke or root beer floats are also sold at Aloha Isle, as well as

pineapple spears and chips. Hot and cold beverages, including juice, are also available.

Auntie Gravity's Galactic Goodies
Tomorrowland - $

This snack option is located on the edge of Tomorrowland and Fantasyland. Soft serve ice cream is featured. You can get chocolate, vanilla, or swirl in a cone, cup, sundae, or float. Cereal, muffins, and fruit are also sold. If you'd prefer, you can grab a smoothie- there are several flavors available. Flavored iced coffees are also sold, as are other cold drinks and hot beverages.

Cheshire Cafe
Fantasyland - $

Muffins and whole fruit make a great quick snack, and you can pick those up here. Cereal with milk is also sold. There are some great beverages available, including slushes and iced coffee. Hot and fountain drinks are also on the menu.

Churros Stand
Frontierland - $

A churro is a long, thin, Spanish doughnut. Churros have quickly become a theme park favorite. If you want to try this delicious treat, stop by Frontierland. This cart sells churros, Mickey Pretzels, and dips. Bottled cold beverages are also available.

Cool Ship
Tomorrowland - $

The misters at Cool Ship will help you to get your temperature down on a hot day. While you enjoy the mist, order a Mickey Pretzel. Fountain beverages and bottled water are also sold.

Egg Roll Stand
Adventureland - $

One thing that is nice about Walt Disney World is that you can find snacks that are not traditional theme park choices. You can pick up a pork and shrimp egg roll or a vegetable version in Adventureland. This snack cart also sells corn dogs and bottled beverages.

Gaston's Tavern
Fantasyland - $

When Main Street Bakery was converted into a Starbucks, many people feared that the Warm Cinnamon Rolls with the gooey icing were a thing of the past. They aren't gone, they've just moved to New Fantasyland in the back of the park. Gaston's Tavern has the rolls, chocolate croissants, fruit, hummus with chips, and other items. The restaurant's signature beverage is LeFou's Brew. Other hot and cold beverages are also sold. If you're lucky, you just might catch the big guy himself near the fountain with his statue.

Liberty Square Market
Liberty Square - $

Few things are more refreshing than cold watermelon on a hot day. You can pick some up here. Liberty Square Market has other healthy choices, including grapes, whole fruit, pickles, and trail mix. Cookies and chips are also sold. Bottled drinks are available as well.

Maurice's Amazing Popping Machine
Fantasyland - $

You won't be surprised to learn that Maurice's Amazing Popping Machine sells popcorn, but you might be surprised to learn that this cart is a great place to get your Mickey bar or other ice cream treat. Bottled beverages are also sold. Maurice's Amazing Popping Machine is located in Enchanted Forest.

Plaza Ice Cream Parlor
Main Street, U.S.A. - $

If you've ever wondered what an ice cream parlor of yesteryear looked like, you won't have to wonder any longer. Plaza Ice Cream Parlor is truly nostalgic. They take their ice cream seriously. It is hand scooped and available in a cup or cone. You can also get a sundae or a float. If you don't eat dairy, ask for Rice Dream or Tofutti. Fat-free and no-sugar-added options are also available.

Prince Eric's Village Market
Fantasyland - $

There are some great snack options that have opened in New Fantasyland. Prince Eric's Village Market features healthy choices. You can enjoy fresh fruit, trail mix, or hummus and chips. If you need to cool off try shaved ice in your choice of several flavors. Honest Tea, Fuze, and other cold beverages are available as well.

Sleepy Hollow
Liberty Square - $

There are some delicious sweet treats available here. You can get funnel cake, with or without strawberries and whipped cream. They also sell waffles, including waffle sandwiches. Sleepy Hollow carries ice cream, as well as hot and cold beverages.

Storybook Treats
Fantasyland - $

While Storybook Treats sounds like it might be located in Storybook Circus, it's actually located in the original Fantasyland. It used to be called Mrs. Pott's Cupboard. You can find soft serve ice cream here available in a dish, cone, or a sundae creation. You can also get a float or a milkshake. Hot and cold beverages are also available.

Sunshine Tree Terrace
Adventureland - $

Soft serve ice cream, chips, and cookies make up the snack options here. Try the Citrus Swirl, it's a combination of vanilla ice cream and orange slush. Sunshine Tree Terrace is located near the Enchanted Tiki Room. There are more flavors of slushes and other hot and cold beverages for sale here as well.

Turkey Legs
Frontierland - $

For some people a jumbo turkey leg is the perfect snack, others make a meal out of one. You can find them at this cart in Frontierland. Chips and cookies are also sold here, as well as bottled cold drinks.

Westwood Ho
Frontierland - $

Westwood Ho might look like a log cabin, but it is really a snack and beverage stand. You can pick up a corn dog or chips here. You can also get frozen lemonade, fountain drinks, Honest Tea or Honest Ade, or hot beverages at this location.

Beverages

Auntie Gravity's Galactic Goodies
Tomorrowland - $

There is a lot to like at Auntie Gravity's if you need to cool off. Not only do they have soft serve ice cream and a few breakfast items, they also have some delicious cold beverages. You can enjoy a smoothie or an iced coffee float. Mocha and latte iced coffees are also served, as are hot beverages and fountain drinks.

Cheshire Cafe
Fantasyland - $

This option has some nice cold beverage choices for a hot day. Try a slush or a flavored iced coffee. Lemonade, juice, and other hot and cold drinks are sold here as well. There is also a limited selection of breakfast items.

Gaston's Tavern
Fantasyland - $

The name of the game here is LeFou's Brew. The tavern's signature beverage is made of frozen apple juice and toasted marshmallow, with a passion fruit and mango foam. It is available in a souvenir cup if you want. You can also get hot and cold drinks, as well as snack items.

The Lunching Pad
Tomorrowland - $

If you like frozen carbonated beverages, you'll want to stop by The Lunching Pad. There are several choices featuring fruit flavors or Coke. You can also quench your thirst with a fountain drink or another cold beverage. Snack items are for sale as well.

Main Street Bakery
Main Street, U.S.A. - $

If you are familiar with Starbucks, you'll know what to expect at Main Street Bakery. The location carries all of your favorite coffees, teas, and re-freshers. Seasonal beverages are sold as well. Even though Starbucks coffee is featured, the location still has the same charm as the original Main Street Bakery. You can also order pastries and Artisan breakfast sandwiches.

Prince Eric's Village Market
Fantasyland - $

This location sells healthy snacks and beverages. Fresh fruit is available, as well as shaved ice, which is almost like a beverage. You can also buy Honest Tea and Honest Ade, Fuze, V8 and other juices, lemonade, and bottled water.

Sleepy Hollow
Liberty Square - $

While waffle sandwiches and funnel cakes are featured here, there are some good beverage choices as well. You can grab your morning cappuccino or espresso. French vanilla iced coffee and the Liberty Swirl Slush (made with strawberry and blue raspberry Fanta) are also available. Other hot and cold beverages are on the menu as well.

Storybook Treats
Fantasyland - $

You might think that Storybook Treats is a great place to get a soft serve ice cream sundae. It is, and it is also a great place to get a milkshake or a float. Fountain drinks and hot beverages are also sold.

Sunshine Tree Terrace
Adventureland - $

Here you can get coffee, floats, and All Natural Lemonade topped with Wild Berry Foam. There are different types of slushes, iced coffee, hot coffees, and other hot and cold beverages. You can also purchase the classic Orange Bird Souvenir Cup and fill it with the beverage of your choice. Ice cream (including Citrus Swirl), chips, and cookies are also sold.

Westwood Ho
Frontierland - $

This is another great place to grab a quick drink in a hurry. You can cool off with a lemonade slush, or try an Honest Tea or Honest Ade. Fountain beverages and water are available, and if you're hungry as well as thirsty, order a corn dog and chips.

TWENTY-EIGHT

A BRIEF INTRODUCTION TO EPCOT

The second theme park to join Walt Disney World was Epcot, which opened on October 1, 1982. Spaceship Earth is the park's main icon. The "giant golf ball" is more than just a focal piece, it contains a ride that allows guests to go back in time through the history of communications.

Epcot is broken up into two main sections: Future World and World Showcase. Those areas are then divided even further. In Future World you can blast off to Mars, design and then ride in a concept car, or go on a hang gliding adventure. World Showcase features eleven pavilions that represent different countries from around the globe. You can experience their cultures, shop for souvenirs that represent each country, and try food from around the world. Several of the attractions at Epcot are educational. That does not mean that the kids will want to stay away! Disney allows them to have fun while they learn something. End your day with IllumiNations: Reflections of Earth. The show features fireworks, lasers, and special effects, all set to music.

There are two annual special events that are held at Epcot. The Epcot International Flower & Garden Festival takes place throughout the park. You'll see topiaries of some of your favorite Disney characters, enjoy celebrity workshops, and dance to the sounds of some of the top musical acts of the 60's through the 80's with the Flower Power Concert Series. The Epcot International Flower & Garden Festival starts in early March and runs daily until mid-May.

The second special event held annually is the Epcot International Food & Wine Festival. It runs mid-September through mid-November. Those of age can sample wine and other drinks from around the world, and everyone can taste foods that are not normally sold in the park. There are plenty of special presentations and meals with celebrity chefs throughout the event, and guests can enjoy the Eat to the Beat Concert Series. Both special events are included in park admission, but some activities at the festivals cost extra.

TWENTY-NINE

FULL SERVICE AND CHARACTER DINING AT EPCOT

Full Service Dining

Chefs de France
World Showcase, France - $$

If you want to feel like you stepped out of a theme park and into a brasserie in Paris, you will want to check out Chefs de France. This popular restaurant is great for couples looking for romance, but it is also family friendly. The restaurant was founded by celebrity chefs Paul Bocuse, Gaston Lenotre, and Roger Verge. Large windows allow for a great view and a lot of natural light during the day. There are pictures of the founders near the entrance and colorful paintings on the ceiling.

The menu at Chefs de France is fresh and simple. It will change from time to time, based on what is in season. Start your meal with escargot, French onion soup, or a cheese platter. Entrees include chicken, duck, beef, and a macaroni and cheese dish with a French twist. Finish you meal with creme brulee or fresh sorbet. There is an extensive wine menu (you are, after all, dining in France) and other alcoholic and non-alcoholic beverages are available as well. Chefs de France is open daily for lunch and dinner.

Coral Reef Restaurant
Future World West - $$

BEST TIP

The ambiance at Coral Reef Restaurant is a lot of fun. It gives the illusion that you are under water. There is a living coral reef on one wall. When you enter you will be given a list of fish and other sea creatures to look for in the tank, there are more than 85 species. Ask for a table close to the aquarium when you check-in for your reservation.

Coral Reef Restaurant is primarily a seafood place, but they do have other options. You can order an Appetizer for Two and try several different creations, or be daring and start your meal with the Charbroiled Octopus. Seafood entrees include lobster, salmon, shrimp, and mahi mahi. If you're not in the mood for seafood you can order beef, chicken, or a vegetarian dish. Try The Chocolate Wave or Coconut-Mango Chiffon Cake for dessert. There are sparkling or white wines and specialty cocktails, as well as other beverages. Coral Reef Restaurant is open daily for lunch and dinner.

La Hacienda de San Angel
World Showcase, Mexico - $$

La Hacienda de San Angel serves fresh Mexican food, not the Americanized version that some have grown to expect at a Mexican restaurant. Sometimes the restaurant looks closed when it is really open, so if you're not sure, ask someone.

Fresh is the word to describe the food. The corn tortillas are made in-house daily and there are several different salsa options to start off your meal. Entrees include pork loin, shrimp, New York Strip, and chicken dishes. They come with corn tortillas and rice. Desserts include Tamal de Dulce and Mexican Ice Cream. For those 21 and older there are specialty margaritas and a large selection of tequila. Other drinks are also available. La Hacienda de San Angel is open daily for dinner.

Le Cellier Steakhouse
World Showcase, Canada - $$$ FAN PICK

Le Cellier Steakhouse can be one of the harder to get reservations at Walt Disney World. This signature restaurant is designed to resemble a wine cellar. It is underground, which means that there are no windows. The space is intimate, with stone arches and subtle lighting. Vintage bottles of wine serve as a decoration.

If you are a steak lover, you will want to visit Le Cellier. It is one the best steakhouses that you will find at Walt Disney World. The extensive list of appetizers includes Canadian Cheddar Cheese Soup, Seared Scallops, and an artisanal cheese platter. You might also want to try the poutine, there are three different varieties and the dish is more than just French fries. If you're not in the mood for steak you can order venison, a veal chop, or the Roasted Forest Mushrooms. Save room for dessert! Maple Creme Brulee and Meyer Lemon Curd Torte are just two of the choices. Since Le Cellier is a wine cellar, you will be able to find the perfect wine to accompany your meal. Other alcoholic and non-alcoholic drinks are also available. Le Cellier is open daily for lunch and dinner.

Monsieur Paul
World Showcase, France - $$$

In 2012, Bistro de Paris closed. The restaurant reopened in 2013 with a new name, Monsieur Paul. The Paul in the name is Paul Bocuse, who is one of the most famous French chefs of all time. (He is also one of the chefs who founded Chefs de France.) Monsieur Paul can be hard to find, the entrance is behind Chefs de France. There is an elevator to this second floor eatery, but if you want you can take the stairs. The wall is filled with pictures from the chef's much celebrated career. The dining area is elegant, with chandeliers, candles, and bold colors. The view of World Showcase is spectacular.

It is the menu that sets Monsieur Paul apart. You can order from the Prix Fixe menu or a la carte. The menu is in French with English translations underneath. Entrees include range-free chicken, roasted duck breast, and red snapper. Vegetarians, there may be no meatless entrees on the menu so be sure to ask your server before you order. There are several desserts with a French twist to them. There is an extensive wine list, and other beverages are also available. Monsieur Paul is open daily for dinner.

Nine Dragons Restaurant
World Showcase, China - $$

Quite simply, Nine Dragons Restaurant's interior is stunning. It is more than your average strip mall Chinese restaurant. The details are amazing. You'll want to take a good look at the glass mural that features two dragons. The intricate woodwork is also something that you should notice. There is a display of glass Chinese artwork, ask a cast member to explain the meanings behind the items. The restaurant is lit with Chinese lanterns. Ask for a table by a window to enjoy a nice view of World Showcase.

The menu at Nine Dragons combines Cantonese, Hunan, Kiangche Mongolian, and Szechuan specialties. You can start with egg rolls, pot stickers, or an appetizer trio. For your entree try Kung Pao Chicken, Canton Pepper Beef, or Vegetable and Tofu Stir-Fry. You'll find all of your favorite Chinese dishes available, and a few that you may not be as familiar with. Chinese Ginger Cake makes a great dessert. If you're over 21 you might want to try a specialty cocktail or frozen daiquiri. Red, white, sweet, and sparkling wines are sold, as well as non-alcoholic specialty drinks and other beverages. Nine Dragons is open daily for lunch and dinner.

Restaurant Marrakesh
World Showcase, Morocco - $$

If you've ever wanted to dine inside a palace, you need to try Restaurant Marrakesh. The building looks a bit plain on the outside, but inside it is gorgeous. You'll feel like you're a personal guest of the

King of Morocco. Every inch of the restaurant's interior is decorated, you'll even want to take a look at the ceiling. From time to time the diners will be entertained by Moroccan musicians. After they play a song or two, a belly dancer will perform. It's tastefully done and she might invite the children to join her so that she can teach them a few moves.

If you're not familiar with Moroccan food, you might want to ask your server for recommendations. You'll find several couscous dishes (couscous is a pasta, not a grain), Shish Kebab, chicken, and lamb. If you're not sure what to order you might want to try the Sultan Sampler or the Taste of Morocco - Berber Feast. Desserts include Bastilla (a flaky pastry dish) and a baklava assortment. There are specialty drinks and Moroccan beer available, as well as other beverages. Restaurant Marrakesh is open daily for lunch and dinner.

Rose & Crown Pub & Dining Room
World Showcase, United Kingdom - $$

A friendly, relaxed British pub is the best way to describe this restaurant. The pub is in the front and the restaurant is in the back. There is both indoor and outdoor seating. If you time your reservation correctly, you might have a great seat for IllumiNations. When you check in, let the cast member know that you would like a table where you can see the nightly show. There may not be one available, those tables are coveted.

The menu features British standards and comfort foods. You'll find Fish and Chips, Corned Beef and Cabbage, Grilled New York Strip Steak, and Vegetable Curry. As you would expect at a pub there are plenty of choices for ales, lagers, and stouts. You can also order Scotch flights or pours. There are specialty cocktails like Leaping Leprechaun as well. Non-alcoholic beverages are also available. Even though there is a pub atmosphere, the restaurant is family friendly. Rose & Crown Pub & Dining Room is open daily for lunch and dinner.

San Angel Inn Restaurante
World Showcase, Mexico - $$

The theme of San Angel Inn Restaurante is unique. Although it is an indoor restaurant, you will feel like you are dining outside in the evening. Where else can you eat with a Mayan pyramid in the background? When you check in, ask for a table near the river. You'll be less crowded (the tables are close together) and you'll be able to watch the boats for the Gran Fiesta Tour Starring The Three Caballeros as they float by.

San Angel Inn Restaurante serves authentic Mexican food, not the Tex-Mex food that is made in so many restaurants. You'll find chicken, fish, pork, and New York strip, served in traditional Mexican dishes. If you're not sure what you want to order, consider the Traditional Prix-Fixe Mexican lunch or dinner. Desserts include Helado de Dulce de Leche and Crema Bavaria. Mexican wines, beers, margaritas, and tequilas are available for those 21 and up. San Angel Inn Restaurante is open daily for lunch and dinner.

Spice Road Table
World Showcase, Morocco - $

In January of 2014, Spice Road Table opened. It is a tapas restaurant, featuring small plates so you can try plenty of different dishes. The atmosphere is relaxed, with shelves filled with knickknacks that you would expect to find in Morocco. There is both indoor and outdoor seating. The outdoor seating area overlooks World Showcase Lagoon, creating coveted spots to watch IllumiNations. Reservations are not accepted.

The menu features items like Lamb Slider, Rice Stuffed Grape Leaves, and Moroccan Merguez Sausage. If you're not sure what to try, order a sampler. For dessert you can try chef created ice cream or maybe you'd prefer the Almond and Rosewater Cake. Spice Road Table also has a large selection of Mediterranean beers, specialty drinks, and wines.

Other hot and cold beverages are also available. Spice Road Table is open daily for lunch and dinner.

Teppan Edo
World Showcase, Japan - $$

Teppan Edo is more than just food. It is part performance, with the chefs creating your meals right before your eyes. There are several small dining rooms and guests might share a table with another party. Each table seats up to eight people. The cook top is in the center on one side of the table.

The menu at Teppan Edo features all of your favorite Japanese dishes. You can pick a meat and vegetable and it will be prepared right in front of you. Entrees come with a side of rice and udon noodles. If you're in the mood for sushi you can get that at Teppan Edo as well. The classic Chocolate Ginger Cake offers the perfect ending to your meal. For a beverage you can order sake, Japanese beer, wine, or a cocktail. Other beverages are also sold. Teppan Edo is open daily for lunch and dinner.

Tokyo Dining
World Showcase, Japan - $$

Tokyo Dining and Teppan Edo share a waiting area. While some of the menu items may be the same, they are two very different restaurants. Tokyo Dining has a contemporary feel to it. You can watch the sushi chefs work, or enjoy the view of World Showcase out the windows.

The menu has plenty of sushi options. Tempura is also a possibility. You could instead order something from the Japanese-style Grill. The Green Tea Pudding makes a great dessert. Enjoy a Japanese beer, sake, or a sake cocktail, or try a different beverage. Tokyo Dining is open daily for lunch and dinner.

Tutto Gusto Wine Cellar
World Showcase, Italy - $$

Quaint is the perfect word to describe this location. Reservations are not accepted and there is not a lot of seating available. If you plan to stop by you might want to try it at an off-time. The lighting is low and the setting is best described as intimate.

While Tutto Gusto Wine Cellar is more for drinks than it is for a meal, there are some filling food items available here. You can order a panini or an Italian specialty such as ravioli or meatballs parmigiana. You can also find luscious desserts such as Cannoli and Nutella Chocolate Cake. Of course the wine is the real star here, with over 200 different bottles to choose from. If you're not sure where to start, you might want to order a flight. There are also cocktails and other beverage choices. Tutto Gusto Wine Cellar is open daily for lunch and dinner.

Tutto Italia Ristorante
World Showcase, Italy - $$

Tutto Italia Ristorante serves delicious Italian favorites in an atmosphere that might make you forget you're in a theme park for a little while. Chandeliers hang from the paneled ceiling, and there are murals on the walls. The waitstaff is dressed as you'd expect in a five star restaurant, but don't worry, there is no dress code.

The menu at Tutto Italia Ristorante is quite extensive. You can start your meal with a Caesar salad, minestrone soup, or antipasto. There are so many great appetizers that you'll have a hard time deciding. The tough choices continue with the entrees. You'll find fettuccine, lasagna, gnocchetti, ravioli, spaghetti, and many other incredible choices. Cannoli, tiramisu, and gelati are just three of the desserts. There are several specialty cocktails offered, as well as beer, wine, and other beverages. Tutto Italia Ristorante is open daily for lunch and dinner.

Via Napoli Ristorante e Pizzeria
World Showcase, Italy - $$

The first thing that you'll notice about Via Napoli Ristorante e Pizzeria is the size. The eating area is huge. There are high arched ceilings and murals on the walls. The large windows allow plenty of light to pour in if you eat at the right time. There is a long table in the center of the room, which allows guests to be seated with other parties. If this is something that you are not comfortable with, ask to be seated at one of the smaller tables. You can see the pizza ovens and the chefs working on their creations. The ovens are named after Italy's three active volcanoes.

The star at Via Napoli Ristorante e Pizzeria is the food. They serve arguably the best pizza at Walt Disney World. Don't jump right to the pizza and forget to check out the appetizers. Start with Mozzarella Caprese, Calamari Fritti, or a bowl of authentic Italian Minestrone. Then get ready for the pizza. You can order individual, large (serves 2-3), or Mezzo Metro (serves 3-5). You can build your own or try a signature pie. The pizza is so authentic that the restaurant uses flour imported from Southern Italy. If you're in the mood for something else, Via Napoli also serves classics like Lasagna Verde and Linguini alla Scoglio. Try to save room for dessert. Selections include Tiramisu and several Gelato options. Those 21 and older can try La Rossa, which is an Italian lager. Other Italian beers and wines, as well as specialty cocktails are also served. Non-alcoholic fruit juice coolers and other beverages are available as well. Via Napoli Ristorante e Pizzeria is open daily for lunch and dinner.

Character and Buffet Dining

Akershus Royal Banquet Hall
World Showcase, Norway - $$$

Akershus Royal Banquet Hall is a great alternative to Cinderella's Royal Table at the Magic Kingdom. It's an easier to get reservation and it only requires one credit on the Disney Dining Plan. You'll still feel like you're dining in a castle and you'll still get to meet princesses. Akershus Royal Banquet Hall may feature Snow White, Cinderella, Belle, Mulan, Aurora, Jasmine, Ariel, or Mary Poppins. It is "Princess Storybook Dining" at its finest. The high ceilings, arches, and elegant details will make you feel like you are inside a castle. A complimentary imaging package is included.

The food at Akershus Royal Banquet Hall is served buffet style. For breakfast you'll find the normal buffet choices of breakfast meats, potatoes, and baked goods. Norwegian breakfast offerings include Smoked Salmon, Glassmeister Herring, and Jalsburg Cheese. Coffee and other beverages are available at breakfast. Lunch and dinner begin with "A Taste of Norway", an appetizer platter with meats, cheese, seafood, and salads. Entrees include pasta, beef, lamb, chicken, and Traditional Kjøttkake (Norwegian Meatballs). Dessert is served family style and includes Norwegian inspired Chocolate Mousse and Apple Cake. If you're over 21 you might want to try the Viking Coffee. Other beverages are also available. Akershus Royal Banquet Hall is open daily for breakfast, lunch, and dinner.

Biergarten Restaurant
World Showcase, Germany - $$$

In Germany they celebrate Oktoberfest for 16 days each year. At Walt Disney World, they celebrate it daily at Biergarten Restaurant. You'll feel like you are dining in the middle of a German village. The restaurant uses long tables so your party may be seated with other guests.

There is live singing and dancing to add to your dining experience. You might find yourself dancing along as well.

The food at Biergarten Restaurant is served buffet style. The buffet may contain German dishes like Bayrischer Kraut Salat, Breaded Pork Schnitzel Vienna Style, and Double-smoked Pork on Sauerkraut, as well as more familiar foods like Macaroni and Cheese. There are also scrumptious desserts, including freshly baked Apple Strudel. Those of age can choose from a selection of German beers and wines. Biergarten Restaurant is open daily for lunch and dinner.

The Garden Grill
Future World West - $$$

The Garden Grill is a character meal that has a unique feature to it. The restaurant slowly rotates while you eat. You'll pass by several different scenes, including a farmhouse and a rainforest. For the best view of the scenes, you might want to ask to be seated at a booth instead of at a table. The Garden Grill is a character meal that is hosted by Chip 'n Dale. Other characters may include Farmer Mickey and Pluto.

The food at The Garden Grill is served family style, which means that the dishes will be brought to the table and you will then serve yourselves. It is all-you-can-eat, so if there is something that you enjoy, feel free to ask for more. Sustainable Fish of the Day, Roasted All-Natural Turkey Breast, and Garden Fresh Vegetables are just some of the dishes that you will be offered. Your meal will end with Fresh-baked Harvest Skillet Cake, made with seasonal fruit. The Garden Grill is open daily for dinner.

THIRTY

QUICK SERVICE DINING AT EPCOT

Electric Umbrella
Future World East - $

At Electric Umbrella you can expect bright lights and colors. The name of the restaurant adds to the theme, with umbrella shaped lights throughout the eatery. There is plenty of both indoor and outdoor seating. The menu features standards, some with creative twists. You can order a Macaroni and Cheese Burger, a Meatball Sub, or a Vegetarian Flatbread. Other entrees are also available. Cheesecake and brownies are among the dessert options. The restaurant sells beer and hot and cold beverages. Electric Umbrella is open daily for lunch and dinner.

Katsura Grill
World Showcase, Japan - $

A day at Epcot can be exhausting. If you need a retreat while you enjoy your meal, you might want to check out Katsura Grill. The location is beautiful and is as tranquil as you can get in a theme park. There is indoor seating, but if it's a nice day you might want to grab an outdoor table instead. Katsura Grill offers sushi, udon, teriyaki, and other Japanese favorites. Those of age can order sake, plum wine, or Kirin Draft Beer. Tea and other beverages are available as well. Katsura Grill is open daily for lunch and dinner.

La Cantina de San Angel
World Showcase, Mexico - $

The location of this Mexican restaurant is beautiful. You can sit and stare at the water, or you can watch as people walk by the Mayan pyramid. All of your Mexican favorites are on the menu: tacos, empanadas, nachos, and Mexican sandwiches are some of the choices. For dessert you might want to grab a churro or a frozen fruit treat. La Cantina de San Angel has some great choices for the 21 and up crowd, including frozen margaritas. Other beverages are also available. There is covered seating outside of the restaurant and it can get crowded. La Cantina de San Angel is open daily for lunch and dinner.

Les Halles Boulangerie & Patisserie
World Showcase, France - $

There are plenty of delicious sandwich options with a French flair at this eatery. You can start your meal with a bowl of soup or a salad. From there you can order half a baguette, a cheese plate, or try a sandwich. Some of the creative choices include Brie Aux Pommes (brie cheese with cranberries and apples) and Poulet au Pistou (chicken breast with cheese, onion, tomato, and pesto). Save room for dessert! With chocolate tarts, eclairs, and Napoleons on the menu, you'll have a hard time deciding which one to try. At Les Halles Boulangerie & Patisserie you'll find wine and other alcoholic choices, as well as your favorite coffee creation and other hot and cold drinks. Les Halles Boulangerie & Patisserie is open daily for lunch and dinner.

Liberty Inn
World Showcase, The American Adventure - $

Take a trip back in time at this colonial themed restaurant. The atmosphere will make you feel as if you've stepped into an American history book. Brick walls, simple designs, and cast member costumes all help to create the mood. While the theme may take you back to the American Revolution, the food won't. You'll find theme park staples like burgers and chicken nuggets, along with New York Strip. If you follow a kosher diet, this is where you will want to eat. Don't forget to end your meal with apple pie! You can enjoy a Samuel Adams or another type of ale. Other drinks are sold as well. There is plenty of indoor and outdoor seating. If you time your meal correctly you might be able to enjoy The Spirit of America Fife and Drum Corps, or any entertainment taking place in the America Gardens Theater. Liberty Inn is open daily for lunch and dinner.

Lotus Blossom Cafe
World Showcase, China - $

If you are in the mood for Chinese standards, then Lotus Blossom Cafe might be the restaurant for you. The decor is simple, yet elegant. There is limited outdoor covered seating, and some tables have a nice view of the Japan pavilion. The menu features classic dishes such as Shrimp Fried Rice with Egg Roll, Hong Kong Style Vegetable Curry over Rice, and Orange Chicken. Those of age can sip a glass of plum wine or enjoy a draft beer. There are also smoothies for all ages, as well as tea and other beverages. Lotus Blossom Cafe is open daily for lunch and dinner.

Refreshment Port
Showcase Plaza - $

If you're looking for Refreshment Port, head toward Canada. That is the closest country to this quick service option. While Refreshment

Port sells mostly snacks, you can also grab chicken nuggets for a quick meal here. Snack items include soft serve ice cream and croissant donuts. There are specialty coffee drinks with alcohol, and other hot and cold beverages. There is no seating. Refreshment Port is open daily for lunch and dinner.

Sommerfest
World Showcase, Germany - $

This popular outdoor eatery works hard to transport you to Germany. The walls in the area are painted to look like a German village. There is limited outdoor seating and the tables fill up quickly. The food at Sommerfest includes the German classics Frankfurters and Bratwurst, plus a German meatloaf sandwich. Don't forget the sides! The Nudel Gratin is more than just macaroni and cheese. With Apple Strudel and Black Forest Cake on the dessert menu, you will want to save room for something sweet at the end of your meal. German beer, schnapps, and wine are sold, as well as other alcoholic and non-alcoholic beverages. Sommerfest is open daily for lunch and dinner.

Sunshine Seasons
Future World West - $

If you take the Living with the Land boat ride at Epcot, you will have a peak inside the greenhouses at the park. Some of that food ends up being served at Sunshine Seasons. There are four different stations to order from. You can't mix and match stations, rather everything must be ordered from the same line. If you're at the restaurant for breakfast you can order eggs, bacon, French toast, or a breakfast panini, among other choices. For lunch and dinner at the Asian Wok Shop you'll find stir fry and noodle bowls. The Sandwich Shop & Bakery features fresh sandwiches on Artisan breads. At the Wood-Fired Grill Shop you can order rotisserie chicken, fresh fish, and other items. The final station is the Soup & Salad Shop. There are also Grab & Go bakery items. Hot and cold beverages are served, and there is plenty of indoor seating. Sunshine Seasons is open daily for breakfast, lunch, and dinner.

Tangierine Cafe
World Showcase Morocco - $

There is a simple beauty at Tangierine Cafe. The architecture alone is reason enough to stop by. The King of Morocco assisted in developing the entire pavilion so you know that everything is authentic as can be. The food will make you want to stay. The menu includes the Mediterranean Falafel Wrap, a Shawarma Lamb Platter, and the Moroccan Kefta Sandwich. There are pastries in a case in the back, and baklava is usually one of them. The restaurant serves draft beer and Moroccan wine by the glass. There is a non-alcoholic frozen fruit beverage on the menu, as well as other hot and cold beverages. There is plenty of indoor and outdoor seating. Tangierine Cafe is open daily for lunch and dinner.

Yorkshire County Fish Shop
World Showcase, United Kingdom - $

If you want fish and chips, stop by Yorkshire County Fish Shop. You can get two strips of fresh fish, served with authentic British chips. You might also want to try an English Bay Sugar Cookie. Those of age can buy ale or lager. Other beverages are also available. There is outdoor seating in the area. Yorkshire County Fish Shop is open daily for lunch and dinner.

THIRTY-ONE

SNACKS AND BEVERAGES AT EPCOT

Snacks

Crepes de Chefs de France
World Showcase, France - $

Located near Les Chefs de France you'll find a hidden gem. This kiosk sells different types of sweet crepes and soft serve ice cream. You can also get your coffee fix, French beer, or another cold drink.

Fife & Drum Tavern
World Showcase, The American Adventure - $

Despite the name, Fife & Drum Tavern is not a tavern. It is instead a snack stand where you can buy turkey legs, popcorn, pretzels, and soft serve ice cream. The kiosk also sells slushes and other cold beverages. Beer and wine are sold as well.

Funnel Cake
World Showcase, The American Adventure - $

Funnel cakes and theme parks are a perfect combination. At this stand you can get your funnel cake; add apples, chocolate sauce, or ice cream if you so desire. Pumpkin Spice Funnel Cake might be available. Pick up a funnel cake kit to take home. Bottled water is also sold.

Gelati
World Showcase, Italy - $

Gelato is the Italian word for ice cream. You can get two scoops of this delicious treat in a cone or a cup. Also on the menu are gelato creations, featuring cookies, strawberries, or espresso. Other desserts are also sold. If you're over 21, you might want to try a frozen Italian Margarita or the Primavera. Wine, beer, coffee, and other beverages are available as well.

Kabuki Cafe
World Showcase, Japan - $

Kakigori is a frozen Japanese treat that is made with shaved ice and fruit toppings. You can find it at Kabuki Cafe. They also sell sushi and edamame. Beer, plum wine, and sake are sold, as are non-alcoholic hot and cold beverages, including the Japanese soda Ramune.

Kringla Bakeri Og Kafe
World Showcase, Norway - $ FAN PICK

Pastries and other sweet items make great snacks, and you can find some delicious choices at Kringla Bakeri Og Kafe. For something a little bit different try the Lefse. It's potato bread served with cinnamon butter. If you want something a little more familiar, grab a sweet pretzel with almonds or chocolate. There are so many incredible choices that you might want to order several pastries and share. Sandwiches are also sold. Beverages range from orange juice to milk to Viking Coffee. There are other alcoholic and non-alcoholic beverages available as well.

L'Artisan des Glaces
World Showcase, France - $

This small shop is hard to find but well worth the effort. It features hand-crafted ice cream and sorbets. There are ten ice cream flavors to choose from and six types of sorbet. The ice cream is softer than most hand-scooped ice cream. You can buy it in a cone or a dish, or you might want to try it in an ice cream sandwich. There is also an Ice Cream Martini for those of age. It is served in a martini glass.

Popcorn in Canada
World Showcase, Canada - $

The name pretty much says it all. Popcorn is sold (in a souvenir bucket if you'd like). Beer, wine, a North Bay Smoothie and other beverages are also available.

Promenade Refreshments
Showcase Plaza - $

This snack stand sells pretzels and cheese sauce, popcorn, and soft serve ice cream. If you're really hungry you might want to order a hot dog and chips. Floats and frozen drinks are also available, as are beer and other cold beverages. The menu at Promenade Refreshments might change seasonally.

Refreshment Cool Post
World Showcase, Outpost - $

On your Epcot map between China and Germany, you'll see an area listed as "Outpost". The spot has an African theme, and it is where you will find Refreshment Cool Post. The kids will want to play on the nearby drums as you order. The menu changes seasonally and may include soft serve ice cream, chips, hot dogs, and other snack items. There are Phineas and Ferb offerings like The Doofenslurper for the little ones. Slushes, beer, and other hot and cold beverages are also available.

Refreshment Port
Showcase Plaza - $

If you've heard about the Croissant Doughnut and know that you have to try it, you'll want to stop by Refreshment Port. They also have soft serve ice cream and chicken nuggets. There are hot specialty alcoholic beverages served here, as well as coffee, tea, and cold fountain drinks.

Beverages

Block & Hans
World Showcase, The American Adventure - $

If you think that pretzels and beer go together, then you'll want to check out Block & Hans. In addition to Mickey and other pretzels, this kiosk features craft beers and bottled water.

Club Cool
Future World West – free, $

Club Cool is a great place to stop by on a hot day. You can cool off in the AC and enjoy free Coca-Cola products from around the world. There are eight different choices, and someone in your party will need to try Beverly. The cups are small and you will not be allowed to fill up your empty drink bottle. Coke memorabilia and frozen Coke are offered for sale.

Espresso Coffee and Pastries
Showcase Plaza and other locations - $

There are several locations in World Showcase where you can order your favorite coffee creation. Specialty cocktails are also sold. Grab a pastry as well to compliment your beverage.

Fountain View
Future World West - $

If you can't get by without your daily Starbucks fix, you'll want to head to Fountain View. They carry all of your favorites. Order a Caramel Frappuccino, a White Chocolate Mocha, or a Cinnamon Dolce Latte. Dozens of drinks are available. Pastries and a few sandwiches are sold as well.

Joy of Tea
World Showcase, China - $

Tea makes good Chinese food taste even better. You can get both at Joy of Tea. The stand has a few food options and several beverage choices. You can try hot tea, cold tea, or a tea slush. There are also specialty drinks, some of which contain tea. Other beverages are available as well.

La Cava del Tequila
World Showcase, Mexico - $

Did you ever think that a theme park would have a lounge that serves over 100 different types of tequila? If you're not sure which one to try, you might want to order a flight. Specialty cocktails and other beverages are also sold. You can order chips with guacamole or salsa as a side if you'd like.

Les Vins de Chefs de France
World Showcase, France - $

Order wine by the glass here. Regional wines and champagne are featured. There are also specialty cocktails and French beer.

Margarita Stand
World Showcase, Mexico - $

You'll find frozen and unique margaritas at this stand. Tequila, beer, and other beverages are also available.

Morocco Coffee & Pastries
World Showcase, Morocco - $

There are some unique coffee choices here, and some with alcohol added. Specialty cocktails with a Moroccan flair are also sold. Non-alcoholic choices include Moroccan Mint Tea and Moorish, which is espresso with cinnamon and nutmeg added. There are other hot and cold beverages available, as well as delicious pastries.

Test Track Cool Wash
Future World East - $

Look behind the misters near the Test Track exit and you'll find this quick option. Frozen Coca-Cola and Raspberry Lemonade are sold. You can also buy bottled cold beverages and chips. Test Track Cool Wash is hard to miss, but you might not realize that beverages are sold here unless you get close.

Tutto Gusto Wine Cellar
World Showcase, Italy - $$

If you stop at Tutto Gusto Wine Cellar, you may never want to leave. Over 200 different types of wine are sold. Cocktails, draft beer, and appetizers are available as well.

UK Beer Cart
World Showcase, United Kingdom - $

Cool down on a hot day with a pint. You can order ale or cider here. If you'd like, you can get it in a souvenir stein.

THIRTY-TWO

A BRIEF INTRODUCTION TO DISNEY'S HOLLYWOOD STUDIOS

The smallest of the four Walt Disney World theme parks is Disney's Hollywood Studios. It opened on May 1, 1989 as Disney-MGM Studios, the name was changed in 2008. It celebrates the Golden Age of Hollywood. Rumors abound about changes that may be coming to the park, but so far nothing official has been announced by Disney. The park's main icon is the Sorcerer Hat, which is based on a segment from the 1940 film *Fantasia*. There is a gift shop located under the Hat.

What Disney's Hollywood Studios lacks in size, it makes up for in punch. The park is home to two of the most famous Walt Disney World thrill rides: Rock 'n' Roller Coaster Starring Aerosmith and The Twilight Zone Tower of Terror. There is plenty for the under 40 inch crowd to do as well. The lines for Toy Story Midway Mania! grow long early in the day; it is one of the most popular family rides at Walt Disney World. Disney's Hollywood Studios is where you can see some of the best live shows in any of the parks and learn a few of the behind-the-scenes tricks that are used to create movie magic. Dining choices at Disney's Hollywood Studios range from classy to whimsical. Some of the most creatively themed restaurants can be found in the park. You'll want to end your evening with Fantasmic!, a live show that features actors, fireworks, and water projection screens. Seating goes fast, so grab a spot early.

Each May and June, Disney's Hollywood Studios hosts the annual Star Wars Weekends. Guests can meet celebrities from the films, take pictures with Star Wars characters, and ride Star Tours - The Adventures Continue. There are bonus live shows, a daily parade, and fireworks to end the day. Most events for Star Wars Weekends are included in park admission.

THIRTY-THREE

FULL SERVICE AND CHARACTER DINING AT DISNEY'S HOLLYWOOD STUDIOS

Full Service Dining

50's Prime Time Cafe
Echo Lake - $$

FAN PICK

50's Prime Time Cafe is one of the most creatively themed restaurants at Walt Disney World. It is made to look like an old-fashioned kitchen, the type that you might see on a 1950's TV sitcom. There are black and white televisions throughout the restaurant where clips from TV shows from 1955 play. You'll be served by a member of your "family", and you will be reminded that you need to finish your vegetables if you want dessert, and that your elbows do not belong on the table. It's all done in good fun.

The menu at 50's Prime Time Cafe features comfort foods with a family twist. You can try Mom's Old-fashioned Pot Roast, Cousin Ann's Traditional Meatloaf, or Grandma's Chicken Pot Pie. Dad gets in on the action when it comes to dessert, with Dad's Brownie Sundae. Other desserts are also sold. Dad is also in charge of Dad's Liquor Cabinet. Specialty cocktails, wine by the glass, draft and craft beers are all available. Milkshakes, malts, lemonade, and other beverages are also available. 50's Prime Time Cafe is open daily for lunch and dinner.

The Hollywood Brown Derby
Hollywood Boulevard - $$$

This popular eatery is a replica of the original Brown Derby restaurant in Hollywood. The walls are covered with caricatures of the rich and famous. The atmosphere is laid back and relaxed, while being classy at the same time. You don't have to be famous in order to get a taste of what it is like to be a celebrity. There is plenty of indoor seating, but because of the popularity of this signature restaurant, you will want to make a reservation. You won't believe that you are eating inside of a theme park.

The must try item on The Hollywood Brown Derby menu is "Our Famous Cobb Salad". It is sold as either an appetizer or an entree. Other dishes include lamb, salmon, beef, duck, and an Asia noodle bowl. Once it's time for dessert, for one price you can sample three different items. One being the signature Brown Derby Original! Mini Grapefruit Cake. A large selection of teas are sold, and if you're over 21, you can have a classic cocktail or order the World Traveler Flight and sample three different wine selections from around the world. The Hollywood Brown Derby is open daily for lunch and dinner.

Mama Melrose's Ristorante Italiano
Streets of America - $$

If you're looking for delicious Italian food, you'll want to reserve a table at Mama Melrose's Ristorante Italiano. Bring your appetite because the portions are huge. The ambiance is casual, with beamed ceilings that are decorated with grape vines and white lights. The restaurant is not always easy to find, head towards Muppet*Vision 3D. It is in the same general area. There are plenty of Italian favorites on the menu. You can start your meal with Crispy Calamari or Fresh Mozzarella with Vine-ripened Tomatoes. Some of the entrees available are pasta, chicken, pork chops, and several different varieties of flatbread pizza. Tiramisu Semifreddo and Chocolate Cannoli Cake are among the dessert choic-es. Mama Melrose's has espresso, cappuccino, and other hot and cold drinks. They also sell specialty and dessert cocktails. Mama Melrose's Ristorante Italiano is open daily for lunch and dinner.

Sci-Fi Dine-In Theater Restaurant
Commissary Lane - $$

Sci-Fi Dine-In Theater is one of the more uniquely themed res-taurants that you will find at Walt Disney World, or anywhere else in Orlando. The idea is simple. You and your party are at a drive-in theater having dinner in your car under the stars. The tables are made to look like convertibles and you will face the drive-in movie screen at the front. Trailers from old black and white science fiction movies like *Plan 9 From Outer Space* play on the screen while you dine. It is a fun restaurant, but be warned, it is very dark inside. You might need the flashlight app on your phone in order to read the menu.

The food selections are on the simple side. There are several different burger choices, as well as ribs, steak, and a Vegetarian Sheppard's Pie. Sci-Fi Dine-In Theater Restaurant is known for the milkshakes; they are available in vanilla, chocolate, strawberry, or Oreo cookie. Beer, wine, and specialty cocktails with fun names like Long Island Lunar Tea are also sold, and other beverages are available. Sci-Fi Dine-In Theater Restaurant is open daily for lunch and dinner.

Character and Buffet Dining

Hollywood & Vine
Echo Lake - $$$

If you have preschoolers you will want to consider making a reservation at Hollywood & Vine. Breakfast and lunch are both character meals, featuring favorites such as Handy Manny from Disney Junior. There's plenty of music and the kids are encouraged to sing and dance along. Go ahead and join them; you know the words. Remember when making your reservation that there are no characters at dinner.

Meals at Hollywood & Vine are served buffet-style. Breakfast features made-to-order omelets, breakfast meats, cereal, fresh fruit, yogurt, pastries, and other items. There is a special buffet for the kids at breakfast, with Mickey Waffles and a couple of other familiar items. The lunch buffet features chicken, seafood, and a make-your-own-pasta bar. The dinner buffet has several of the same items as lunch and also carved meats. There are plenty of sides for both lunch and dinner. There is also a large selection of desserts that you can choose from. The children's buffet for lunch and dinner has chicken, mac and cheese, and vegetables. Hollywood & Vine is open daily for breakfast, lunch, and dinner. But remember, only breakfast and lunch include Disney Junior characters.

THIRTY-FOUR

QUICK SERVICE DINING AT DISNEY'S HOLLYWOOD STUDIOS

ABC Commissary
Commissary Lane - $

At ABC Commissary, the theme is art deco and there are movie posters and televisions to add to the decor. The restaurant can get busy on crowded days. The food has an international touch, with choices like Couscous Quinoa & Arugula Salad, Asian Salad, and a Fish Platter. There are also burgers, seafood, and a chicken club sandwich. Chocolate Mousse and a Strawberry Parfait (made without added sugar) are on the dessert menu. There are hot and cold beverages, including beer and wine. ABC Commissary also has kosher choices. There is plenty of indoor seating and a few outdoor tables as well. ABC Commissary is open daily for lunch and dinner.

Backlot Express
Echo Lake - $

Located between Indiana Jones Epic Stunt Spectacular! and Star Tours - The Adventures Continue is Backlot Express. You'll see hundreds of movie props while you feast on burgers, chicken nuggets, sandwiches, or hot dogs. There is both indoor and outdoor seating available. Hot and cold beverages are sold here, as well as beer and wine by the glass. Backlot Express is open daily for lunch and dinner.

Min and Bill's Dockside Diner
Echo Lake - $

That's not a real ship you'll see on Echo Lake, it's a quick service restaurant. Min and Bill's Dockside Diner features specialty sandwiches such as a sausage sandwich with onions and peppers, and a frankfurter on a pretzel roll. Turkey legs, chips, and cookies are sold. You can also order a hot or cold beverage. There are several different beers on the menu, as well as an alcoholic frozen lemonade. There is limited outdoor seating. Min and Bill's Dockside Diner is open daily for lunch and dinner, but hours may vary.

Pizza Planet Arcade
Streets of America - $

Toy Story fans will want to check out Pizza Planet Arcade. It is based on the pizza restaurant depicted in the first *Toy Story* movie. There are two floors. Downstairs you will order and you can also grab a table or play arcade games. There is more seating upstairs, and it is quieter because there are no games to play. Outdoor seating is also available. The simple menu offers: individual pan pizzas with a side Caesar salad, or a meatball sub. There are a couple of dessert items that change from time to time. You can also order hot and cold beverages, or draft beer. Pizza Planet Arcade is open daily for lunch and dinner.

Starring Rolls Cafe
Sunset Boulevard - $ **FAN PICK**

Starring Rolls Cafe tends to get busy as soon as the park opens for the day. The reason is simple. The eatery features a great selection of muffins, pastries, and other baked goods. You can also grab a bagel with cream cheese, fresh fruit, yogurt, and other breakfast items. When it's time for lunch, you can get sandwiches, sushi, and more delicious baked goods. You can order your morning latte, cappuccino, or espresso, or try another coffee drink. Juice and other cold beverages are also sold, as well as wine. There is limited outdoor seating and the tables will go quickly on crowded days. Starring Rolls Cafe is open daily for breakfast and lunch.

Studio Catering Co.
Streets of America - $

In the back of the park near Lights, Motors, Action! Extreme Stunt Show, you'll find Studio Catering Co. It is an open-aired restaurant but the seating area is covered and pretty well protected from the elements. The menu features mostly sandwiches and wraps, with choices such as Spicy Buffalo Chicken Sandwich, Grilled Vegetable Sandwich, Chicken Caesar Wrap, and Sloppy Joe. Coffee, juice, and other cold drinks are sold, as well as beer, wine, and sangria. Studio Catering Co. is open daily for lunch and dinner.

Sunset Ranch Market
Sunset Boulevard - $

Sunset Ranch Market is not one specific quick service option. It is a group of outdoor counter service restaurants that are together in one place. There is a covered seating area and other tables have umbrellas. If the members of your party can't decide where to eat, this might be a good choice because there are several options. The following Sunset Ranch Market eateries are good places to grab a meal.

Catalina Eddie's

Are you thinking quick Italian food? You can order an individual cheese or pepperoni pizza, a Caesar salad with Chicken, or a Hot Italian Deli Sandwich. Desserts are house-made and could include Banana Parfait or Vanilla Cake with Chocolate Custard. Hot and cold drinks, as well as bottled beer are also sold. Catalina Eddie's is open daily for lunch and dinner.

Fairfax Fare

If you need to eat something quickly for breakfast, you can get it here. They sell egg and cheese English muffins with either sausage or bacon. They also have fruit, cereal, yogurt, danish, and cinnamon rolls. Juice and hot and cold beverages are available for breakfast. For lunch and dinner, the name of the game at Fairfax Fare is BBQ. You can order chicken, spare ribs, pork, and other choices. Sides include coleslaw and baked beans. If you're in the mood for a turkey leg, you can grab those at Fairfax Fare as well. They also serve hot dogs. Desserts include Banana Parfait and Vanilla Cake. Hot and cold drinks, including beer, are sold. Fairfax Fare is open daily for breakfast, lunch, and dinner.

Rosie's All-American Cafe

A third meal option at Sunset Ranch Market is Rosie's All-American Cafe. They sell cheeseburgers, vegetable burgers, and chicken nuggets. You can try cake or a Banana Parfait for dessert. Juice, hot and cold beverages, and bottled beer are also sold. Rosie's All-American Cafe is open daily for lunch and dinner.

THIRTY-FIVE

SNACKS AND BEVERAGES AT DISNEY'S HOLLYWOOD STUDIOS

Snacks

Backlot Cantina
Streets of America - $

Head to the giant Coke bottles in the back of the park! You'll find them behind Pixar Place and next to Backlot Tour. Not only will you be able to cool off with the misters, you can also grab an ice cream bar at the snack stand. They also sell fresh fruit, chips, and cold beverages.

Dinosaur Gertie's Ice Cream of Extinction
Echo Lake - $

You can't miss Dinosaur Gertie! This snack option is based on the 1914 short film *Gertie the Dinosaur*, which had a large influence on

Walt Disney. The Disney's Hollywood Studios version is an ice cream stand, featuring soft serve in a cup or a waffle cone. Ice cream bars and sandwiches are also sold, as well as chips and cold drinks. Dinosaur Gertie's Ice Cream of Extinction is open seasonally.

Herbie's Drive-In
Streets of America - $

If you want to grab something to eat before catching Lights, Motors, Action! Extreme Stunt Show, you should check out this kiosk. Based on the *Herbie the Love Bug* series, this stand sells popcorn, corn dogs, chips, and other snacks. Cold beverages and frozen drinks (with or without alcohol) are also available.

Hey Howdy Hey Take Away
Pixar Place - $

The line for Toy Story Midway Mania! can grow long quickly, so grab a snack before your wait. Hey Howdy Hey Take Away has popcorn, chips, hot dogs, whole fruit, and trail mix. They also serve danish and cinnamon rolls in the morning. Standing in line can also make you thirsty, so grab a frozen drink before you get in that line. The Wheezy's Breezy Freezy comes in several different flavors. Those of age can have a shot added. Other cold beverages and coffee are also served.

Hollywood Hills Theater
Sunset Boulevard - $

Fantasmic! is a must see show. The problem is that the theater fills up quickly, so arriving early is necessary. After you have found your seat, what do you do if you get hungry? The answer is simple, just head to a Hollywood Hills Theater snack kiosk. You can pick up items such as a conewich, popcorn, cotton candy, chips, fruit, and other snacks. They also sell ice cream bars, cold drinks, beer, and wine.

Ice Cold Snack Stand
Park Entrance - $

Ice Cold Snack Stand carries more than just frozen snacks. While it is true that you can get a cold drink or an ice cream bar at the park's entrance, there are other choices as well. If you need your morning coffee or cappuccino, you can get it here. Other snacks include muffins, cinnamon rolls, chips, and granola bars. Don't hit the park hungry, grab something to eat so that you'll have the energy to face the day.

KRNR Station
Sunset Boulevard - $

After riding Rock 'n' Roller Coaster you deserve a reward, and what better reward is there than ice cream? At the KRNR Station kiosk you can get soft serve ice cream in a waffle cone or a cup. Floats and smoothies are also available. Frozen lemonade, cold drinks, and coffee are sold here as well.

Min and Bill's Dockside Diner
Echo Lake - $

There are a couple of quick meals sold at Min and Bill's. There are also some snack options. Grab some chips or try a chocolate chip cookie. You can cool off with a shake or frozen lemonade. Other hot and cold choices, including a few alcoholic beverages, are also available. Min and Bill's is open daily. Hours may vary.

Oasis Canteen
Echo Lake - $

Theme parks and funnel cakes seem to go hand in hand. At Oasis Canteen you can order yours with or without ice cream or strawberries on top. They also sell soft serve in a waffle cone at the kiosk. You can pick up a float or another cold beverage. Draft beer is also sold.

Pretzel Garden
Mobile

This mobile kiosk can often be found in the Streets of America. Mickey Pretzels, with or without dipping sauce, are sold. You can also try a jalapeno cheese pretzel or a cream cheese pretzel. Other snacks and cold beverages are available as well.

Studios Popcorn
Hollywood Boulevard - $

Head towards the Sorcerer Hat if you want some popcorn! This stand also sells whole fruit, granola bars, and cold drinks, including draft beer.

Sunset Ranch Market
Sunset Boulevard - $

Sunset Ranch is not one specific restaurant, rather it is a group of quick service meal and snack options. Located on the way to Tower of Terror, the area has plenty of outdoor seating.

Anaheim Produce

This is a great place to grab a healthy snack. You'll find fresh and cut fruit, trail mix, celery or carrots with dip, and other options. You can also buy chips or a Mickey Pretzel with cheese. You might want to purchase a frozen lemonade or frozen margarita, or maybe you'd rather enjoy another cold beverage.

Hollywood Scoops

What better way to cool off on a hot day than with hand-scooped ice cream? Hollywood Scoops sells it by the cup or cone, or you can get a sundae. Ice cream sandwiches on fresh baked cookies are also sold.

Toluca Legs Turkey Co.

Some people think of turkey legs as a snack. Others will have one for a meal. That is what you will find at Toluca Legs Turkey Co.- jumbo turkey legs. They also sell pork shank with chips. You can buy a cold fountain beverage, water, or bottled beer here as well.

Beverages

Hey Howdy Hey Take Away
Pixar Place - $

Pixar Place gets crowded quickly, so you might want to grab something to drink before getting into a long line. Try a Wheezy's Breezy Freezy sold in several different flavors. Have a shot added if you're of age. Other cold beverages and snacks are sold here as well.

High Octane Refreshments
Streets of America - $

Right next to Studio Catering Co. you'll find the perfect place to grab a quick drink - or maybe a long, slow one. High Octane Refreshments has a full bar, but it's still family friendly. There are plenty of beer and wine choices, as well as specialty alcoholic and non-alcoholic cocktails and other choices.

The Hollywood Brown Derby Lounge
Hollywood Boulevard - $

Can't get a reservation at the Hollywood Brown Derby? See if there is a seat available at the lounge next door instead. Appetizers are available, including "Our Famous Cobb Salad". You can also enjoy a specialty martini, premium beer, or wine by the glass. Celebrity Flights are also sold, allowing you to taste three different drinks that complement each other. Non-alcoholic specialties are also available.

Ice Cold Snack Stand
Park Entrance - $

You don't want to hit the park without your morning coffee. Pick it up before you pass through the gate at this stand. You can also order cold beverages here, and you might want to grab a snack as well.

Joffrey's Coffee
Pixar Place and Streets of America - $

There are two different kiosks where you can buy Joffrey's Coffee at Disney's Hollywood Studios. One is located in Pixar Place, near Toy

Story Midway Mania. The other is located in Streets of America, near the *Cars* meet and greet area. Both locations serve coffee, espresso, tea, and other hot and cold drinks. A limited number of pastries are sold as well.

Peevy's Polar Pipeline
Echo Lake - $

Frozen beverages in several different flavors are available at Peevy's Polar Pipeline. Juice and bottled drinks are sold as well. Healthy snacks and ice cream bars are also available.

Tower of Terror Coffee Cart
Sunset Boulevard - $

This is a good place to pick up your favorite hot beverage. You can get cappuccino, espresso, or other delicious drinks. Cold beverages, including coffee choices, are also sold at the kiosk. If you need something to go with your coffee, try a muffin or a pastry.

Tune-In Lounge
Echo Lake - $ FAN PICK

This family-friendly lounge is located next to 50's Prime Time Cafe. There is a full bar with specialty drinks such as Grandma's Picnic Punch and Uncle Tim's Summer Breeze. The menu from 50's Prime Time Cafe is available. So, if you couldn't get a reservation and you have a craving for meatloaf, you might want to stop by.

The Writer's Stop
Streets of America - $

Start your day with your favorite coffee creation and a muffin. They serve cappuccino, espresso, and a host of other hot and cold beverages. The Writer's Stop also serves bakery items.

THIRTY-SIX

A BRIEF INTRODUCTION TO DISNEY'S ANIMAL KINGDOM

Disney's Animal Kingdom opened on April 22, 1998. The park is currently changing. In January, 2014, Camp Minnie-Mickey closed. A few days later, ground broke for Avatar Land (also known as Pandora). The new area is expected to open in 2017.

There are six different lands at Disney's Animal Kingdom. Space-wise, it is the largest of the Walt Disney World parks. It is not difficult to get from one section of the park to another with one exception. To get to Rafiki's Planet Watch, you'll need to take the Wildlife Express Train from Africa.

The main icon at Disney's Animal Kingdom is The Tree of Life. It's located in the Discovery Island section of the park, but it can be seen from many different places. It houses the 3-D film It's Tough to Be a Bug, which is based on characters from the 1998 movie *A Bug's Life*. The film runs continuously. You will want to take notice of the animals that are carved into The Tree of Life. Over 300 different species are represented.

Some of the highlights at Disney's Animal Kingdom are Expedition Everest - Legend of the Forbidden Mountain, DINOSAUR, and Kilimanjaro Safaris. You will also want to explore the trails that will allow you to see animals in their Disney-created habitats.

Dining at Disney's Animal Kingdom can start when you arrive since Rainforest Cafe is located at the entrance. Inside the park you'll find Asian, African, and American dishes. Those with special dietary needs will want to stop by Gardens Kiosk and ask for information on the park's restaurants.

Over the years, some guests have said that Disney's Animal Kingdom is not a "full day park" because of the lack of an end-of-the-day experience. That is soon set to change. Rivers of Light will be a nighttime extravaganza that features live music, water screens, and plenty of surprises. It is expected to open sometime in 2016.

THIRTY-SEVEN

FULL SERVICE AND CHARACTER DINING AT DISNEY'S ANIMAL KINGDOM

Full Service Dining

Rainforest Cafe
Oasis - $$

It is hard to miss Rainforest Cafe. You will see it to the left as you enter the park. Rainforest Cafe is an international chain that fits right in at Walt Disney World. The restaurant is filled with audio-animatronic animals that are based on what you might find in a real rainforest. There are elephants, tigers, butterflies, and plenty of monkeys. Every few minutes a storm moves in, but don't worry, you won't get wet. The fake thunder and lightning causes the animals to react. Rainforest Cafe is loud and can be overwhelming for some children, but overall it is family friendly and fun.

The menu is quite extensive at Rainforest Cafe. Many of the items are given names that match the restaurant's theme. Breakfast features traditional foods with creative names like Benedict Bamba and Pie of the Viper. At lunch and dinner, you'll find selections such as Jungle Chop Salad or Planet Earth Pasta. The menu features shrimp and other seafood items, chicken, beef, pasta, and several types of burgers. The restaurant's signature dessert is the Sparkling Volcano. It is made of chocolate brownie cake and vanilla ice cream, which is then topped with caramel and chocolate sauces. A sparkler decoration is added to the top. The Sparkling Volcano is meant to be shared. The restaurant offers a large selection of both alcoholic and non-alcoholic specialty drinks. Other beverages are also available. Rainforest Cafe is open daily for breakfast, lunch, and dinner.

Yak & Yeti Restaurant
Asia - $$

Located in the heart of Asia, Yak & Yeti features pan-Asian cuisine. Do not confuse it with the counter service options Yak & Yeti Local Foods Cafes or Yak & Yeti Quality Beverages. The interior of the restaurant is relaxed and busy at the same time. There are statues, knick-knacks, and Asian-style paintings galore. You might want to ask for a seat upstairs by a window, you'll have a great view of other park guests as they pass by below.

The menu at Yak & Yeti Restaurant is filled with items that you would expect to find at a pan-Asian restaurant, with appetizers such as Wok-Fried Green Beans and Ahi Tuna Salad. Entrees include Stir-Fried Beef and Broccoli, Crispy Honey Chicken, and Vegetable Lo Mein. Try Fried Wontons or Mango Pie for dessert. There are several specialty drinks on the menu, as well as a few international beers. Yak & Yeti Restaurant is open daily for lunch and dinner.

Character and Buffet Dining

Tusker House Restaurant
Africa - $$$

If you're looking for character dining at Disney's Animal Kingdom, make your reservation at Tusker House Restaurant. Just make sure that you book it for breakfast or lunch, because dinner does not have characters. The character meals include a visit from Donald and friends (possibly Mickey, Daisy, and Goofy) all dressed up and ready to head out on a safari.

The restaurant has the look and feel of an outdoor African market. While the food has an African flair, you'll find something for even the pickiest eater because there are so many choices. The breakfast buffet features everything from Mickey Waffles to Mealie Pap (it's a type of African porridge). Make sure you try the Jungle Juice! For lunch you'll find sirloin on the buffet, as well as couscous, pork loin, chicken, and samosa. If you book your reservation for dinner, you can enjoy carved meats with all the fixings, baked salmon, or stew. You and your kids can also create a unique PB&J sandwich. While it seems like Tusker House is heavy on the meat, the restaurant also prides itself on the variety of vegetarian options available. Tusker House Restaurant serves breakfast, lunch, and dinner daily, but remember that only breakfast and lunch include Donald and his friends.

THIRTY-EIGHT

QUICK SERVICE DINING AT DISNEY'S ANIMAL KINGDOM

Bradley Falls
Asia - $

If you want to sit down and enjoy a casual meal you will probably not want to stop at Bradley Falls. It is a kiosk and there is no seating. What you will find at Bradley Falls is a small selection of vegetarian offerings. You can order a falafel sandwich with chips, samosa with slaw, or hummus with vegetables and a pita on the side. There is also an Asian salad, and a seasonal fruit salad might be available. Bradley Falls is open seasonally for lunch and dinner.

Flame Tree Barbecue
Discovery Island - $ FAN PICK

Flame Tree Barbecue is one of the most popular counter service restaurants at Walt Disney World. The food and the service are outstanding.

You can order ribs, pork, chicken, or a turkey leg. If you'd prefer a healthier selection, order the fresh fruit plate. Flame Tree Barbecue has covered outdoor seating that overlooks the Discovery River. Tables tend to fill up quickly on busy days, especially around traditional meal times. Beer and wine are sold. Flame Tree Barbecue is open daily for lunch and dinner.

Mr. Kamal's
Asia - $

The kiosk known as Mr. Kamal's has undergone changes for the better. It no longer serves fried chicken nuggets and corn dog nuggets. The new menu is much healthier, featuring vegetarian and Indian cuisine. You can now order hummus, samosa, or a falafel sandwich. Cold beverages are also available. Mr. Kamal's is open seasonally for lunch and dinner.

Pizzafari
Discovery Island - $

If you want to sit down in the AC and enjoy a counter service meal, you should check out Pizzafari. There are six rooms, giving you a fighting chance to find a table. Outdoor seating is also available. The walls are brightly painted, with murals of everything from peacocks to polar bears. Individual pizzas are featured. Cheese, vegetable, and pepperoni are available, all served with a Caesar Salad on the side. Sandwiches and salads are sold as well, and the restaurant offers kosher items. The restaurant also has a breakfast menu featuring eggs, cereal and milk, and the Spinach & Goat Cheese Frittata. Pizzafari is open daily for breakfast, lunch, and dinner.

Restaurantosaurus
Dinoland U.S.A. - $

Pay attention to the details at Restaurantosaurus. The theme is creative; a group of paleontology students turned their dorm into a restaurant. All of the rooms are different and there are puns galore. There is plenty of indoor seating, and there are more tables outside. The food is fairly standard for a theme park; you'll find chicken nuggets, hot dogs, burgers, and sandwiches. Restaurantosaurus is open daily for lunch and dinner.

Tamu Tamu Refreshments
Africa - $

If you want to try something a little bit different, Tamu Tamu Refreshments could be a good choice. This outdoor option may look rundown, but that's just part of the fun. Outdoor seating is available behind the building. You'll find a couple of curry and rice options, plus a roasted chicken salad. Tamu Tamu Refreshments is open seasonally for breakfast and daily for lunch and dinner.

Yak & Yeti Local Food Cafes
Asia - $

If you're looking to satisfy your craving for good Mandarin food in a hurry, Yak & Yeti Local Foods Cafes is the right choice for you. Not to be confused with the two other Yak & Yeti options, Local Foods Cafes is an outdoor counter service restaurant. There is outdoor seating, you may want to plan your meal for when the sun is not directly overhead because not all tables are covered. The menu consists of such standards as beef lo mein and sweet-and-sour chicken. The portions are huge, so you won't go away hungry. Yak & Yeti Local Food Cafes is open daily for lunch and dinner.

THIRTY-NINE

SNACKS AND BEVERAGES AT DISNEY'S ANIMAL KINGDOM

Snacks

Anandapur Ice Cream Truck
Asia - $

Stop and take a peek at the Anandapur Ice Cream Truck, even if you're not in the mood for ice cream. It is located not too far from Expedition Everest and the details are amazing. The truck is mostly blue and it is covered with intricate paintings of animals, many of which you might see in the park. Soft serve ice cream is sold in a waffle cone or as a float. You can also purchase cold drinks.

Beastly Kiosk
Discovery Island - $

If you're looking for a pretzel, head to Beastly Kiosk. This small stand sells soft and Jalapeno cheese pretzels, along with dipping sauces. You can also buy cold drinks. Meals (usually corn dogs with a side) are sold seasonally as well.

Dino-Bite Snacks
Dinoland U.S.A. - $

Next to Restaurantosaurus, you'll find Dino-Bite Snacks. They sell hand-scooped ice cream and churros. You can also purchase fresh baked cookies and hot and cold drinks.

Dino Diner
Dinoland U.S.A. - $

The Disney Imagineers obviously had fun when creating Dino Diner. It is designed to look like a trailer, but it has a dinosaur head, scales, and tail. The selection of snacks is small; they offer chips and cinnamon glazed nuts. Beer, frozen beverages, and cold drinks are also served. Dino Diner serves lunch seasonally.

Discovery Island Ice Cream
Discovery Island - $

Haagen-Dazs and Edy's ice cream are served in a waffle cone at this kiosk. The kids might want to try the Bugs Sundae, which includes gummy worms and chocolate cookie crumbs for dirt. Cold drinks are also sold.

Harambe Fruit Market
Africa - $

What tastes better than cold fruit on a hot day? Harambe Fruit Market sells whole and cut seasonal fruits. Mickey Pretzels and Jalapeno cheese filled pretzels are sold as well. You can also purchase juice or water.

Gardens Kiosk
Discovery Island - $

Gardens Kiosk is part snack stand and part information center. You can purchase gluten-free and vegan baked goods and snacks here. You can also find out information on all of the restaurants in the park, so that those with allergies and special dietary restrictions can make well-informed choices ahead of time. If you follow a special diet or have food allergies, make this your first stop in the park.

Harambe Popcorn
Discovery Island - $

Popcorn and cinnamon-glazed nuts are sold here. You can also purchase cold beverages, including Jungle Juice and beer.

Mr. Kamal's
Asia - $

Mr. Kamal's is similar to Bradley Falls. Both kiosks serve vegetarian options such as edamame beans and hummus with chips. If you're looking for a healthy snack, you might want to give Mr. Kamal's a try.

Trilo-Bites
Dinoland U.S.A. - $

Trilo-Bites is another snack kiosk. You can buy waffles here, with or without ice cream. You can also enjoy a waffle bowl sundae, a float, or a milkshake. Other cold drinks and beer are also sold. Trilo-Bites serves lunch seasonally.

Beverages

Dawa Bar
Africa - $

Dawa Bar sells specialty cocktails, wine, and domestic African beers (including Tusker Lager). Cocktails include creations such as Lost on Safari and Sugar Cane Mojito. There is covered outdoor seating.

Drinkwallah
Asia - $

Wouldn't a frozen drink taste terrific on a hot day? You can order yours at Drinkwallah. They also sell fruit and other snacks.

Isle of Java
Discovery Island - $

Get your morning coffee fix right after you enter the park! Isle of Java sells cappuccino, espresso, coffee, and iced coffee. You can also purchase frozen drinks and other cold beverages, as well as baked goods.

Kusafiri Coffee Shop & Bakery
Africa - $

Here is another place where you can buy coffee, iced coffee, cappuccino, and espresso. There are plenty of bakery choices to accompany your daily habit. Juice and cold drinks are also sold. Those 21 and older might want to try Amarula Schokoleti, which is hot chocolate with Amarula.

Royal Anandapur Tea Company
Asia - $

This is a great place to go if you want hot or iced coffee or tea. Grab a latte, cappuccino, espresso, or another favorite. You can also pick up a pastry to go with your chai latte.

Upcountry
Asia - $

Upcountry kiosk features frozen drinks and other beverages. Alcoholic specialties include the Frozen Emperor Margarita and the Yak Attack. Beer is also available. For something without alcohol, you might want to try a frozen coffee creation, a frozen lemonade, or order another cold drink. Chips, pretzels, and a couple of other food items are also sold at Upcountry.

Yak & Yeti Quality Beverages
Asia - $

The third Yak & Yeti option, this walk-up lounge features draft beers, specialty drinks, and other hot and cold beverages. There are also chips, an Asian Chicken Sandwich, and a Mandarin Chicken Salad on the menu, so it's possible to grab a quick meal here as well. There is covered outdoor seating.

FORTY

A BRIEF INTRODUCTION TO THE DISNEY WATER PARKS

There are two water parks at Walt Disney World. The first of the current water parks to open was Disney's Typhoon Lagoon, which opened on June 1, 1989. The story behind the park is that a typhoon hit a tropical paradise, which is why you will see wrecked ships, surfboards, and fishing gear everywhere. The icon of the park is the shrimp boat Miss Tilly, which sits on top of Mount Mayday. Typhoon Lagoon is home to the largest wave pool in North America, and guests can experience a geyser from Mount Mayday every half hour. Crush 'n' Gusher is a water roller coaster that offers three different experiences. Shark Reef provides guests with a chance to swim with the sharks. There are plenty of other slides and areas for the whole family. You can even sign up for surfing lessons.

On April 1, 1995, Disney's Blizzard Beach opened. The legend states that there was a freak snowstorm in Florida, so a ski resort was built. Of course the snow melted, and the resort was turned into a water park. Mount Gushmore is the central icon, and many of the slides are based there. You can take a chairlift to the top and brave the 120 foot slope of Summit Plummet. Teamboat Springs is a family raft ride. There are plenty of other slides for thrill seekers and also for those looking for a more relaxing ride. Melt-Away Bay is the park's wave pool.

Many of the dining locations at the Disney water parks are seasonal. The stands will not be open when there won't be enough guests at the park to financially justify keeping them open. There are no full service restaurants in either park.

One popular offering at the Disney water parks is the refillable mug program. This is not the same program that you will find at the resort hotels; you must purchase these separately. For one fee you can buy a souvenir mug and keep refilling it throughout the day. The refill stations are marked clearly on the map.

Since Central Florida is hot and humid all summer long, the water parks are popular destinations. They will often fill to capacity on peak days, so plan to arrive early.

Longtime Walt Disney World fans might remember another water park. Disney's River Country opened on June 20, 1976, and it closed permanently at the end of the 2001 season.

Forty-One

DISNEY'S BLIZZARD BEACH DINING

Meals

Avalunch
Quick Service - $

Head past the Chairlift after you enter the park and you'll find Avalunch on the right. The menu features different hot dog creations, turkey legs, and a chicken salad. Fresh fruit, chips, cheesecake, and a few other items are also sold. Draft beer, fountain drinks, and water are available as well. Avalunch is a drink refill station. Outdoor seating is available. Avalunch is open seasonally for lunch and snacks.

Cooling Hut
Quick Service - $

There are a couple of sandwich options at this location that can make a filling meal. You can choose between a tuna sandwich or a chicken wrap. Either one comes with chips. There are also some great snack choices at Cooling Hut. You can get pretzels, popcorn, nachos, or ice cream bars. Draft beer, coffee, and cold beverages are available. Cooling Hut is a drink refill station. There is no seating. Cooling Hut is open seasonally for lunch and snacks.

Lottawatta Lodge
Quick Service - $

Lottawatta Lodge is the largest restaurant at Blizzard Beach. Choose from pizza, burgers, wraps, and sandwiches. Ice cream in a bowl, cup, or sundae makes a great dessert. Beer and wine are sold, as are other hot and cold beverages. Lottawatta Lodge is a drink refill station. Outdoor seating is available. Lottawatta Lodge is open daily for lunch and snacks.

Warming Hut
Quick Service - $

This location features sandwiches and nachos. You'll find a Pulled Pork Sandwich, a Jerk Chicken Sandwich, and a Meatball Sub among the choices. They come with a side of coleslaw or chips. Pulled pork and jerk chicken are also toppings for the nachos. Ice cream bars, soft serve ice cream, and other sweet treats are sold. Beer and other cold beverages are available. Warming Hut is a drink refill station. Outdoor seating is available. Warming Hut is open seasonally for lunch and snacks.

Snacks and Beverages

Frostbite Freddy's Frozen Freshments
Quick Service - $

Of course a place with the word "Frostbite" in the name has to sell ice cream. You can pick up a Mickey Bar or a Mickey Ice Cream Sandwich here. Other ice cream treats are sold as well. For the 21 and up crowd, there are frozen margaritas and other specialty drinks. Non-alcoholic choices include frozen lemonade and smoothies. Frostbite Freddy's Frozen Freshments is open seasonally.

Frosty the Joe Man
Quick Service - $

The "Joe" in this case stands for coffee, and that's just what you'll find here. Just because you're spending a day out in the hot sun does not mean that you should give up your daily caffeine. You can order cappuccino, espresso, and other hot beverages. Iced versions are available as well. You can also buy a frozen drink or a pastry. Frosty the Joe Man is open seasonally.

Funnel Cakes at Disney's Blizzard Beach Water Park
Quick Service - $

As the name implies, here you can order funnel cakes, topped with ice cream and chocolate sauce if so desired. Other snack options include pretzels, cotton candy, and fried ice cream. Bottled water is also sold. Funnel Cakes at Disney's Blizzard Beach Water Park is open seasonally.

I.C. Expeditions
Quick Service - $

Take a break from your fun in the water and head to I.C. Expeditions at some point during your day. You can order ice cream bars, soft serve ice cream cones, or sundaes. The star of I.C. Expeditions is the Sand Pail. It is a sundae that comes with waffle pieces, sprinkles, cookie pieces, toppings, and other goodies. It is served in a pail with a shovel for a spoon, and it is large enough to share. Ice cream floats, bottled water, and fountain drinks are also sold. I.C. Expeditions is a drink refill station. Outdoor seating is available. I.C. Expeditions is open daily.

Mini Donuts at Disney's Blizzard Beach Water Park
Quick Service - $

FAN PICK

You will not want to pass by this small kiosk at the front of the park. You can buy mini donuts in packs of six or twelve. They come with your choice of dipping sauce. Hot beverages and frozen lemonade are also available. Mini Donuts at Disney's Blizzard Beach Water Park is open seasonally.

Polar Pub
Quick Service - $

While this open-air lounge is made with those 21 and older in mind, it is still family friendly. Choose from creations such as the Grapefruit Margarita, the Blue Blizzard, and the Grey Goose Le Citron Slush. Wine, beer, and plenty of other cocktails are available. For a special non-alcoholic beverage, try the Gator Freeze. Chips, bottled water, and Monster Energy Drink are sold here as well. Polar Pub is open seasonally.

Snow Balls
Quick Service - $

Sometimes you want to grab something quick and refreshing. That is what you will find at this kiosk. Snow Balls (also known as Arctic Expedition) sells several flavors of shaved ice. Mickey Bars and other ice cream treats are also avialable. Snow Balls is open seasonally.

FORTY-TWO

DISNEY'S TYPHOON LAGOON DINING

Meals

Crush 'n' Gusher Hot Dog Cart
Quick Service - $

On the way to Crush 'n' Gusher, you'll find this stand. You can pick up hot dogs, turkey legs, and sandwiches. Chips, ice cream bars, and cold drinks are also sold. Crush 'n' Gusher Hot Dog Cart is a drink refill station. It is open daily for lunch and snacks.

Leaning Palms
Quick Service - $

The largest eatery at Typhoon Lagoon is Leaning Palms. Look for the yellow building that, well, leans! There is a good selection of entrees, including burgers, hot dogs, chicken nuggets, and personal pizzas. For something that is unexpected in a water park, you might want to try the

Turkey Pesto Sandwich. Other sandwiches are also available. For dessert you can enjoy Key Lime Pie, Chocolate Cake, a Chocolate Chip Cookie, or a fruit cup. Beer and wine are sold, as are other hot and cold beverages. Leaning Palms is a drink refill station. Outdoor seating is available. Leaning Palms is open daily for lunch and snacks.

Lowtide Lou's
Quick Service - $

There are three main lunch choices at Lowtide Lou's. You can order a tuna sandwich, a chicken wrap, or Turkey Pesto. All come with chips. For dessert there are Mickey Ice Cream Bars and other frozen treats. Quench your thirst with frozen lemonade or another cold drink. Beer and wine are also available. Lowtide Lou's is a drink refill station. It is open seasonally for lunch and snacks.

Snack Shack
Quick Service - $

While the name of this walk-up window implies that it is for snacks, this location is also a great place to grab lunch. You might want to try a Caesar Salad with Chicken. Sandwiches include Tuna, Turkey Pesto, and Chicken Wrap, and they come with chips. Soft serve ice cream and ice cream bars are sold, along with other desserts. For those over 21, Strawberry Margaritas and Pina Coladas are available. Fountain drinks and bottled water are sold as well. Snack Shack is open seasonally for lunch and snacks.

Surf Doggies
Quick Service - $

At Surf Doggies you'll find hot dogs and turkey legs for lunch. There are also some snack choices, including nachos, pretzels, and chips.

Fountain drinks and bottled water are served as well. Surf Doggies is a drink refill station. It is open daily for lunch and snacks.

Typhoon Tilly's
Quick Service - $

If you're in the mood for seafood, head to Typhoon Tilly's. You'll find a shrimp or fish basket, served with fries. Also available are a Barbecued Pulled Pork Sandwich, the Turkey Pesto Sandwich, and other items. Two of the dessert choices are Chocolate Cake and Key Lime Pie. Specialty drinks are sold, as are beer, wine, and other hot and cold beverages. Typhoon Tilly's is a drink refill station. Outdoor seating is available. Typhoon Tilly's is open seasonally for lunch and snacks.

Snacks and Beverages

Arctic Dots
Quick Service - $

This is where you can get a cup of those little balls of ice cream that are popular at some theme parks. Several flavors are available. You can get small, large, or layered. You can also pick up a chocolate chip cookie. Arctic Dots is open seasonally.

Coffee Hut
Quick Service - $

You're not going to want to give up your favorite specialty coffee just because you are at a water park. Coffee Hut has espresso, cappuccino, and flavored lattes. Frozen drinks and other hot beverages are available as well. There are also pastries, because nothing tastes better with a cup of coffee than delicious, sweet baked goods. Coffee Hut is open seasonally.

Funnel Cakes at Disney's Typhoon Lagoon Water Park
Quick Service - $

Spending all day in the water will make you hungry, so grab a funnel cake! You can get one with or without ice cream and chocolate sauce. Also sold here are snow cones, pretzels, and fried ice cream. If you're thirsty, bottled water is available. Funnel Cakes at Disney's Typhoon Lagoon Water Park is open seasonally.

Happy Landings Ice Cream
Quick Service - $

Plan to take an ice cream break while you're at Typhoon Lagoon. Happy Landings Ice Cream is the place where you'll want to go. You can order soft serve in a cone, dish, or sundae. If you're extremely hungry or feel like sharing, try the Sand Pail. It is soft serve chocolate and vanilla ice cream topped with cookie pieces, waffle cone bits, sprinkles, and lots of other toppings. It is served in a pail, and you're given a shovel to use as your spoon. Floats, fountain drinks, and bottled water are also served. Outdoor seating is available. Happy Landings Ice Cream is open daily.

Let's Go Slurpin'
Quick Service - $

This open air lounge has a full bar, but there are choices for all ages. Specialty drinks include creations such as Tropical Splash, Mango Margarita, and Typhoon Tilly. For a delicious treat without alcohol, order the Gator Freeze. Cream cheese and jalapeno pretzels are also available. There is limited seating at the bar. Let's Go Slurpin' is open daily.

Mini Donuts at Disney's Typhoon Lagoon Water Park
Quick Service - $

Mini donuts make a great quick snack. You can order them in a pack of four, eight, or twelve. Don't forget the dipping sauce! You can also get hot and cold beverages, including frozen lemonade. Mini Donuts at Disney's Typhoon Lagoon Water Park is open seasonally.

FORTY-THREE

A BRIEF INTRODUCTION TO DOWNTOWN DISNEY

Downtown Disney opened on March 22, 1975. There is no fee to enter, making it a great place to spend an off-day from the parks. Many people are not sure exactly what Downtown Disney is. It is often referred to as a "shopping and entertainment district".

At Downtown Disney you will find stores, restaurants, and more. If you're hungry, the area has everything from quick snacks to fine dining. There are unique shopping experiences, including the largest Disney character store on the planet. You'll find souvenirs that you never got around to picking up in the parks. You can bowl, catch the latest movie, or see Walt Disney World from high in the air in a tethered balloon. There is live entertainment in the evenings. This is also where you'll find La Nouba by Cirque du Soleil, House of Blues, and DisneyQuest.

On March 14, 2013, Walt Disney World announced major refurbishment plans for Downtown Disney. The name will eventually be changed to Disney Springs, and the number of stores and restaurants will double. The transformation is currently underway, and it is expected to be completed in 2016. Until the work is finished, the area will still be referred to as Downtown Disney.

Currently there are three sections to Downtown Disney: West Side, Pleasure Island, and Marketplace. A lot of the construction is taking place at Pleasure Island, which will eventually be replaced. With Disney Springs there will be four sections. West Side and Marketplace will still be there, and they will be joined by Towne Center and The Landing.

Self parking at Downtown Disney is free. If you're taking a Disney bus, you'll need to take it from a resort hotel. The Disney buses do not usually travel between the theme parks and Downtown Disney.

FORTY-FOUR

FINE AND FULL SERVICE DINING AT DOWNTOWN DISNEY

Fine Dining

The Dining Room at Wolfgang Puck Grand Cafe
West Side - $$$

If you're looking for a quiet, romantic dinner away from the theme park madness, look no further than The Dining Room. Located upstairs above Wolfgang Puck Grand Cafe, this signature restaurant offers delicious food and incredible views. There are several different dining options at Downtown Disney with Wolfgang Puck's name on them, and this is the most formal of the choices.

The menu at The Dining Room at Wolfgang Puck Grand Cafe features the creations of the celebrity chef. You might want to start your meal with Wasabi Pea Crusted Crab Cakes or Hamachi Sashimi Skewers. Soup and salad are also sold. Entrees include Miso Glazed Salmon, Seasonal Fish, and Sichuan NY Strip "Au Piovre". Sushi is also available. If you're not sure what to order, try the Austrian 3-Course Tour or the California 4-Course Tour. Cheesecake, Carrot Cake, and Key Lime Pie are three of the dessert choices. Specialty cocktails include Coco Chanel and Pinkberry Martini. There is an extensive wine list. Other alcoholic and non-alcoholic beverages are also served. The Dining Room at Wolfgang Puck Grand Cafe is open daily for dinner.

Fulton's Crab House
Pleasure Island - $$, $$$

You can't beat the combination of fresh food and great atmosphere, and that is exactly what you will find at this signature restaurant. Fulton's Crab House is located in a replica turn of the century paddle riverboat. It's named The Express Lilly, after Walt Disney's wife. The atmosphere is perfect for a romantic dinner, but the restaurant is also family friendly. The ambiance is incredible inside and out; you'll really feel like you're on a riverboat. Make a reservation near sunset and request an outdoor table for a view that you will never forget.

According to the restaurant's website, you can expect "Fresh Seasonal Foods from Ports Worldwide". There's also plenty of beef on the menu, to compliment the seafood. Start your lunch with New England Clam

Chowder, a Crab Cake appetizer, or order something from the Raw Bar. Lunch also features entree salads such as Ahi Tuna Cobb. There are plenty of sandwich choices including Crab Cake BLT, Florida Grouper Sandwich, and Fulton's Steakhouse Burger. If you'd like, you can create a soup and sandwich combo. At dinner, Fulton's Crab House really shines. Fish Tacos, Calamari, and a Lobster Corn Dog are just a few of the hot appetizers. If you're not sure what to order from the Raw Bar, try Fulton's Seafood Tower. Soups and salads are also available. There are so many entrees that you might have a hard time deciding. Some of the choices are crab cakes, snapper, lobster, ribs, filet mignon, ribeye, and even pasta. Sorbet is the perfect light dessert after a filling meal. Fulton's Crab House has an award winning wine list; many wines are available by the glass. Craft beers are also sold, as are specialty cocktails including Fulton's Seasonal Manhattan, Fulton's Cappuccino, and Strawberry Cheesecake Martini. Other alcoholic and non-alcoholic beverages are also sold. Fulton's Crab House is open daily for lunch and dinner.

Wolfgang Puck Grand Cafe
West Side - $$$

The second of the Wolfgang Puck eateries is Wolfgang Puck Grand Cafe. This signature restaurant is located in the same building as The Dining Room, but has a more casual feel. Bright colors and geometric lighting fixtures add an eclectic vibe to the dining area. The walls are covered with artwork. When you enter, you'll pass both the sushi bar and the open pizza kitchen. Request a table near a window for great views of Village Lake.

The menu at Wolfgang Puck Grand Cafe features the creations of one of the most famous chefs in the world. His motto is "live, love, eat", and there is plenty to love on the menu. Start with the signature item- Butternut Squash Soup. You might try Grilled Italian Sausage or Garlic & White Bean Hummus to begin your meal as well. There are entree salads if you want to keep your meal light. Other entrees include pork, chicken, steak, and pasta. The Wood Fired Pizzas are individual sized. You can also order your favorite sushi creation. Sandwiches are served at lunchtime as well. Try a slice of Florida Key Lime Pie or Classic Carrot Cake for dessert. There are many signature cocktail choices, including Wildberry Lemonade, Tropical Sunburst, and Lemon Goose-tini. You can skip the alcohol with the Nada Colada or a Fruit Blast. There's an international wine list to choose from as well. Other alcoholic and non-alcoholic beverages are also available. Wolfgang Puck Grand Cafe is open daily for lunch and dinner.

Full Service Dining

AMC Downtown Disney 24 Dine-In Theatres
West Side - $

Also known as Fork and Screen, AMC Downtown Disney 24 Dine-In Theatres takes the expression "dinner and a movie" to a whole new level. Once you purchase your ticket you can pick which seats you'd like. Depending on the theater, there are two or four seats per group. Relax in the lobby for a few minutes while you wait for your seating. You'll then be escorted to the theater to sit in comfortable chairs with a table in front of you. There is plenty of room and, since each theater has limited seating, there is an at-home, intimate feel to the experience. A call button will allow you to get in touch with your server when needed. All guests must be 18 or older, or accompanied by an adult over 21.

The food at Fork and Screen is much more creative than the traditional movie theater popcorn and candy. You can start with a plate of Buffalo Chicken Wings or the Seafood Sampler. Entrees include burgers, fish, chicken, wraps, tacos, quesadillas, and flatbread pizzas. Since dessert will help you make it through the latest thriller they have some great options, including sundaes and carrot cake. Don't forget your drink! There's a full bar, which features specialties like Blue Laguna, Pomegranate Martini, and Oreo Mudslide. Other alcoholic and non-alcoholic beverages are also sold. AMC Downtown Disney 24 Dine-In Theatres is open daily for lunch and dinner.

Bongos Cuban Cafe
West Side - $$

Enjoy a meal in Cuba without ever leaving Central Florida. Bongos Cuban Cafe will transform you to a Havana nightclub from the 1950's, at least for a little while. If you're not sure which building it is, just look for the giant pineapple. The restaurant is the creation of Gloria and Emilio Estefan, and there are images of the singer throughout. You'll also find palm trees, Spanish sayings, and, of course, bongos as part of the decor. There is plenty of indoor seating, or for an excellent view you might ask to be seated outside. On Friday and Saturday evenings, there is live music and dancing.

The food at Bongos is Cuban with a little bit of Caribbean flair thrown in from time to time. You can start your meal with soup or a salad. If you're not sure which appetizer to order, you might want to try the "Bongos Combo", which serves two. Lunch offers a variety of sandwiches from the classic Sandwich Cubano to the Cuban Club Sandwich. Burgers, skirt steak, chicken, and other dishes are also available, (all with a Cuban twist). For your dinner entree you might want to try The Cuban Tour, Bongos Famous Fried Shredded Beef, or Cuban Style Milanese Chicken Breast. For dessert your whole party can split a churros platter. Bongos Cuban Cafe has lots of specialty cocktails for adults. World Famous Mojitos and Bongoritas are both available, as well as beer, wine, sangria, and other alcoholic and non-alcoholic beverages. Bongos Cuban Cafe is open daily for lunch and dinner.

Crossroads at House of Blues
West Side - $$

If you like art and good food, you'll want to check out Crossroads at House of Blues. The restaurant is popular with tourists and locals alike. The lighting is low and the walls are filled with eclectic artwork, instruments, and other salutes to the arts. On Friday and Saturday evenings, there is live blues music, featuring local and national artists. If you are planning to attend a concert at the House of Blues Music Hall, make a dinner reservation at Crossroads before the show. Ordering an entree will allow you to "Pass the Line" so that you will be admitted before other concertgoers. The restaurant tends to be noisy, so this is not where you'll find a quiet meal.

The menu at Crossroads at House of Blues was created by celebrity chef Aaron Sanchez of Food Network fame. Appetizers for lunch or dinner include Cornbread with Maple Butter, Crossroads Quesadilla, and various flatbread options. You might also want to order one of the several varieties of Street Tacos. Next, you'll choose entrees from fried chicken, jambalaya, ribs, shrimp and grits, sandwiches, signature burgers, or other items. Desserts include Bourbon Bread Pudding, Triple Chocolate Cheesecake, and Chef's Choice Ice Cream. Beer, wine, and other alcoholic and non-alcoholic beverages are available.

On Sunday mornings at 10:30 and Sunday afternoons at 1:00, the Sunday Gospel Brunch is held at Crossroads. Live gospel music is performed while you enjoy an all-you-can-eat buffet. Food items include omelets, scrambled eggs, biscuits and gravy, BBQ chicken, prime rib, chicken jambalaya, and bread pudding. Gospel music superstar Kirk Franklin helped to create and produce the show, and he will occasionally make an appearance. Crossroads at House of Blues is open daily for lunch and dinner, and Sundays for brunch.

Paradiso 37, Taste of the Americas
Pleasure Island - $$

The "37" in the name refers to 37 countries in North, Central, and South America. The "Taste of the Americas" part refers to the mixed cuisine that is served. You'll find a blend of flavors from all of the Americas. At lunchtime the restaurant is a great spot for a semi-quiet meal. It really comes alive at night with live music starting at 6:00pm. While there is a nightclub feel in the evenings, kids are still welcome. Both indoor and covered outdoor seating is available.

The menu is the same for lunch and dinner. You might want to start your meal with North American Corn Dogs, P37 Nachos, or Caribbean Crab and Fish Fritters. There's a great variety of entrees. There are several types of burritos, or you might want to try the contrasting tastes of the Bacon and Pineapple Burger. Other burgers, steak, chicken, seafood, and enchiladas are also served. If you're in the mood for dessert, selections include Seasonal Fruit Empanadas, Paradiso 37 Chocolate Stack, and Chilean Sopapillas. If you're hot, thirsty, and of age, you can order "the world's coldest beer". It's kept at 29 degrees, and you can see the thermometer that proves it. There's an international wine menu and plenty of tequila. The Tequila Tower features over 50 choices. You can order margaritas by the pitcher or tequila flights so that you can taste several varieties. Summer Time, Pain Killer, and Pisco Sour are a few of the specialty cocktails. The menu explains where each drink originates. Other alcoholic and non-alcoholic beverages are also available. Paradiso 37, Taste of the Americas is open daily for lunch and dinner.

Planet Hollywood
West Side - $$

It's hard to miss Planet Hollywood. The building is a giant blue planet. If you love movies, you'll want to make a reservation here. There is movie memorabilia everywhere! You'll find props and costumes from hundreds of movies along the walls and in cases. Cars, motorcycles, ships, and even Woody hang overhead. Rock videos and movie clips play while you dine. Planet Hollywood is quite popular, so you'll want to make a reservation. Since it's loud and flashy inside, this isn't the place for a quiet meal. While you wait for your meal or after you're done, take a stroll around all three floors of the restaurant. That way, you can have a better look at the props and memorabilia.

The menu at Planet Hollywood is as diverse as its decorations. Appetizers run from A to Z with the Avocado Stack to Zucchini Strips. You'll also find Parmesan Spinach Dip, Buffalo Wings, Sliders, and other appetizers. Or, try the VIP Platter which serves four, to share several different appetizers. If you want salad, try the Hollywood Bowl or the Southwestern Salad. Entrees include seafood, steak, burgers, fajitas, pasta, chicken, sandwiches, and other choices. The L.A. Lasagna deserves special mention because the classic dish is fried. For dessert, try a Cool Planet Banana Split or another ice cream treat. There are also several types of cheesecake and White Chocolate Bread Pudding. Specialty cocktails include selections such as The Dark Knight, Iron Man, and Legally Blonde. Beer, wine, and other alcoholic beverages are also served. Non-alcoholic drinks include milkshakes, frappes, smoothies, coffee, tea, and other hot and cold choices. Planet Hollywood is open daily for lunch and dinner.

Portobello Country Italian Trattoria
Pleasure Island - $$$

Unlike many Disney restaurants, the atmosphere at Portobello is not overly flashy. The eating area is mostly earth tones, which contrast nicely with the white tablecloths. Simple pictures adorn the walls. The large bar shows off the restaurant's wine selection. If you'd prefer to eat outdoors, you'll have a nice view of Village Lake and Fulton's Crab House.

Portobello Country Italian Trattoria features seasonal Italian foods. The menu will change from time to time based on what is fresh. Local ingredients are incorporated as well. Start your lunch or dinner with Mozzarella Stuffed Rice Balls, Shrimp Spiedino, or Portobello Mushroom (you knew that had to be on the menu.) Soups and salads are also sold. For your entrée, you might want to order an individual sized pizza, as there are many creations to choose from. Pasta choices might include Gnocchi, Black Fettucine with Shrimp, and Spaghetti with Meatballs. If you don't want pizza or pasta you can order steak, chicken, seafood, or pork. The portions at Portobello Country Italian Trattoria are large, but you should save room for dessert. With options like Chocolate Paradis, Biramisu (it's tiramisu with beer), and Authentic Italian Gelato & Sorbet, you'll be glad that you decided to indulge. Specialty cocktails include Raspbasilico, Stregarita, and Italian Manhattan. Wine is served by the glass, half bottle, or bottle. There are also domestic and imported beers. If you don't want the alcohol you can order an Italian soda or Local Honey Lemonade. Other alcoholic and non-alcoholic beverages are also available. Portobello Country Italian Trattoria is open daily for lunch and dinner.

Raglan Road Irish Pub and Restaurant
Pleasure Island - $, $$

FAN PICK

Whoever thought that there would be a traditional Irish pub in Central Florida? Raglan Road is bigger than most pubs found in Ireland, but everything else is as authentic as can be. The 130-year-old bars were imported from Ireland. There is live music and authentic Irish dancing most nights, and the place can get loud. The menu is the creation of Master Chef Kevin Dundon, who put his own spin on many classic dishes. While the "Pub" part of the name is taken seriously, kids are welcome.

At Raglan Road Irish Pub and Restaurant, you'll find all of your favorite Irish classics, but with fun names. Appetizers include Heaven on Earth (ribs), Dalkey Duo (cocktail sausages), and Kiss Before Shrimp (it's heavy on the garlic). For your main course, you can order Fish & Chips, Keen Eye for the Shepherd's Pie, Raglan Risotto, Bangers & Booz, or Kevin's Heavenly Ham. Lamb, pork, beef, seafood, and other dishes are also served. The desserts are as delicious as the rest of the food, with choices like Strawberry and Apple Crumble, Trifle Sinful, and Dunbrody Kiss, which is billed as "Chef Dundon's gift to America". Since it's an authentic Irish pub, there is a huge selection of draft beers, ales, and lagers. Order an imported or domestic pint, or try a flight instead. Specialty drinks include An Irish Red Eye, The Dubliner, and One For The Road. Wine and other alcoholic beverages are also served. Raglan Road Irish Pub and Restaurant is open daily for lunch and dinner.

Rainforest Cafe at Downtown Disney Marketplace Marketplace - $$

This is one of two Rainforest Cafe locations at Walt Disney World. The other restaurant is located at Disney's Animal Kingdom. The restaurant is part of an international chain, and it fits in quite well at Walt Disney World. The Downtown Disney version is easy to find, just head towards the giant volcano (it erupts at night). Inside you'll find a rainforest theme, complete with audio-animatronic animals, vines, real fish, and other surprises. There are "storms" from time to time. The lights will flash, and it's fun to watch the animals react. Rainforest Cafe is loud, and it's a great place for most kids. If your children don't like loud noises, you might want to stay away. There's a gift shop where you can browse while you're waiting for your table.

Many of the menu items have fun themed names. You might want to begin your meal with Jungle Chop Salad or Lava Nachos for Two.

Entrees have names like Taste of the Wild, and Planet Earth Pasta. You'll find seafood, burgers, steak, pasta, sandwiches, and other selections. The chain's signature dessert is the Sparkling Volcano. It's made out of chocolate brownie cake (shaped like a volcano), vanilla ice cream, whipped cream, and both chocolate and caramel sauces. It's topped with a decorative sparkler and it is large enough for at least three people. Specialty drinks include Margarilla, Tropical Toucan, and Panama Punch. Other alcoholic drinks are also served. There are non-alcoholic specialties, as well as other beverages. Rainforest Cafe at Downtown Disney Marketplace is open daily for lunch and dinner.

Splitsville Luxury Lanes
West Side - $$

You'll rethink what a bowling alley is supposed to be like when you visit Splitsville Luxury Lanes. There are 30 lanes on two floors. There's live music and dancing. You can play billiards or visit the gift shop. If you don't bowl, don't let that keep you away. You do not have to bowl in order to eat. The walls feature murals that will remind you that you're at Walt Disney World and in Florida. There is both indoor and outdoor seating.

The food is what makes Splitsville such a popular spot for tourists and locals alike. Celebrity chef, Tim Cushman, seems to have thought of everything. Appetizers include diverse selections such as Cheeseburger Sliders, Edamame, and Alley Nachos. Ever think of ordering sushi in a bowling alley? You can see where it's made and then place your order. You can dine on pizza, burgers, noodle bowls, sandwiches, pork, chicken, salmon, steak, and other items. The menu also features 16 choices with a "GF" symbol next to them. That stands for "gluten-free", making it easy for those who need to keep an eye on gluten. Desserts include Super Sundae and Giant Cake. When they say giant, they mean it. Specialty cocktails include 7/10 Dirty, Snickertini, and Birthday Cake. Another interesting beverage option allows you to "customize your drink" with Coca-Cola Freestyle. Other alcoholic and non-alcoholic beverages are also available. Splitsville Luxury Lanes is open daily for lunch, dinner, and bowling.

T-REX
Marketplace - $$

You'll head back over 200 million years and party with the dinosaurs when you enter T-REX. The restaurant was created by the same group responsible for Rainforest Cafe, and both places are loud and a lot of fun. Be warned that there are several larger than life creatures throughout the place (including a moving octopus over the bar), so if your kids scare easily this may not be the place for them. There are four different themed rooms that you might dine in. You could sit in an ice cave, or maybe enjoy a meteor shower. The Paleo Zone allows kids to dig for fossils while waiting for the meal. You can even make your own dinosaur to take home at Build-A-Dino By Build-A-Bear Workshop. It's located in the gift shop.

Like Rainforest Cafe, many of the menu items have fun names. Appetizers include Footprints Flatbread, Megalosaurus Mozzarella, and the Supersaurus Sampler, which is enough food for four. The entree names are just as creative. You'll find Layers of the Earth Lasagna,

Gigantosaurus Burger, and Cretaceous Chicken Fried Steak all listed. You can order pasta, burgers, sandwiches, chicken, steak, ribs, salad, seafood, and other items to feast on. Chocolate Extinction is the restaurant's signature dessert. It is made of chocolate fudge cake, ice cream, sauces, whipped cream, and Butterfinger pieces. It serves four. Other desserts include Ice Age Indulgence and Cosmic Key Lime Pie. Even though the restaurant is great for kids, adult beverages are served. A popular specialty is the Cotton-tini, which is made with cotton candy. Other specialties include Caveman Punch and Prehistoric Sunset. Beer, wine, and other alcoholic beverages are also sold. Non-alcoholic choices include Strawberry-Asaurus Lemonade and The Ultimate Prehistoric Smoothie, as well as other drinks. T-REX is open daily for lunch and dinner.

FORTY-FIVE

QUICK SERVICE DINING AT DOWNTOWN DISNEY

Bongos Cuban Cafe Express
West Side - $

In the mood for some authentic Cuban food, but don't have time for a sit down restaurant? Stop by Bongos Cuban Cafe Express! Located right by the full service restaurant. You can still order your Traditional Sandwich Cubano, Cuban Frita, or Arroz con Pollo, but you won't need to take a couple of hours out of your day for your meal. Beverages are available. Bongos Cuban Cafe Express is open daily for lunch and dinner.

Cookes of Dublin
Pleasure Island - $

Enjoy authentic Irish family recipes at Cookes of Dublin. The batter recipe is a closely guarded secret, and the food is not cooked until you order it. That may take a few extra minutes, but the wait will be worth it. You can try the special family batter with The Original One & One (Fish & Chips) or Battered Burger & Chips. You'll also find Irish classics such as Beef and Lamb Pie, Fisherman's Pie, and Mini Irish Sausages. If you want something to dip your chips in, try Irish Vintage Cheese and Bacon Dip, or Garlic Mayo. For dessert you might want the Strawberry Shortcake (as soon as you see it you'll know why). There are also cupcakes, ice cream, and "Doh Bar" Fried Candy Bars. Non-alcoholic beverages are sold. There is a small amount of indoor and covered outdoor seating. Cookes of Dublin is open daily for lunch and dinner.

Earl of Sandwich Marketplace - $

FAN PICK

Plan your meal at an off-time if possible because Earl of Sandwich is extremely popular. The staff is good at keeping the line moving, even when the restaurant is packed. The eatery is a tribute to John Montagu, who forever changed the way that we eat by inventing the sandwich back in 1762. Earl of Sandwich claims to have "The World's Greatest Hot Sandwich". Breakfast features different types of egg and cheese sandwiches, fruit and yogurt parfaits, oatmeal, bagels, and some bakery items. At lunch and dinner the hot sandwiches are the star. They're made to order. Choices include The Original 1762, The Earl's Club, Tuna Melt, and Caprese. Wraps are also available. You can add soup, salad, and sides like coleslaw or potato salad. You might want to grab a dessert before you checkout; cookies, brownie sandwiches, and cupcakes are a few of the choices. Beverages include Earl's Grey Lemonade, coffee, smoothies, and fountain drinks. Earl of Sandwich is considered by many to be one of the best food bargains at Walt Disney World. There is indoor and outdoor seating, and spots go quickly during peak times. Earl of Sandwich is open daily for breakfast, lunch, and dinner.

The Express at Wolfgang Puck Grand Cafe West Side - $

If you want to try the recipes of one of the world's most famous chef's, but you're in a hurry, The Express at Wolfgang Puck Grand Cafe is your solution. It's one of four Wolfgang Puck restaurants at

Downtown Disney and one of two quick service options. You can still enjoy your Butternut Squash Soup or California Roll, but you won't have to make a reservation or wait for a table. You can order an individual pizza, Chicken Pot Pie, Chinois Chicken Salad, or Pesto Chicken Salad Sandwich. Beverages are available as well. The Express at Wolfgang Puck Grand Cafe is open daily for lunch and dinner.

FoodQuest
West Side - $

DisneyQuest Interactive Indoor Theme Park is five floors of fun for those who love video games, virtual reality, and adventure. It requires a separate ticket. Once you're in DisneyQuest, what do you do if you get hungry? You stop by FoodQuest. You can order flatbread pizza, sandwiches, wraps, burgers, and other things that will help you refuel. Ice cream bars and cupcakes are sold for dessert or as a snack. Beer and wine are available to those of age. Other beverages include fountain drinks, coffee, tea, juice, milk, and water. FoodQuest is open daily for lunch, dinner, and snacks.

Marketplace Snacks
Marketplace - $

If you're looking for a quick lunch or dinner, don't let the name Marketplace Snacks fool you. You can order a veggie or an Italian wrap. Chili Cheese hot dogs are also served. Beer, wine, and cold beverages are available as well. Marketplace Snacks is open daily for lunch, dinner, snacks, and beverages.

The Smokehouse
West Side - $

The Smokehouse is a quick meal option at House of Blues. But don't be surprised if you find the setting so relaxing that you decide to stay for a while. Outdoor seating is available, and there is often live music. Barbecue is the name of the game here. You'll find pulled pork or chicken, ribs, and even turkey legs. Of course baked beans and coleslaw are available sides. Cookies, brownies, and candy are sold for dessert. If you're 21 or older you can order a cocktail, a glass of wine, or a beer. Fountain drinks and other beverages are also served. The Smokehouse is open daily for lunch and dinner.

Wolfgang Puck Express at Downtown Disney Marketplace
Marketplace - $

The final Wolfgang Puck offering is Wolfgang Puck Express at Downtown Disney Marketplace. There is a unique feature to this choice. Unlike the other three Wolfgang Puck restaurants, this one serves breakfast. You can start your day with eggs, Belgian or chocolate chip waffles, omelets, a breakfast pizza, or other items. Lunch and dinner feature "Wolfgang Classics" like Cavatappi Chicken Alfredo and Bacon Wrapped Meatloaf. You can also get pizza, sandwiches, salads, and other items. Desserts include Vanilla Bean Cheesecake and Creme Brulee with Berries. Beer, wine, fountain drinks, and other beverages are sold. There is indoor and outdoor seating. Wolfgang Puck Express at Downtown Disney Marketplace is open daily for breakfast, lunch, and dinner.

Food Trucks

In 2013, the first food trucks opened at Downtown Disney. Each truck serves a limited number of items that are Disney classics. The trucks are themed and brightly decorated. The hours of operation may vary, and since they are mobile, the locations can change as well. There have also been hints that Disney will add more food trucks in the future.

Fantasy Fare
Mobile - $

Hand dipped corn dogs are a popular item at Disneyland Resort in California. At Fantasy Fare, they're now sold in Central Florida as well. Croque Monsieur from Disneyland Resort Paris and Glass Noodle Salad with Chicken from Hong Kong Disneyland Resort are also featured. Cold drinks are available. Fantasy Fare is open on select days for lunch and dinner.

Namaste Cafe
Mobile - $

The tastes of Disney's Animal Kingdom are featured at this food truck. The menu includes Slow Cooked Beef Short Ribs, Tandori Spiced Shrimp, and Butter Chicken. All three entrees are served with Basmati Rice, Naan Bread, and Pickled Vegetables. Cold drinks are also sold. Namaste Cafe is open on select days for lunch and dinner.

Superstar Catering
Mobile - $

A "Star Studded Menu" is featured at Superstar Catering. You can find selections from Disney's Hollywood Studios here. The items available are Beef, Spinach and Feta Meatball Sandwich, Lamb Meatball Flatbread Sandwich, and Turkey Sausage Meatballs. Cold drinks are available. Superstar Catering is open on select days for lunch and dinner.

World Showcase of Flavors
Mobile - $

The idea for World Showcase of Flavors is brilliant. It features three dishes that are served at the Epcot International Food & Wine Festival.

The choices are Grass Fed Beef Sliders, Lobster Roll, and Pierogies with Kielbasa and Caramelized Onions. Wine is also available, with suggested pairings for each dish. Cold drinks are sold as well. World Showcase of Flavors is open on select days for lunch and dinner.

FORTY-SIX

SNACKS AND BEVERAGES AT DOWNTOWN DISNEY

Snacks

Downtown Snow Company
Marketplace - $

Wouldn't a little bit of snow be nice on a hot summer's day? That's what you can get at Downtown Snow Company. The kiosk sells Snow Shaved Ice in various flavors. You can add toppings if you'd like. Glazed roasted nuts are also sold. Beverages include iced tea, juice, and water.

Ghirardelli Ice Cream & Chocolate Shop
Marketplace - $

FAN PICK

Chocolate and ice cream! What more could you want in a snack? The sundaes at Ghirardelli are legendary, with choices like The Treasure Island Warm Brownie Sundae, Espresso Escape, and The Strike It Rich Butterscotch Hot Fudge Sundae. If you'd prefer, you can order a sundae with your choice of ice cream and toppings. You can also order a cone or a cup. If you love chocolate, but don't want ice cream, try a brownie or a cookie. Floats and shakes are served, as well as several hot creations, many of which include chocolate. You can also order cold coffee drinks and other beverages. There is indoor and outdoor seating, but tables go quickly.

Haagen-Dazs Kiosk
West Side - $

Fourteen popular flavors of Haagen-Dazs are sold here. Order your favorite in a cup, or try a hand-dipped cone for a little extra decadence. Sundaes are available as well, or you can pick up a shake or a coffee frappe.

Goofy's Candy Company
Marketplace - $ FAN PICK

While Goofy's Candy Company is technically a store and not a restaurant, there are so many snack options that it deserves a mention. You'll find plenty of candy, and also covered apples, crisped rice treats, and other sweet items. You can also create your own snack. You pick a treat, choose what it will be dipped in, add a topping, and then decide what should be drizzled on top. A cast member will then create it for you while you watch. If you're thirsty, you can also order Goofy's Glaciers. These frozen drinks are available in eight flavors, and you can mix them if you want.

Wetzel's Pretzels
Marketplace - $

When you're in a hurry, a pretzel can be the perfect snack. You'll find many great choices at Wetzel's Pretzels. In addition to the original pretzel, you can order a creation such as Sinful Cinnamon or Sour Cream & Onion. Pretzel Bitz are also sold. Add a dip and you'll be full in no time. Frozen granita, lemonade, and other cold drinks are available as well.

Wetzel's Pretzels Kiosk
West Side - $

Wetzel's Pretzels and Haagen-Dazs used to share a space in Downtown Disney. With all the changes, that location closed to make way for Starbucks. Now the two brands have kiosks right next to each other on the Cirque du Soleil side of DisneyQuest. This kiosk features original, cheese, and flavored pretzels, bitz, and dips. Lemonade and other beverages are also sold.

Beverages

Cap'n Jack's Margarita Bar
Marketplace - $

While Cap'n Jack's Restaurant may be gone (an early casualty of Disney Springs), you can still order some of the specialty drinks at Cap'n Jack's Margarita Bar. A few of the selections are Marina Margarita, 1800 Margarita, and Rum Runner. The frozen Strawberry Margarita, a Cap'n Jack's classic, is also served, as are beer, wine, and other alcoholic and non-alcoholic choices. There is limited outdoor seating.

Forty Thirst Street Express
Marketplace - $

Joffrey's coffee is featured here. You can order your favorite hot or cold creation, and if you're of age you can add a kick to your beverage. Frozen drinks are also sold.

The Front Porch
West Side - $

Enjoy a drink and live music outside of House of Blues. The lounge and the seating are all outdoors and performances may be canceled if the weather turns ugly. Enjoy beer, wine, or a cocktail while you relax for a little while.

Lava Lounge
Marketplace - $

Where else can you grab a cool drink inside of a volcano? Appetizers are served and you might also be able to order off the Rainforest Cafe menu. Specialty cocktails such as Mongoose Mai Tai, Island Freeze, and Hawaiian Orchid Martini are served, as well as other alcoholic and non-alcoholic beverages. Covered outdoor seating is available.

MacGUFFINS
West Side - $

MacGUFFINS proves that there's more to movie theater beverages than oversized fountain drinks! The lounge is located in the lobby of AMC Downtown Disney. You can order a meal or a snack to accompany your drink. Cocktails include Cosmopolitan, Blue Laguna, and Velvet Hammer. Other alcoholic and non-alcoholic drinks are also served and you can take everything into the theater with you when it's time for your flick.

Starbucks at Downtown Disney Marketplace
Marketplace - $

Here you can find breakfast sandwiches and pastries all day, as well as all of the drinks that Starbucks is known for. This outside kiosk sells

Caffe Misto, Shaken Passion Iced Tea, Vanilla Bean Creme, and all your other favorites. Look in front of World of Disney for this walk up location.

Starbucks at Downtown Disney West Side
West Side - $

All of your favorite Starbucks beverages are sold here, but there is also something unique to look for. This location features the Clover Bar, which sells reserve coffees that are brewed to order. Some rare coffees and blends are available. If you just want to get a Caramel Macchiato, they serve those as well. You can also order breakfast sandwiches and pastries all day. There is an interactive "chalk" screen, which allows guests to doodle on pictures taken seconds earlier in the restaurant, or on the live stream from Disneyland in California. Enjoy your beverage in the air conditioning, or sit outside by the fire.

FORTY-SEVEN

ESPN WIDE WORLD OF SPORTS COMPLEX

While the ESPN Wide World of Sports Complex may not be a part of most Walt Disney World Vacations, it still deserves a mention. The area covers over 220 acres and the complex is host to over 200 sporting events throughout the year. It is where Spring Training takes place for the Atlanta Braves. The games are played in Champion Stadium. There are concession stands throughout the complex. You can visit the Welcome Center and the ESPN Clubhouse Shop. There is an admission fee to enter. The amount varies depending on what is taking place at the time. Parking is free.

ESPN Wide World of Sports Grill
Quick Service - $

Come in out of the heat and sit for a while in air conditioned comfort. ESPN Wide World of Sports Grill features the type of dishes that you might expect to find at a stadium. Cold sandwiches include tuna salad, a BLT, and a veggie pita. Burgers, pulled pork, and Pastrami on Rye are among the hot sandwiches. Wings, nachos, hot dogs, and individual pizzas are also on the menu. Ice cream and cookies are among the desserts. There's a bar with selections for those of age, and coffee, tea, and other hot and cold beverages are sold as well. Watch the latest game while you eat. Before you leave, make sure that you have your picture taken behind the replica ESPN Sports Center desk.

Food Trucks
Mobile - $

For some sporting events, food trucks will show up at ESPN Wide World of Sports Complex. One truck is the ESPNWWOS Truck, but other trucks that are not owned by Disney might be there as well. The menus and the number of trucks will vary depending on the event.

FORTY-EIGHT

A BRIEF INTRODUCTION TO THE WALT DISNEY WORLD RESORTS

Part of planning a Walt Disney World vacation is deciding where you are going to stay. There are plenty of hotel rooms that are located on Disney property. Each Disney-owned resort has its own unique theme, ranging from whimsical to luxurious. There are four main pricing classifications for the Walt Disney World Resorts: Value, Moderate, Deluxe, and Deluxe Villa. There is also a campground. The time of year will affect the price.

There are some perks that Disney gives to people who stay on property. Disney's Magical Express is a service that picks guests up at the airport and then takes them back once their vacations are over. Extra Magic Hours allow guests to spend time in a select park when it is not open to the general public. The Disney Dining Plan is a way for guests to try different Walt Disney World restaurants while paying a set price. Not all hotels that are located on Disney property are owned by Walt Disney World, and the benefits will vary at those hotels.

All of the resorts have unique themed pools which match the theme of the resort. The more expensive the resort, the more elaborate the pools. There are also playgrounds, free movies under the stars, and walking trails at the resorts. Some have fitness centers. The rooms have free Wi-Fi and there is free transportation to the parks.

Dining at the Disney resorts is as diverse as the resorts themselves. Food courts are popular quick service options. Much of the food is prepared ahead of time so you can grab your meal and go. Some of the best signature dining experiences in all of Central Florida can be found at the Walt Disney World resorts. The chefs truly take pride in their creations and the atmosphere is more relaxed than in the full service theme park restaurants. There are also lounges and pool bars, which are family friendly. With the exception of Shades of Green, you do not need to be staying at a particular resort in order to dine there.

FORTY-NINE

DISNEY'S ALL-STAR MOVIES RESORT

Value

This Value resort is a salute to some Disney classics. The movies featured are *101 Dalmatians, Fantasia, Herbie: The Love Bug, The Mighty Ducks,* and *Toy Story.* They are depicted by larger than life statues and other nods to the films. The resort is a bit out of the way; the closest park is Disney's Blizzard Beach Water Park. It is part of the Animal Kingdom Resort Area. In-room pizza delivery is available until 1:00am.

World Premiere Food Court
Quick Service - $

This food court opens early and it remains open until midnight. The theme will make you feel like you have stepped inside a movie theater for a premier. Breakfast is served until 11:00am. There are five different stations from which you can order. Breakfast features omelets, pancakes, Mickey Waffles, and other morning foods. For lunch and dinner you can get individual pizzas, pasta, burgers, pork, chicken, beef, seafood, sandwiches, and other items. There is a bakery station and ice cream is also sold. Pizza, burgers, sandwiches, bakery items, and ice cream are among the late night choices. Beverages are also available. World Premiere Food Court is open daily for breakfast, lunch, dinner, and snacks.

Silver Screen Spirits Pool Bar
Pool Bar - $

Cool off at the Fantasia Pool by grabbing a drink at the Silver Screen Spirits Pool Bar. Try a frozen Mango Margarita or Black Cherry Lemonade on the rocks. There are plenty of specialty drinks to choose from, as well as beer, wine, and sangria. Non-alcoholic specialties include the Lava Smoothie and the Orange Freeze. Silver Screen Spirits Pool Bar is open daily for beverages.

FIFTY

DISNEY'S ALL-STAR
MUSIC RESORT

Value

This Value resort is a salute to different types of music. There are nods to Broadway, calypso, country, jazz, and rock and roll. Larger than life cowboy boots, guitars, drums, and other music related items are everywhere. There is, of course, a guitar shaped pool. The closest park is Disney's Blizzard Beach. The resort is part of the Animal Kingdom Resort Area. In-room pizza delivery is available until 1:00am.

Intermission Food Court
Quick Service - $

One thing that is nice about the food courts is that they have a large variety of options. Intermission Food Court is no exception. The colors are bright and you'll see stars everywhere, including giant depictions of legendary musicians. The eatery opens early for breakfast, which is served until 11:00am. Choices include Mickey Waffles, omelets, pancakes, baked goods, and plenty of other breakfast items. There are bountiful choices for lunch and dinner, including burgers, pizza, quesadillas, salads, and pasta. Save room for dessert! You can order an ice cream sundae, cake, or another sweet treat. The restaurant stays open until midnight, so grab a late night snack after a long day in a park. Beverages are also available. Intermission Food Court is open daily for breakfast, lunch, dinner, and snacks.

Singing Spirits Pool Bar
Pool Bar - $

Located at the Calypso Pool, this outdoor location has a full bar. You can try Skinnygirl Coconut Mojito, Moscato Colada, or Island Moonshine. Non-alcoholic drinks are available as well. Singing Spirits Pool Bar is open daily for beverages.

FIFTY-ONE

DISNEY'S ALL-STAR SPORTS RESORT

Value

This Value resort is designed for people who love both sports and all things Disney. Baseball, basketball, football, tennis, and surfing are featured. Where else can you see a football helmet that is several stories tall, or Huey, Dewey, and Louie playing baseball? Disney's All-Star Sports Resort is the closest of the three All-Star Resorts to Disney's Blizzard Beach. It is part of the Animal Kingdom Resort Area. In-room pizza delivery is available until 1:00am.

End Zone Food Court
Quick Service - $

This is a terrific place to grab a quick meal or a snack. You'll feel like you're dining in a sports stadium. You can start your day with breakfast meats, eggs, Mickey Waffles, pancakes, pastries, or other early morning items. Breakfast is served until 11:00am. There is plenty to choose from for lunch or dinner. Make-your-own salad, nachos, pizza, sandwiches, burgers, pasta, and hot dogs are just a few of the entrees. A smoothie will help you cool off on a hot day. Dessert items include gelato, Mickey Ice Cream Bars, and bakery treats. End Zone Food Court remains open until midnight with a large selection of late night snacks, including pizza and burgers. Beverages are also available. End Zone Food Court is open daily for breakfast, lunch, dinner, and snacks.

Grandstand Spirits Pool Bar
Pool Bar - $

Located by the Surfboard Bay Pool, this watering hole has a full bar. Moscato Colada, Citrus Blast, and Superfruit Sangria are just a few of the choices. There are also non-alcoholic drinks available. Grandstand Spirits Pool Bar is open daily for beverages.

FIFTY-TWO

DISNEY'S ANIMAL KINGDOM LODGE

Deluxe

There is a natural feel to the beauty found at this Deluxe resort. On the property for Disney's Animal Kingdom Lodge there are four savannas, which are home to over 200 species. If you need some adult time, there are supervised activities for the children. You'll want to take the kids to Uwanja Camp; it's a water play area designed with the whole family in mind. You can also sign up for a sunrise safari. There is so much to see and do at Disney's Animal Kingdom Lodge that you might decide to take a day off from the theme parks and spend some time just exploring. Disney's Animal Kingdom Lodge is home to the world's largest African wine collection outside of Africa. It is part of the Animal Kingdom Resort Area. Room service is available until midnight.

Jiko - The Cooking Place
Fine Dining - $$$

There is something truly special about this signature dining experience. The flavors of Africa are served in fresh items that you won't find elsewhere in Central Florida. The setting is unique, with large windows that allow a gorgeous view, birds flying overhead, and walls filled with bottles of African wines. There's an open kitchen so you can watch as the chefs prepare your meal. While the attention to detail is obvious, nothing is overdone. There are also some fun Hidden Mickeys to look for. The restaurant has a dress code.

While the atmosphere at Jiko - The Cooking Place is incredible, it is the food that you will best remember it for. The dishes have an African flair, but there is something for everyone on the menu. Start your meal with a wood-fired flatbread. You might then want to try an artisanal cheese. The menu changes from time to time so that only the freshest foods will be served. It could include such specialties as "Nigerian-style" Pan-roasted Local Whole Fish, Tangine Chicken, Spicy Botswana-style "Seswaa" Beef Short Rib, and Vegetable and Tofu Sambusas. There are also incredible dessert selections, such as Chocolate and Tea Safari, Kenyan Coffee Creme Brulee, and Milk Tart. Only African wines are served, and there is quite a selection. There are also after dinner drinks, specialty teas, and other alcoholic or non-alcoholic beverages available. Jiko - The Cooking Place is open daily for dinner.

Jiko - The Cooking Place is also the home of Jiko Wine Tasting. Each Wednesday, those 21 and older can sample three African wines, accompanied by a selection of cheese. Reservations are recommended and can be made by calling 407-WDW-DINE (407-939-3463).

Sanaa
Full Service - $$

Sanaa is located in the Kidani Village section of Disney's Animal Kingdom Lodge. The word "sanaa" means "art" in Swahili and you'll soon see why it is the perfect name for this eatery. The atmosphere at the restaurant is beautiful, with bold colors and simple designs. The best part of the ambiance is the view that you'll have of the savanna. Ask for a window table when you check in. The animals freely roam outside, giving you a chance to watch them as you dine.

The food at Sanaa is just as wonderful as the view. Start with a choice of breads with accompaniments, or try the Appetizers Sampler for Two. The entrees may include Tandoori Lamb, Grilled New York Strip, Today's Sustainable Fish, and Sanaa Vegetarian Sampler. Tanzanian Chocolate Mousse and Warm Bamboo Rice Pudding are just two of the possible desserts. There are specialty cocktails such as Magical Star Cocktail and African Starr Mojito. Non-alcoholic choices include Mango Lassi Smoothie, Press Pot Coffee, and Loose Leaf Tea Offerings. You can also enjoy fountain beverages and other drinks. Sanaa is open daily for lunch and dinner.

Boma - Flavors of Africa Buffet - $$

FAN PICK

Boma - Flavors of Africa has the feel of an open African market. Even the ceiling is decorated. Stacked jars double as pillars. There are animal statues that serve as decorations. Although the name implies only African food, there is a good mixture of African and American dishes. The food is served buffet style.

For breakfast at Boma, the buffet features well known items such as omelets, pancakes, and hand carved meats. You can also find less familiar choices like French Toast Bread Pudding, Pap and Chakalaka, and African Pastries. Press Pot with Kenyan Coffee and other hot drinks, as well as various juices, milk, fountain drinks, and other beverages are available. For dinner, you might want to start with the Butternut Squash Soup. There are several other soups that you might decide to sample, plus there are salads and other sides on the buffet. Spice-crusted Beef Striploin, Whole Durban-style Roasted Chicken, Mater Paneer and Fufu are a few of the entree choices. For dessert, grab a Zebra Dome and a Kenyan Coffee Tart. The buffet has a separate area for children. There are specialty cocktails, such as the Rye Manhattan and the Truffle Olive

Martini. Non-alcoholic hot and cold beverages are available as well. Boma - Flavors of Africa is open daily for breakfast and dinner.

The Mara
Quick Service - $

The Mara is named after a river in Kenya and Tanzania and is part of the name of a national reserve. This quick service eatery takes the name seriously by creating the feel of a rainforest inside. There are murals on the walls and the pillars in the restaurant are designed to look like trees. There is indoor and outdoor seating. While there are plenty of African inspired dishes, the menu also features American favorites. Breakfast includes such items as the African-inspired Breakfast Platter, the Bobotie Platter, and Mickey Waffles. For lunch or dinner you might want the Falafel Pita or the Mara Salad with Chicken, or maybe you'd prefer an Angus Bacon Cheeseburger or a flatbread pizza. There are bakery items served throughout the day, as well as coffee creations, smoothies, and other beverages. The Mara is open daily for breakfast, lunch, dinner, and snacks.

Maji Pool Bar
Pool Bar - $

Located inside Kidani Village, this pool bar carries more than just beverages. It can be a great place to grab a snack or a quick meal while you relax in the sun. Offerings include Pressed Pork, Ham and Swiss Sandwich, Vegetarian Falafel, and Tandoori Chicken Caesar Salad. You can also order chips, fruit, or dessert. Some of the alcoholic choices are Moscato Colada, Mango Margarita, and Banana Cabana. There are non-alcoholic specialty drinks and other beverages available as well. Maji Pool Bar is open daily for beverages and snacks.

Uzima Springs Pool Bar
Pool Bar - $

Built to resemble a thatched hut, this watering hole has a full bar for those 21 and older. It is located by the Uzima Pool. Specialty drinks such as Skinny Coconut Mojito and Island Moon-shine are featured, as are African beers and wines. There are non-alcoholic specialties and other beverages sold as well. Uzima Springs Pool Bar is open daily for beverages.

Cape Town Lounge and Wine Bar
Lounge - $

Since Disney's Animal Kingdom Lodge has the world's largest collection of African wines found outside of Africa, it makes sense that there is a wine bar. Located near Jiko - The Cooking Place, you can grab a drink while you wait for your reservation. If you don't have a reservation, you can enjoy a meal in the lounge; the Jiko menu is available. There is a full bar, which serves specialty drinks, draft beers, and of course, African wines. Even though it is a lounge it is family friendly, with non-alcoholic choices like Minnie Mouse and Sunriser. Cape Town Lounge and Wine Bar is open each evening.

Sanaa Lounge
Lounge - $$

Grab a drink then head outdoors to see which animals are roaming about, or sit down and relax for a little while. African wines, beers, and specialty cocktails are served, as are flights and other beverages. You can enjoy an appetizer such as Potato and Pea Samosas or Lamb Kefta Sliders with your drink. Sanaa Lounge is open daily for snacks and beverages.

Victoria Falls Lounge
Lounge - $

This lounge is a great place to relax for a little while after a crazy day in the parks. You can munch on Roasted Nuts with African Spices or Crisp Breads and Dips, while enjoying a cool drink. There are plenty of specialty cocktails to choose from, including Pimm's Punch and Blue "Glow-tini". There are specialty beers, African wines, and other selections as well. Non-alcoholic specialties include Pomegranate Splash and Coconut Elixir. Victoria Falls Lounge is open each evening.

FIFTY-THREE

DISNEY'S ART OF ANIMATION RESORT

Value

In 2012, Walt Disney World opened its newest Value resort. Disney's Art of Animation is a salute to four Disney animated classics; *Cars*, *Finding Nemo*, *The Lion King*, and *The Little Mermaid*. You'll find giant characters from the movies at the resort. The Big Blue Pool is the largest pool at any of the Walt Disney World resort hotels. The closest theme park is Disney's Hollywood Studios. Art of Animation is part of the Wide World of Sports Resort Area. In-room pizza delivery is available until midnight.

Landscape of Flavors
Quick Service - $

This food court gives nods to all four movies that are represented at the resort. The colors are bright, and there are plenty of choices, including grab and go items if you're in a hurry. For breakfast you can create your own yogurt parfait or fruit bowl. There are waffles shaped like your choice of three different characters. Cereal, eggs, pancakes, breakfast meats, sandwiches, and plenty of other early morning items are also sold. Lunch and dinner feature traditional entrees like pizza, burgers, and sandwiches. You could step out of the box a bit with selections such as Mongolian Grill Beef Stir Fry or Tandoori Boneless Chicken Thigh. Desserts include bakery items, Mickey Oreo Cupcakes, and gelato. There are plenty of beverage options. Late night snacks are available until midnight. Landscape of Flavors is open daily for breakfast, lunch, dinner, and snacks.

The Drop Off Pool Bar
Pool Bar - $

The Big Blue Pool is Walt Disney World's largest resort pool, and while you're enjoying some time in the water you might get thirsty. The Drop Off has a full bar. Specialty drinks include Citrus Infusion, Banana Cabana, and Captain's Mai Tai. There are non-alcoholic specialty drinks and other choices available as well. The Drop Off Pool Bar is open daily for beverages.

FIFTY-FOUR

DISNEY'S BEACH CLUB RESORT

Deluxe

Located in the Epcot Resort Area, Disney's Beach Club is a Deluxe resort. It is designed to resemble an old-fashioned hotel in New England. Located along Crescent Lake, it's a quick walk to Disney's Yacht Club or BoardWalk, making it easy to enjoy the many restaurants and shopping in those hotels. The lobby at Disney's Beach Club Resort is relaxed, and the rooms are spacious and offer a simple elegance. The International Gateway entrance to Epcot is a short walk away. It is also possible to walk to Disney's Hollywood Studios from the resort, although the walk is much longer. Boats are available to take you to and from either park as well. Room service is available 24 hours a day.

Beaches & Cream Soda Shop
Full Service - $

FAN PICK

Step back in time to an old-fashioned soda and ice cream shop at Beaches & Cream. There are a few booths; the rest of the seating is tables with chairs. Small details like beach balls and ice cream cones are used to decorate the restaurant. There is a jukebox to add to the atmosphere. Even the menu has a retro feel.

While Beaches & Cream Soda Shop may be known as an ice cream parlor, do not dismiss the other food. You'll find simple, filling meals here. Some of the highlights are the Bacon Angus Beef Burger, the Grilled Cheese and Tomato Bisque, the Beaches Rachel Sandwich, and the Vegetarian Falafel. Most entrees come with your choice of fruit or French fries. There are shakes, ice cream sodas, and floats available. Make sure that you save room for the ice cream! Some of the best sundaes at Walt Disney World are served at Beaches & Cream. You can order a classic sundae, made the way that you want it, or you can try one of the specialty creations. The signature sundae is the Kitchen Sink. It serves four and contains eights scoops of ice cream, and, according to the menu, "every topping we have". It is served, of course, in a large bowl that is shaped to resemble a kitchen sink. Beaches & Cream Soda Shop is open daily for lunch and dinner.

Cape May Cafe
Buffet and Character Dining - $$, $$$

Bright and open, the New England beach town theme continues at Cape May Cafe. Beach umbrellas are used as decorations. There are two dining rooms, the larger one is closer to the buffet. Breakfast is a character meal with Goofy, Minnie, and Donald dressed ready for a day at the beach. While there are no characters at dinner, the restaurant is a great place to get away from the craziness of Epcot, without having to go too far.

Breakfast features cereals, bagels, pastries, scrambled eggs, potatoes, breakfast meats, cheddar grits, and other offerings. The dinner buffet is where seafood lovers will want to go. Steamed clams, mussels, snow crab legs, shrimp, and salmon are some of the seafood choices. Chicken, pasta, and carved strip loin are also available. There are plenty of sides, salads, and soups to go along with your meal. For dessert, grab a pastry or two. There is a separate buffet for the kids. Cape May Cafe is open daily for breakfast and dinner.

Beach Club Marketplace
Quick Service - $

While you may think at first that you are just walking into a store, don't let the souvenirs stop you from reaching the quick service counter located in the back. Breakfast is served until 11:00am and it features eggs, breakfast sandwiches, and pastries. You can also get your morning coffee. Lunch and dinner are also available. If you're in a hurry, you can get a grab and go sandwich. You can also have a sandwich prepared for you the way that you want it. Some of the choices include turkey, ham and cheese, and roast beef. If you're not in the mood for a sandwich, try a flatbread pizza instead. Since the eatery is located in the Beach Club, you might try the New England Clam Chowder. There are plenty of pastries sold to satisfy your sweet tooth. If you're hungry late at night, the restaurant stays open until 11:00pm. Beach Club Marketplace is open daily for breakfast, lunch, dinner, and snacks.

Hurricane Hanna's Waterside Bar and Grill
Quick Service - $

Hurricane Hanna's is more than just a pool bar. There is a seating area away from the pool and you can enjoy an outdoor meal even if you're not planning to go for a swim. The entrees include Hanna's 1/3 lb Bacon Angus Cheeseburger, Vegetarian Quinoa Wrap, and the Lobster, Shrimp and Scallop Roll. If you'd rather have a snack, you can grab hummus and vegetables, fruit, or an ice cream treat. Cocktails sold include a Mango Margarita and the Skinny Coconut Mojito. Non-alcoholic beverages include fountain drinks, coffee and other hot choices, and a Frozen Strawberry Colada. Hurricane Hanna's Waterside Bar and Grill is open daily for lunch, dinner, snacks, and beverages.

Martha's Vineyard
Lounge - $

This comfortable lounge is a great place to relax after a long day in the parks. Appetizers are available including Lump Crab Cake and Martha's Vineyard Salad. You also might want to enjoy the Cape May Cafe Chowder; it will hit the spot. If you're really hungry, order the Taste of Cape May. It includes snow crabs, clams, and other favorites. From the full bar, you might want to try Bahama Mama, Blue "Glow-tini", or another specialty drink. Imported wines are sold, as is draft beer. Non-alcoholic beverages are also available. Martha's Vineyard is open each evening.

FIFTY-FIVE

DISNEY'S BOARDWALK INN

Deluxe

Located in the Epcot Resort Area, this Deluxe resort is part hotel and part entertainment district. Created to resemble famous boardwalks like those found in Atlantic City and Coney Island, the area offers shopping, entertainment, and signature dining. The International Gateway entrance to Epcot is an easy walk away and there is also a walking path to Disney's Hollywood Studios. You can take a boat to either park. At night, Disney's BoardWalk comes alive. Street performers entertain crowds for free each night from 7:00-10:00. (If the weather is bad, they'll be inside the hotel.) Carnival style games are played and there are two nightclubs in the area. You can also watch the fireworks portion of IllumiNations and Wishes can sometimes be seen in the distance. In the hotel's lobby you'll find a miniature carousel and roller coaster. If you're interested in learning more about this fascinating hotel, take the free BoardWalk Ballyhoo Guided Tour. It takes place Wednesday through Saturday. A new BoardWalk restaurant, Trattoria al Forno, is set to open in December, 2014. The full service option will feature simple Italian foods and classic desserts. Over 100 Italian wines will be served. Room service at Disney's BoardWalk Inn is available until midnight.

Flying Fish Cafe
Fine Dining - $$$

Flying Fish Cafe is one of the best restaurants that you will find at Walt Disney World. This signature dining experience is unforgettable! The atmosphere is fun, with fish and parachutes near the ceiling and amusement park murals on the walls. The kitchen is open so you'll be able to see the chefs as they work their own special kind of Disney magic. The atmosphere combines charm and elegance with a dash of fun. There is a dress code.

While Flying Fish Cafe is primarily a seafood restaurant, it can accommodate other tastes as well. You can start off with sushi (vegetarian is available), or maybe you'd prefer a crab cake. There are several artisanal cheeses to choose from, or you might want to just order the platter. There is also a great selection of salads and soups. The entrees may change, depending on what is fresh and what the chefs have recently created. Options could include Oak-grilled Scottish Loch Duart Salmon, "Surf & Surf", and Idaho Potato-wrapped Red Snapper. Not in the mood for seafood? Order Char-crusted Angus New York Strip Steak instead. The sides change seasonally. Don't let your special dining needs stop you from trying Flying Fish Cafe. The restaurant is vegetarian friendly (just ask your server what you can eat), and they will also try to accommodate any other requests. Make sure that you arrive hungry, because you will not want to skip dessert. With choices such as Caramelized Banana Napoleon, Sinful Dark Chocolate Delice Creation, and White Chocolate and Raspberry Creme Brulee, you'll end your meal with a smile on your face. There is a full bar and other beverages are available. Flying Fish Cafe is open daily for dinner.

There are also two special dining events that are held at Flying Fish Cafe. Chef's Tasting Wine Dinner allows a limited number of guests to sit at the chef's counter and enjoy a five course meal, complete with wine pairings. Dining with a Disney Imagineer allows you and your party to share a meal with someone who makes the magic happen. Either event requires a separate reservation.

Big River Grille & Brewing Works
Full Service - $$

Big River Grille & Brewing Works houses the only working microbrewery on Walt Disney World property. Even though beer is being brewed, the restaurant is still family friendly. Inside you'll see the brewing kettles. The indoor dining area has a modern pub feel to it. There is a bar where you can sit, or you can opt for a table. If the weather is nice, you might request to be seated outdoors. You'll have an incredible view of Crescent Lake while you dine. Reservations are not accepted.

The menu at Big River Grille & Brewing Works features familiar favorites. You might want to start with a bowl of Beer Cheese Soup, or maybe you'd prefer a salad. Nachos and a few other choices are also available for appetizers. The entrees include Blackened Mahi Mahi Sandwich, Big Brew Cheeseburger, and Flame-Grilled Meatloaf. Steak, chicken, pasta, and other choices are also on the menu. Chocolate lovers will want to try the Chocolate Confusion. New York Cheesecake is available for dessert as well. Those 21 and up can try the house-made beers. If you can't decide which one you want, a sampler is available. There are also specialty cocktails and other alcoholic and non-alcoholic beverages sold. Big River Grille & Brewing Works is open daily for lunch and dinner.

ESPN Club
Full Service - $

ESPN Club's atmosphere makes you will feel like you are dining in a ballpark. It is a fun place to eat and catch a game at the same time. Giant televisions play the current must-see games and let you catch the latest scores. You can sit at the bar or at a table in the "stadium" dining room. There are a few outdoor tables as well. Each evening there is a live sports show with prizes. There is also an arcade next door. ESPN Club does not accept reservations and lines can grow long when there is an important game on.

The food at ESPN Club is best described as ballpark food with creative twists. Appetizers include Overtime Fries, Pub Nachos For Two, and "Boo-Yah!" Chili. For entrees there are creative choices such as Chicago Meets Pittsburgh: Extreme Roast Beef Sandwich, PB & J Burger, and Championship Chicken Sandwich. There are plenty of other sandwiches and burgers on the menu, as well as fish and steak. Dessert won't disappoint either, with choices like Vanilla-Sour Cream Cheesecake and Warm Bourbon-Pecan Brownie. As you'd expect at a sports bar, there are dozens of beers available. The sports theme doesn't stop with the specialty drinks; there are choices such as the Espy and the MVP Margarita. There are also plenty of non-alcoholic beverages available. ESPN Club is open daily for lunch and dinner.

BoardWalk Bakery
Quick Service - $ FAN PICK

In 2013, BoardWalk Bakery was closed for several months for renovation. The result is a great place to grab a quick meal or a delightful baked item. You can also pick up a snack here at the end of your day. The open kitchen allows you to watch the bakers as they work on their creations. For breakfast, you can order an omelet and biscuit combo or an egg bowl. Lunch and dinner feature sandwiches such as pork, turkey, roast beef, or mozzarella. Of course you can order bakery items at any time. Bagels, croissants, muffins, cupcakes, and tarts are just a few of the choices. Cappuccino, espresso, regular coffee, fountain drinks, and other beverages are available as well. BoardWalk Bakery is open daily for breakfast, lunch, dinner, and snacks.

BoardWalk Hot Dog Cart
Quick Service - $

Also known as BoardWalk To Go, this stand has more options than you might expect. While it, of course, sells hot dogs, you can also get chicken, fried ravioli, pulled pork, and even a meatball sub. Nachos, onion rings, and other sides are served as well. Bottled, frozen, and fountain beverages are sold. There is seating in the area. BoardWalk Hot Dog Cart is open daily for lunch, dinner, and snacks.

Pizza Window
Quick Service - $

This walk-up window sells whole pizzas or pizza by the slice. You can choose pepperoni or cheese, or maybe you'd like to try the BoardWalk Signature Pizza. It's topped with roasted garlic, mushrooms, and spinach. Chocolate cake is available, as is a fruit cup. Sangria, beer, water, and fountain drinks are sold as well. Pizza Window is open until midnight, so grab a late night pie after you leave Epcot. There is outdoor seating in the area. Pizza Window is open daily for lunch, dinner, and snacks.

Seashore Sweets
Snacks - $

This candy store also has some great snacks. Hand-scooped ice cream is sold by the cup, cone, or sundae. Cookies, fudge, and other treats are also available. There is seating outside of the store. Seashore Sweets is open daily for snacks.

BoardWalk Joe's Marvelous Margaritas
Snacks and Beverages - $

Despite the word "Joe" in the name, you won't find coffee here. This stand features specialty margaritas. You'll find the Frozen Grand Margarita, the Wildberry Margarita, and the Frozen Pineapple Margarita among the choices. Beer, wine, and sangria are also sold, as are fountain drinks. Snacks include Mickey Pretzels and roasted nuts. BoardWalk Joe's Marvelous Margaritas is open daily for beverages and snacks.

Funnel Cake Cart
Snacks - $

What's a stroll down the BoardWalk without a funnel cake? This kiosk is open evenings. You can buy a funnel cake, with or without ice cream or chocolate. Cotton candy and fried ice cream are also sold. For beverages, you can pick up coffee or soda. Funnel Cake Cart is open evenings for snacks.

Leaping Horse Libations
Pool Bar - $

Even though libations are served here, this spot is family friendly. You can grab a sandwich or a salad if you're hungry. For something less filling, you can buy chips or an ice cream bar. Specialty drinks like Moscato Colada and Island Moon-shine are sold, as well as other alcoholic and non-alcoholic beverages. Leaping Horse Libations is open daily for lunch and beverages.

Belle Vue Lounge
Lounge - $

This old-fashioned lounge is located inside the BoardWalk Inn. Old radio shows play in the background. In the morning, you can enjoy cereal and milk or pick up a pastry before you hit the parks. Coffee, tea, and juice are also sold. In the evenings, you can relax over a drink. There's a full bar; specialties include Truffle Olive Martini and Red Stag Lemonade. There are also non-alcoholic choices. If the weather is nice, enjoy your drink out on the veranda. Belle Vue Lounge is open daily for breakfast and evenings for beverages.

Atlantic Dance Hall
Nightclub - $

This nightclub is strictly for those 21 and older. Your ID will be checked when you arrive. There is a full bar and no food is served. You'll have a chance to dance to your favorite songs and videos from the 1980's up to today. There is a cover charge. Atlantic Dance Hall is also a favorite for private events, including wedding receptions. If there is a special event being held inside, the club will be closed to the general public. Atlantic Dance Hall is open evenings from 9:00pm until 1:45am.

Jellyrolls
Nightclub - $

The other nightclub on Disney's BoardWalk is Jellyrolls. It is also only for those 21 and older. It is a dueling piano bar, where guests have a chance to stump one of two maestros. You can sing along and everyone will have a great time. Jellyrolls is popular with locals as well as tourists. There is a full bar and no food is served. There is a cover charge. Jellyrolls is open evenings from 9:00pm until 2:00am.

FIFTY-SIX

DISNEY'S CARIBBEAN BEACH RESORT

Moderate

Disney's Caribbean Beach Resort is a Moderate resort with a tropical feel. It is built around Barefoot Bay and features six different villages; you'll find rooms in areas like Jamaica and Aruba. You can walk or travel by bus from one village to the next. Rent a boat from the marina, relax in a hammock, or enjoy a game of beach volleyball. There are several pools, a jogging trail, and many other features that make the resort special. It even has its own island, Caribbean Cay. The two main public areas are The Custom House and Old Port Royale Centertown. Disney's Caribbean Beach Resort is located between Epcot and Disney's Typhoon Lagoon Water Park. It is part of the Epcot Resort Area. In-room pizza delivery is available until 11:30pm.

Shutters at Old Port Royale
Full Service - $$

The name of this restaurant is taken seriously. Beautiful shutters are used plentifully as part of the decor. The atmosphere is on the relaxed side, just what you'll need after a long day in a tropical paradise. Pastel colors make the dining room inviting and there is an open kitchen so you can watch the chefs prepare the food. At 9:00pm (except during the Christmas season when it's usually 9:30pm) head outdoors and catch the fireworks from IllumiNations. It's the perfect way to end your meal.

Much of the menu at Shutters at Old Port Royale is Caribbean inspired and you'll find surf and turf items as well. Start your meal with Mahi Bake or Chicken Wings. Entrees include Pasta Piquant (shrimp, chicken, or vegetarian), Today's Sustainable Fish, Caribbean-braised Boneless Beef Short Ribs, and Grilled Beef Rib-Eye. You might want to try the Shutters Chocolate Cake or the Tres Leche for dessert. If you'd like a specialty cocktail, sip on the Magical Star Cocktail or the Shutters Swirl. You can order hot or frozen cappuccino and other coffee drinks, smoothies, and milkshakes. Other alcoholic and non-alcoholic drinks are also sold. Shutters at Old Port Royale is open daily for dinner.

Old Port Royale Food Court
Quick Service - $

You'll feel like you're in an open air market, even though you're indoors. That is part of the fun of this food court. Calypso music plays in the background. The colors are bright and the atmosphere is relaxed. You just might forget that you're trying to grab a quick meal. The restaurant opens early for breakfast. All of your morning favorites can be found, including eggs, pancakes, yogurt, cereal, French toast, bakery items, and Mickey Waffles. You can also grab your morning coffee or a smoothie. Lunch and dinner feature pasta, pizza, burgers, hot dogs, sandwiches, salads, and other items. Soft serve ice cream makes a great snack or dessert. Smoothies, coffee, and other beverages are available. The food court remains open until midnight for late night snacks. Old Port Royale Food Court is open daily for breakfast, lunch, dinner, and snacks.

Banana Cabana Pool Bar
Pool Bar - $

This pool bar is a great place to order a refreshing drink on a hot day. After all, relaxing by the pool can be hard work. Specialty drinks include Moscato Colada and Citrus Blast. There are also non-alcoholic specialties such as Orange Freeze and Lava Smoothie. Other beverages are also sold. Banana Cabana Pool Bar is open daily for beverages.

FIFTY-SEVEN

DISNEY'S CONTEMPORARY RESORT

Deluxe

There are some unique features at Disney's Contemporary Resort that you will not find elsewhere. It is the only resort that the monorail enters. While the system does service two other Deluxe resorts, it actually enters the main building at the Contemporary. The second unique feature that this Deluxe resort offers is a walking trail to the Magic Kingdom. You can take the monorail or a boat if you'd like, but the park is just a few minutes away on foot. The A-Frame main building is one of Walt Disney World's original resorts. There is a slight futuristic feel to the property. Bay Lake Tower is a new addition to the resort. If you want to skip the parks, you can parasail, water ski, rent a watercraft, or hang out by one of the pools. In the evening you might decide to watch the Electrical Water Pageant and then catch the fireworks. The views from the Contemporary are incredible. It is part of the Magic Kingdom Resort Area. The resort also has a great selection of dining options. Room service is available 24 hours a day.

California Grill
Fine Dining - $$$

This signature restaurant is located on the 15th floor of the Tower Building. You will check in on the second floor and a private elevator will take you and your party to the restaurant. Once you're off the elevator you'll see a wall of wine bottles. The atmosphere in the dining area is relaxed and filled with light. The ambiance is a combination of retro and futuristic. One of the best things about California Grill is the view. There are large windows that let you see all that is going on in the world below. There are also two outdoor balconies that provide a breathtaking view of the Magic Kingdom. California Grill is known for its view of the nightly fireworks. The soundtrack is piped into the restaurant, but you'll want to watch from a balcony. You do not have to make a reservation for near the time of the fireworks to enjoy the show, just show your receipt at the check in booth and you'll be allowed back up to enjoy them.

You'd probably expect fresh choices at a restaurant called California Grill, and that is exactly what you will find. The menu changes from time to time; it depends on what is in season. Start your meal with an Oven-dried Tomato Flatbread or Sonoma Goat Cheese Ravioli. There is a large selection of cheese, as well as charcuterie. From there you might want to enjoy some sushi; California Grill serves some of the best on Walt Disney World property. Entrees might include Jumbo Scallops and Grits, Oak-fired Filet of Beef, and Sweet Potato Gnocchi. If you can't decide what to have for dessert, consider the Sundae Sampler or the Seasonal Tasting. One of the things that California Grill is known for is the wine selection. There are over 250 vintages to choose from. If you have a question, just ask. They have sommeliers on staff to help. There are also signature cocktails such as the Sake Martini and the Passion Fruit Margarita. Craft beers and other adult beverages are available as well. Non-alcoholic beverages are also served. California Grill is open daily for dinner.

The Wave... of American Flavors
Buffet and Full Service - $, $$

One glance at the entrance to this restaurant and you'll see why it is called The Wave. The "American Flavors" part of the name is because the restaurant uses local sustainable foods. The menu will change from time to time, depending on what is fresh. In the dining room the wave theme continues on the backs of the chairs and on the ceiling. The location makes it easy to get away from the Magic Kingdom for a couple of hours and still be able to return without any fuss.

Breakfast at The Wave... of American Flavors is offered in two different ways. You can order a la carte or you can partake of the breakfast buffet. The buffet items include eggs, breakfast meats, and other things that you would expect to find on a buffet. It might also contain local fruits, sweet potato pancakes, and multigrain waffles. If you'd prefer to order off the menu, you might find breakfast choices such as Egg White Frittata, Make Your Own Wave Muesli, or Brioche French Toast. The lunch entrees could include Curry Vegetarian Stew, Thompson Farm Country Bacon Cuban on Multigrain Roll, and Today's Sustainable Fish. If your reservation is for dinner, you might want to start with The

Wave Appetizer for Two or Black Bean Chili. Depending on what fresh ingredients are available, entrees could include Lobster Ravioli, Florida Clams, Royal Red Caribbean Shrimp, Ashley Farms Naturally Raised Chicken Breast, and Today's Sustainable Sauteed Fish. Desserts include several flights, so you'll have a chance to sample different treats. There are specialty cocktails with fun names like Under the Florida Moon, Forever Young, and The Wavesicle. Organic beers are also featured. Organic Colombian Press Pot Coffee and other hot and cold beverages are sold. The Wave... of American Flavors is open daily for breakfast, lunch, and dinner.

Chef Mickey's
Character Dining - $$$ FAN PICK

This is one of the most popular character meals at Walt Disney World. What's not to love? You can dine with Mickey, Minnie, Donald, Goofy, and Pluto, all dressed up in their chefs' outfits. There is a lot of interaction with the characters and being able to watch the monorail wiz by adds to the fun. The "Mickeys" here aren't so hidden, you'll find the famous mouse's likeness on the backs of the chairs, on the condiment holders, on the walls, and in plenty of other places. Part of the reason that Chef Mickey's is so popular is because all five classic characters usually do appear.

The food at Chef Mickey's is served buffet style. There are plenty of choices for breakfast. You'll find breakfast meats, eggs, quiche, fruit, cereal, pancakes, potatoes, Mickey Waffles, Minnie's Breakfast Pizza, pastries, and many other items. The dinner buffet includes soups, salads, carved meats, pasta (including Mickey-shaped ravioli), chicken, pizza, vegetables, and other choices. Once it's time for dessert you'll want to check out the sundae bar. You can create your sweet ending however you want it. Specialty cocktails such as Agave Nectar Margarita and Heather & Honey Sidecar are sold. There are also non-alcoholic specialties and other beverages available. Chef Mickey's is open daily for breakfast and dinner.

Contemporary Grounds
Quick Service - $

You know that you need your morning coffee to get your day off on the right foot. Contemporary Grounds is where you can get it. They have coffee, tea, cappuccino, espresso, and other hot beverages. If you would prefer your caffeine cold, they have frozen drinks as well. You can pick up a quick-to-go breakfast sandwich or pastry to eat. Contemporary Grounds opens early and remains open late so you can enjoy a snack at the end of the day. Contemporary Grounds is open daily for breakfast, snacks, and beverages.

Contempo Cafe
Quick Service - $

This is another option for a quick meal or snack. There is plenty of seating, although it can get crowded at traditional mealtimes. Like Chef Mickey's, you can watch the monorail as you eat. You will order at a kiosk and be given a pager. Don't worry, the system is easy to use. When your food is ready, just pick it up. Make sure you check out the mural while you wait for your food. There are also grab and go items available if you're in a hurry. Breakfast offerings include breakfast platters, Mickey Waffles, grits, potatoes, and other items. Bakery goods are available at 6:00am, entrees are served starting at 7:00am. For lunch or dinner you might want to try a flatbread or a burger. Sandwiches and pasta are also available. The restaurant even sells sushi. Make sure that you save room for dessert, because Contempo Cafe is known for its cupcakes. At the end of the evening you can grab a late night snack until midnight. Contempo Cafe is open daily for breakfast, lunch, dinner, and snacks.

Cove Bar
Pool Bar - $

This pool bar is only for those who are staying at Bay Lake Tower. In addition to beverages, there are some entrees and snacks on the menu.

Try a Turkey BLT Wrap or enjoy a hot dog. Sushi, chips, ice cream, fruit, and other items are also available. Cocktails include Captain's Mai Tai and Mango Margarita. There are other alcoholic and non-alcoholic choices served. Cove Bar is open daily for lunch and beverages.

The Sand Bar
Pool Bar - $

This pool bar is unique in that there is an indoor seating area. It's small, but it will give you a chance to get out of the hot summer sun. They serve more than just beverages; in fact, you can order an entire meal here. Cheeseburgers, chili dogs, and wraps are a few of the choices. There are also a few snacks like hummus and vegetables, or Mickey Pretzels. Alcoholic beverages include Banana Cabana and Superfruit Sangria. Fountain drinks and other beverages are also sold. The Sand Bar is open daily for lunch, snacks, and beverages.

California Grill Lounge
Lounge - $$$

If you couldn't get a reservation for California Grill, you might want to see if there is any space available here. Even though it is a lounge, the full California Grill menu is available. You can enjoy sushi, while sipping on wine, then stay for the fireworks. The seats here are coveted, so you should try to plan your stop well before the fireworks to secure your spot. California Grill Lounge is open evenings for dinner and beverages.

Outer Rim
Lounge - $

This lounge offers a relaxing atmosphere and a great view. Enjoy sparkling wine, seasonal beer, or a chocolate stout. There is a full bar and several specialty cocktails, such as Pimm's Punch and Magical Star

Cocktail. There are also non-alcoholic specialties and other beverages served. Outer Rim is open evenings for beverages.

Top of the World
Lounge - $

Accessible to Disney Vacation Club members staying at the resort, this lounge is located on the top floor of Bay Lake Tower. The lounge is known for its view, especially the view of the fireworks. Pizza and snacks are available, and there is a full bar. Top of the World is open evenings for snacks and beverages.

Wave Lounge
Lounge - $

Located next to The Wave... of American Flavors, this lounge has a relaxing atmosphere. Keeping with the restaurant's mission for freshness, you can order appetizers such as Sustainable Fish Taco and Lump Crab-Florida Rock Shrimp Cakes. Enjoy an organic beer, or try a specialty drink. Chocolate Martini and Habanero Lime Margarita are just two of the choices. Other drinks and non-alcoholic specialties are available. Wave Lounge is open evenings for snacks and beverages.

FIFTY-EIGHT

DISNEY'S CORONADO SPRINGS RESORT

Moderate

This Moderate resort celebrates the explorer Don Francisco de Coronado and Spanish-colonial Mexico. Where else can you swim near a Mayan pyramid? It is also home to the largest hot tub at Walt Disney World. Lago Dorado is a 22 acre lake and the resort is also home to a convention center. There's a playground for the kids and a fitness club for the adults. The closest park to Coronado Springs is Disney's Blizzard Beach and it is part of the Animal Kingdom Resort Area. Room service is available for breakfast until 11:00am and for dinner until 11:00pm.

Maya Grill
Full Service - $$

The Mayan motif of the resort continues at Maya Grill. The lighting is a bit on the dramatic side, adding to the mysterious feel of the restaurant. The Mayan themes of sun, fire, and water are featured throughout the space. There is live entertainment Thursday through Sunday evenings.

The food at Maya Grill is Nuevo Latino, but there are plenty of familiar choices. Start your meal with the Empanadas Duo or Southwest Spring Rolls. From there you might want to try a Tex Mex platter such as the San Antonio Fajita Skillet or the Three Amigos. There are several other platters to choose from as well. If you're not in the mood for Tex Mex, that's not a problem; you can order steak, chicken, fish, or pork. The desserts include Coconut Flan and Fried Ice Cream. Specialty coffees, wine, sangria, and other beverages are available. Maya Grill is open daily for dinner.

Cafe Rix
Quick Service - $

If you're hungry and in a hurry, Cafe Rix is the place to stop. They have prepared foods. Find what you want, grab it, and pay for it. Breakfast features muffins, pastries, bagels, donuts, fruit, cereal with milk, and a few other things. Smoothies and hot beverage creations are sold, as well as other morning drinks. For lunch and dinner grab and go salads and wraps are featured. You can also buy fruit, hummus and vegetables, and other snacks. There are some delicious desserts to choose from, including several flavors of gelato. Smoothies, teas, and other beverages are also sold. The eatery stays open until midnight so you can enjoy a snack at the end of the day. Cafe Rix is open daily for breakfast, lunch, dinner, and snacks.

Pepper Market
Quick Service - $

Pepper Market has the feel of an outdoor Mexican market, but you'll get to dine inside and enjoy the air conditioning. The outdoor theme is taken so far that there are umbrellas over some of the tables. There are bright colors and you'll feel like it's fiesta time. Pepper Market has undergone a few changes over the years, finally becoming a food court. There are seven stations to choose from. Mexican and American foods are featured. Breakfast includes the items that you might expect like eggs, omelets, and Mickey Waffles, but there are some surprises as well. The Creme Brulee French Toast is a standout item. You can also get a Mexican Eggs Benedict Burrito, Chorizo Hash and Poached Eggs, or the Breakfast Frittata. Lunch and dinner include a Build Your Own Chef Salad station, tacos, empanadas, flatbread pizzas, ribs, burgers, sandwiches, pasta, and other items. For dessert there are bakery items, cake, and churros. Coffee, tea, fountain drinks, and other beverages are available at all three meals. Pepper Market is open daily for breakfast, lunch, dinner, and snacks.

Siestas Cantina
Pool Bar - $

A special pool needs a special place to grab a bite or a drink and that is what you will find at Siestas Cantina. Enjoy a quick meal with options like Pork Carnitas Tacos, Caprese Roll, and Taco Salad. There's a full bar with specialties such as Margarita al Classico and Coronado Crush. There are also frozen drinks like Funky Monkey and Guava Lava. Siestas Cantina is open daily for lunch and beverages.

Laguna Bar
Lounge - $

This lounge is located outdoors, by Lago Dorado. If you need a beautiful place to unwind after a long day, you'll want to stop by. You'll find creations with names like Mango Blueberry Basil Margarita, Passion Fruit Caipirinha, Coronado Crush, and Cancun Colada. If you want something simpler, they can whip that up as well. Although the location is a bar, it's still family friendly. Laguna Bar is open daily for beverages.

Rix Lounge
Nightclub - $

While the name may imply that this is a place to relax, Rix Lounge is more of a nightclub than a place to wind down. There is a Latin feel to the location and a DJ is on hand on select nights. Rix Lounge is designed for the 21 and up crowd. You can enjoy appetizers such as chicken wings and a veggie plate. Flatbreads are also served. There are plenty of creatively named cocktails that you might want to try. Birthday Caketini, Pomegranate Pop, Earth, Wind, and Fire, Frozen Strawberry Cheesecake, and Beergrita are just a few of the choices. Special events are sometimes held here as well. Unless there is a closed event, Rix Lounge is open evenings for snacks and beverages.

FIFTY-NINE

DISNEY'S FORT WILDERNESS RESORT & CAMPGROUND

Moderate

There are two different types of accommodations at Disney's Fort Wilderness Resort. The first is a working campground. You can bring an RV or a camper, hookups are available. There are also sites where you can pitch a tent. Guests staying at a campsite have access to all the same benefits as other Disney guests. Some of the RV sites allow pets, unlike elsewhere on Disney property. Ask about the pet policy when you make your reservation.

If you'd like to enjoy the beauty of nature but don't feel like roughing it that much, you might want to consider booking one of the cabins at Disney's Fort Wilderness Resort. The Moderate resort has cabins that look rustic, but you'll enjoy modern conveniences. There are walking trails for both the cabins and the campground. There are some other fun features at Fort Wilderness. Visit Tri-Circle-D Ranch to see horses and ponies. Horseback riding and carriage rides can be booked as well. You can rent a boat or try your hand at archery. Disney's Fort Wilderness

Resort is also where you will find Chip 'N Dale's Campfire Sing-a-long. You can watch the Electrical Water Pageant here. Disney's Fort Wilderness Resort is part of the Magic Kingdom Resort Area.

Trail's End Restaurant
Buffet and Full Service - $$

Trail's End Restaurant is a bit on the rustic side and that is only half the fun. Decorations include wooden crates and barrels. Cast iron pots and pans line the walls, helping to create the feel of a simpler time. It is the type of place where you'll want to sit and relax for a while. You can even play checkers outside as you wait.

Breakfast at Trail's End Restaurant is served buffet style. You'll find a lot of the standard fare; eggs, breakfast meats, pastries, bagels, cereal, fresh fruit, and other choices. There are also some unique items here. Mickey Waffles are available plain or with chocolate chips. You'll want to enjoy a pecan cinnamon roll, they're unlike any cinnamon rolls served elsewhere on Disney property. You can create your own yogurt parfait as well. There is also a takeout menu.

Lunch at Trail's End Restaurant is served a la carte. Start with Southern Fried Green Tomatoes or a Smoked Cheese-stuffed Jalapeno. You might want to try the Chicken and Waffles for your entree, or maybe order the Knife & Fork Shrimp Po' Boy instead. Other options include flatbreads, burgers, seafood, and barbequed pork. The Warm Sticky Bun Sundae is a perfect ending to any meal, but the Wilderness S'mores are also hard to resist.

At dinner the restaurant again offers a buffet. You can find down home favorites like fried chicken and BBQ ribs. You can also dine on salad, soup, shrimp, carved meats, pizza, pasta, and a baked potato bar. Leave room for dessert, because the buffet has some delicious choices. Homemade seasonal fruit cobbler is available, as well as soft serve ice cream. Other sweet choices could include cake, cookies, and pudding. There is a takeout menu for dinner, featuring pizza, nachos, and chicken. Trail's End Restaurant is open daily for breakfast, lunch, and dinner.

Hoop-Dee-Doo Musical Revue
Dinner Show - $$$$

Celebrate the Wild West in this two hour dinner show. Located in Pioneer Hall, there's dancing and singing, and guests are encouraged to clap along. The hall where the show is performed is huge and continues with the rustic feel of the resort. The food is served family style all-you-can-eat and is served between acts. You'll find fried chicken, BBQ ribs, potatoes, salad, baked beans, and cornbread. Dessert is strawberry shortcake. For those 21 and older beer, wine, and sangria are available for no extra charge. Coffee, tea, fountain drinks, and lemonade are also included in the price. For an extra fee, you can order a margarita or tequila. Hoop-Dee-Doo Musical Revue runs daily for dinner.

Mickey's Backyard BBQ
Dinner Show - $$$

With classic characters, lots of food, and a fun setting, what's not to love about Mickey's Backyard BBQ? The show is held at the Pavilion, which is a covered outdoor space. There are rope tricks and live country music, and the audience is encouraged to sing and dance along. The characters are all dressed up in their picnic attire and you will have a blast watching them get in on the action. Characters may include Mickey, Minnie, Goofy, Chip, and Dale. The food is all-you-can-eat and may include salad, cornbread, chicken, ribs, burgers, hot dogs, mac and cheese, and corn on the cob. Watermelon and ice cream bars are on hand for dessert. Beer and wine are included in the price for those of age. Fruit punch and soft drinks are also included. Mickey's Backyard BBQ is held on select evenings for dinner.

Meadow Snack Bar
Snacks - $

If you're looking for a light meal or a filling snack, you won't need to look any further. Meadows Snack Bar sells sandwiches and hot dogs.

Pizza is also available and salads are as well. If you want a snack instead of a meal, you can find some healthy options like carrots and celery sticks, or apple slices with caramel sauce. Cake, cobbler, and ice cream bars are also sold. Specialty drinks include Myer's Platinum Rum and Jose Cuervo Margarita. Beer is also available, as are fountain drinks and other beverages. Meadow Snack Bar is open seasonally for lunch, snacks, and beverages.

Crockett's Tavern
Lounge - $

Named after Davy Crockett, this lounge offers a tame version of the "wild" frontier. You can order a pizza here, or you might want to munch on the nachos or the chicken wings. There is a full bar. Specialty drinks include Jameson Irish Coffee and Heather & Honey Sidecar. There is a good selection of red and white wines. Other drinks are also served, including non-alcoholic specialties. Crockett's Tavern is open daily for beverages and snacks.

SIXTY

DISNEY'S GRAND FLORIDIAN RESORT & SPA

Deluxe

If you're looking for the best of the best, you'll want to stay at Disney's Grand Floridian. You'll find luxury around every corner. The design is Victorian and the pace is relaxed. There is often a live orchestra playing in the lobby. You'll enjoy gorgeous views of Cinderella Castle and it is a great place to catch the fireworks at the end of the night. If you're looking to unwind a little bit while on your vacation, you'll want to stop by the world class spa. You can rent a sailboat, go for a jog, send your kids on a pirate cruise, or watch the Electrical Water Pageant. Some of the best dining options in Central Florida are located at Disney's Grand Floridian. If you're visiting during the holidays, check out the giant gingerbread house. Disney's Grand Floridian Resort & Spa is located in the Magic Kingdom Resort Area. Room service is available 24 hours a day.

Citricos
Fine Dining - $$$

Citricos is beautiful and elegant, without being overdone. Large windows offer a great view of the Grand Floridian property. The restaurant is located on the second floor and you might even catch a glimpse of the Magic Kingdom. The dining room is well lit and there is a homey feel to it. The chefs can be seen from some tables as they prepare their creations. This is signature dining that doesn't feel excessive. There is a dress code.

The food at Citricos has a Mediterranean flair. Start your meal with Athena Melon and Parma Prosciutto or the Cheese Course Trio. You also might want a bowl of Carrot and Cilantro Soup or a Masumoto Family Farm Peaches and Baby Greens Salad. Entrees include pork, chicken, beef, swordfish, and tofu creations. Tropical Fruit Creme Brulee would be the perfect dish to end the meal, but so would Chocolate-Banana Torte. Citricos has an award winning wine list. If you can't decide which wine would be perfect, speak with a sommelier. Plenty of other alcoholic and non-alcoholic beverages are available as well. Citricos is open daily for dinner.

There is also a small private dining area at Citricos. This is reserved for what is known as The Chef's Domain at Citricos. Groups of up to 12 guests can dine together. Guests will either choose from the menu or make arrangements in advance for a special meal. Dinner is served at 5:30 and again at 8:30 each evening. Reservations can be made by calling 407-WDW-DINE (407-939-3463). There is a $650 minimum purchase required.

Narcoossee's
Fine Dining - $$$

Another signature restaurant, Narcoossee's has a waterfront beach feel. The building itself is partially over Seven Seas Lagoon, which adds to its charm. There are large windows with shutters above and some fantastic views. Make sure you take a peek at the mural over the bar. You might want to plan your meal near the time of the evening fireworks at the Magic Kingdom. You can watch them from inside the restaurant, or you could head out to the wrap around deck. There is a dress code at Narcoossee's, so you may need to change if you've been in a park all day.

Narcoossee's is a seafood restaurant. Maine Lobster Bisque makes a great start to your meal. You might want to try Crispy Rhode Island Calamari, or Willapa Bay, Washington State Oysters-on-the-Half Shell for an appetizer. Narcoossee's is where you can find a Two-Pound Steamed Maine Lobster. Maybe you'd prefer the Grilled Alaskan Wild-Caught Halibut. Not in the mood for seafood? Other entrees include chicken, New York Strip, filet mignon, and even ravioli. Some of the dessert selections are Narcoossee's "Candy Bar", Almond-crusted Cheesecake, and Plant City Strawberry Shortcake. Adults might want to try the Nutcracker or the Nutty Irishman. Other alcoholic beverages are also available. There is also a large selection of specialty teas. Narcoossee's is open daily for dinner.

Victoria & Albert's
Fine Dining - $$$$

Possibly the best restaurant at Walt Disney World is Victoria & Albert's. It just might be the best restaurant in Central Florida. It is a recipient of the AAA Five Diamond Award, a distinction that it first earned back in 2000. The restaurant itself is breathtaking, with chandeliers, white tablecloths, and elegant servers. The dress code is stricter than at other signature restaurants. This is an adult dining experience-children under ten are not allowed. Expect your meal to take at least two hours, depending on the dining experience that you choose. Meals are a set price and the wine pairing will cost extra.

There are three different dining experiences that you can choose from at Victoria & Albert's. The Dining Room features up to seven courses. The menu changes often, but in the past has included such choices as Octopus "A la Plancha", Yellowtail Snapper, Veal Napoleon, Niman Ranch Lamb, and Colorado Bison. Desserts might include Tanzanian Chocolate Timbale and Caramelized Banana Gateau. For a more intimate experience, try Queen Victoria's Room. There are only four tables and you'll enjoy ten courses. If you really want a special meal, book the Chef's Table. You and your party (up to ten people) will meet the chefs, talk about your food preferences, and a ten course meal will be created just for you. You'll be given a copy of the menu at the end of your meal as a souvenir. Victoria & Albert's has a world class wine collection; there are over 700 bottles to choose from. Make your reservation by calling 407-WDW-DVNA (407-939-3862). Victoria & Albert's is open daily for dinner.

Grand Floridian Cafe
Full Service - $$

Light and bright are two perfect words to describe Grand Floridian Cafe. Large windows allow the sunlight to flood in. The central columns are white, as are the backs of the chairs. Pastels offset the white, making the restaurant more elegant. Grand Floridian Cafe is just a monorail ride away from the Magic Kingdom, but the pace will allow you to leave the rush of the world's most popular theme park behind for a little while.

Breakfast at Grand Floridian Cafe offers some normal choices and some unexpected surprises. You can order eggs, pancakes, Mickey Waffles, and pastries. Some of the more unique breakfast items are Lobster Eggs Benedict, Vanilla-laced French Toast, and Smoked Salmon. For lunch or dinner you might want to start with Chickpea Fritters or Shrimp Cocktail. Try the Grand Floridian Burger or Orecchiette Pasta for your entree. Pork chops, chicken, shrimp, and steak are also available. Consider the Chocolate Fondue or the Key Lime Tart for dessert. If you can't decide on the perfect ending to your meal, order the Dessert Sampler. At all three meals specialty cocktails include Florida Sunshine and Key West. Coffee, tea, and other alcoholic and non-alcoholic beverages are sold. Grand Floridian Cafe is open daily for breakfast, lunch, and dinner.

1900 Park Fare
Character Dining - $$$

There is a carousel theme at this beautiful restaurant. Full-sized carousel horses (and other animals) are part of the decorations. There is also a calliope at the restaurant's entrance to add to the motif. The main dining room is quite large and there are smaller dining areas as well. There is plenty of lighting, and pastel colors add to the whimsical feel.

There are three different character experiences available at 1900 Park Fare. The first one is the Supercalifragilistic Breakfast. You might meet Mary Poppins, Alice, the Mad Hatter, Pooh, and Tigger. The food is served buffet style. There are some signature items at breakfast; they include Floridian Strawberry Soup, Chef's Choice Hash, and Lobster Benedict. You can also get eggs, breakfast meats, pancakes, Mickey Waffles, fresh fruit, cinnamon buns, bagels, and other items. Specialty cocktails for breakfast include Grand Mimosa and Kir Royale. Other beverages are also available.

Dinner at 1900 Park Fare offers the second character dining known as Cinderella's Happily Ever After Dinner. This is a great alternative to Cinderella's Royal Table at the Magic Kingdom. Cinderella and Prince Charming will be there and they just might waltz for their guests. Other characters usually include Lady Tremaine, Anastasia, and Drizella. The food is served buffet style. There are several salads to choose from, and there's a carving station. The signature dishes at dinner include Roasted Root Vegetable Gratin, and Spice-crusted Salmon. There's an international feel to the buffet, with pot stickers, Chicken Marsala, shrimp, sushi, ribs, Guinness Stew, and other choices. Cookies, brownies, cakes, and other sweet treats are also on the buffet. Beverages are available as well.

The third option at 1900 Park Fare is not a traditional meal; it's afternoon tea. Known as Wonderland Tea Party, this experience is only for children ages 4-12; no adults are allowed! The kids will eat a light lunch, drink "tea" (really apple juice), and then decorate a cupcake. They'll play games and have a chance to meet Alice and the Mad Hatter. There's a keepsake photo, and your kids will have a memory that will last a lifetime. Wonderland Tea Party is held on select afternoons. 1900 Park Fare is open daily for breakfast and dinner.

Gasparilla Island Grill
Quick Service - $

With Gasparilla Island Grill, you'll never have to be hungry on your Walt Disney World vacation. The restaurant never closes! There is plenty of indoor seating, but if the weather is nice you might want to sit outside and enjoy the view of Cinderella Castle in the distance. Breakfast is served until 11:00am. You can order hot items such as eggs, breakfast sandwiches, or Mickey Waffles, or you might want to grab a bagel, pastry, or other bakery item and head out to the parks. You can also order your morning coffee at Gasparilla Island Grill. For lunch or dinner you can create your own salad. Sandwiches, flatbreads, and burgers are also available. There are still plenty of bakery choices at lunch and dinner. Grill items are available until 11:30pm. After that you can get pizza, sandwiches, and desserts. Hot and cold beverages are sold throughout the day. Gasparilla Island Grill is open daily for breakfast, lunch, dinner, and snacks.

Beaches Pool Bar & Grill
Pool Bar - $

What could be better than sipping a cold drink while sitting on a white sand beach? How about enjoying sushi at the same time? Beaches Pool Bar & Grill has sushi, salads, burgers, chicken nuggets, and even Beef and Brie Bruschetta. If you want something sweet and a little bit different, try the Pina Colada Cupcake. To satisfy your thirst you can order a Moscato Colada or a Black Cherry Lemonade, or maybe you'd prefer beer or wine. Other alcoholic and non-alcoholic beverages are also sold. Beaches Pool Bar & Grill is open daily for snacks and beverages.

Courtyard Pool Bar
Pool Bar - $

One thing that is nice about Disney's Grand Floridian is that they go above and beyond expectations at every turn. Courtyard Pool Bar is no exception. You can find some filling food choices here, including flatbreads, salads, burgers, and sandwiches. Banana Cabana and Skinny Coconut Mojito are two of the cocktails available. Beer, wine, sangria, and other alcoholic beverages are also sold. For something refreshing without a kick, try the Orange Freeze or the Lava Smoothie. Fountain and other drinks can also be purchased. Courtyard Pool Bar is open daily for snacks and beverages.

Citricos Lounge
Lounge - $$

Want a taste of Citricos, but don't have a reservation? Stop by Citricos Lounge instead. Some of the signature restaurant's menu is available to lounge customers. Tapas include PEI Mussels, Ashley Farms Chicken B'steeya, and Cheese Course Trio. You can also order soup or a salad. Since it is a lounge, you'll find an extensive selection of specialty cocktails, including Citrico's Bellini and Citropolitan. There are international wines and artisanal beers. You can even try aged whiskey. Citricos Lounge is open evenings for snacks and beverages.

Mizner's Lounge
Lounge - $

Enjoy music from the Grand Floridian Society Orchestra as you snack on appetizers and dessert or unwind with a drink. Mizner's Lounge will allow you to do all that at the end of a long day of fun. Appetizers include Hardwood-grilled Berkshire Pork Belly, Veal Bolognese, and an Artisanal Cheese Selection. For dessert you might want to try Lemon-scented Cheesecake or Seasonal Berry Gratin. Platinum Margarita and Belvedere Vodka Martini are just two of the cocktails on the menu. You can also find champagne, wine, beer, and high-end liquors. Cigars are also on the menu. Mizner's Lounge is open evenings for snacks and beverages.

SIXTY-One

DISNEY'S OLD KEY WEST RESORT

Deluxe

There is something special about the Florida Keys. The pace is a little more relaxed than in other parts of the country and it seems that the stress level stays down. That feel is what Disney has recreated at Disney's Old Key West Resort. These Deluxe villas were built for Disney Vacation Club members, but empty rooms are available to the general public. The community is known as Conch Flats and you'll find lush vegetation, squirting "dolphins" in the pool, a marina, and a fitness center. There are three playgrounds, nightly campfires, and a 1.37 mile long jogging trail. Disney's Old Key West Resort isn't too far from Epcot and Typhoon Lagoon. It is part of the Downtown Disney Resort Area. In-room pizza delivery is available until midnight.

Olivia's Cafe
Full Service - $, $$

Named after unlikely restaurateur Olivia Farnsworth, this full service restaurant will feel like home. It's a step back in time to when life seemed a little bit easier. The walls are covered with pictures and there are special touches like oars and other nautical items. The pastels will add to the laid back feel. There is both indoor and outdoor seating.

Breakfast at Olivia's Cafe is a mix of traditional and creative items. You can get pancakes and eggs, but there are also more unique choices like the Conch Republic Omelet and the Breakfast Cuban. You can order your morning cappuccino, espresso, or latte, or start your day with a different type of kick with a Bloody Mary or a Mimosa. Joffrey's coffee, juice, milk, and other beverages are also served. For lunch or dinner you might want to start with the conch fritters or Olivia's House Salad. There are plenty of seafood entrees including Shrimp and Grits, Pan-seared Sea Scallops, and Mallory Square Cobb Salad. If you're not in the mood for seafood you might want to try Olivia's Vegetarian Pasta or Island Barbecue Pork Ribs. There are plenty of sandwiches, and steak and chicken items are also sold. To really feel like you're in the Florida Keys, order the Key Lime Tart for dessert. Among the other dessert choices are Flourless Chocolate Cake, Banana Bread Pudding Sundae, and cheesecake. Olivia's Cafe is open daily for breakfast, lunch, and dinner.

Good's Food To Go
Quick Service - $

Good's Food To Go is part pool bar, part quick service restaurant. It opens early for breakfast. You can order a Croissant Sandwich or a Breakfast Platter. Grits, oatmeal, bagels, pastries, and other breakfast items are also sold. Lunch and dinner feature burgers, hot dogs, sandwiches, chicken nuggets, pizza, soup, and nachos. You can also get pretzels, ice cream, and of course, Key Lime Pie. Beer, coffee, fountain drinks, and other beverages are available. There is outdoor seating in the area. Good's Food To Go is open daily for breakfast, lunch, dinner, and snacks.

Turtle Shack Snack Bar
Pool Bar - $

This is another great option when you want lunch or a snack. Play a game of shuffleboard then grab something to eat. You'll find pizza, hot dogs, and sandwiches on the menu. Snacks include nachos with cheese, ice cream bars, and brownies. Beer and wine are sold, as are smoothies, fountain drinks, juice, and other beverages. Turtle Shack Snack Bar is open seasonally for lunch and snacks.

Gurgling Suitcase Libations & Spirits
Lounge - $

This small lounge exudes charm. Turtle Crawl, Rum Runner, and Sultry Seahorse are three unique specialty cocktails. Other beverages are also available. If you're hungry, take a look at the menu from Olivia's Cafe. It's available as well. Gurgling Suitcase Libations & Spirits is open daily for lunch, dinner, and beverages.

SIXTY-TWO

DISNEY'S POLYNESIAN VILLAGE RESORT

Deluxe

Enjoy a tropical paradise at Disney's Polynesian Village Resort. Located on the shores of Seven Seas Lagoon, you'll find lush vegetation, fire dancers, and even a volcano. Learn the hula or watch Wishes and the Electrical Water Pageant from the beach. This Deluxe resort is simply breathtaking in design. If you want to enjoy a romantic evening for two, take the kids to the Never Land Club; they'll make friends and have a great time. Rent a boat at the marina or relax under a cabana. When you're ready to head to the Magic Kingdom, just hop on the monorail. There are some great dining choices at Disney's Polynesian Village Resort, including one of the best desserts on Walt Disney World property. (see Ohana). The hotel is currently undergoing a major refurbishment, which will be complete sometime in 2015. Part of the refurbishment will include a new food and beverage option called Trader Sam's Grog Grotto. Disney's Polynesian Village Resort is located in the Magic Kingdom Resort Area. Room service is available until midnight.

Kona Cafe
Full Service - $$ FAN PICK

This full service restaurant is located on the second floor of the Great Ceremonial House. The eating area is filled with bright shades of purple, orange, yellow, and other colors. The lighting fixtures have a South Seas feel to them. You can watch the pastry chefs as they create sweet treats. It is an easy restaurant to overlook if you have never been to Walt Disney World. If you make a reservation, you won't be disappointed.

Kona Cafe is a popular breakfast spot. This is where you'll find Tonga Toast, an incredible creation made of French toast, bananas, strawberry compote, and cinnamon and sugar. Kona Cafe also has Macadamia-Pineapple and other pancakes, French toast, eggs, pastries, and other breakfast items. Espresso, cappuccino, Liliko'i Juice, and other beverages are available for breakfast. For lunch, you might want the Polynesian Plate Lunch or the Kona Turkey Sandwich. More sandwiches, noodle bowls, steak, sushi, and other items are also available. Start your dinner with Kona Salad or Maui Onion and White Bean Soup. Entrees include Teriyaki-style New York Strip, Togarashi Spiced Ahi Tuna, and

Pan-Asian Noodles. Duck, chicken, steak, seafood, and sushi are also on the menu. Remember the pastry kitchen that you walked by when you were seated? Desserts for lunch and dinner include Banana-Chocolate Creme Brulee, Jasmine Tea-infused Cheesecake, and the popular Kona Konc. Specialty drinks include Kona Cool Sundown and Tropical Macaw. Beer, wine, sake, and other alcoholic beverages are also sold. Coffee lovers will want to try the 100% Kona Coffee. It's pressed at your table and, if you like it, you can buy a bag to take home with you. Kona Cafe is open daily for breakfast, lunch, and dinner.

'Ohana
Family Style and Character Dining - $$, $$$ FAN PICK

'Ohana is a favorite for tourists and locals alike. The food is served all-you-can-eat family style and it is delicious. The word "Ohana" means family and the servers will become your "cousins" for the meal. The restaurant has Hawaiian Tiki gods, a fire pit, and great views of the Magic Kingdom. Fish and birds are part of the decor overhead. Hula lessons and other activities take place while you wait.

Breakfast at 'Ohana is a character meal called Best Friends Breakfast. It features Lilo and Stitch. Mickey and Pluto might be there as well. Since the food is served family style, it will be brought to your table on platters that you then will share. Offerings include eggs, breakfast meats, Mickey Waffles, potatoes, fruit, and breakfast breads. You'll want to try the POG Juice. There's a lot of character interaction, and everyone is invited to get out of their seats to sing, dance, and join in on the 'Ohana Family Parade. Since this character meal is extremely popular, you'll want to make your reservation well in advance.

While there are no characters at dinner, 'Ohana is still a popular spot for the evening meal. The food will be brought to your table for everyone to share. The offerings that you enjoy might include 'Ohana Pineapple-Coconut Bread, salad, pork dumplings, and chicken wings. The restaurant is known for its entrees of skewered meat cooked over the fire pit. The meat is accompanied by noodles and vegetables. Even though there is a lot of meat served, vegetarians should not shy away.

Let the cousin who checks you in know about your eating habits, and you'll receive delicious meat-free options. Other special dietary needs will also be met. Dessert at 'Ohana is the icing on the cake, so to speak. 'Ohana Bread Pudding a la mode with Bananas-Caramel Sauce is one of the most popular desserts anywhere on Disney property. Time your reservation to watch the fireworks at the Magic Kingdom, the music is piped in so that you can get the full affect. 'Ohana is open daily for breakfast and dinner.

Disney's Spirit of Aloha Show
Dinner Show - $$$$

Spirit of Aloha celebrates the traditions of Hawaii, New Zealand, Samoa, Tahiti, and Tonga. You'll enjoy drummers and dancers. Kids are invited on the stage to learn a few moves. The highlight of the show is a fire dancer. There are three different options when it comes to seating. The better the seat, the more you'll pay. Be warned that the theater is outdoors and the show will be canceled for inclement or cold weather. The food is brought to your table family style. You'll feast on pineapple-coconut bread, salad, BBQ ribs, pulled pork, chicken, and rice. For dessert, you'll receive pineapple bread pudding. Fountain drinks, lemonade, and coffee are included in the price. Those 21 and up can also enjoy beer or wine. Specialty drinks are sold for an extra cost. Disney's Spirit of Aloha Dinner Show is held on select evenings for dinner.

Capt. Cook's
Quick Service - $

There are three special things that you need to know about Capt. Cook's. First, if you didn't make a breakfast reservation for Kona Cafe, you can order Tonga Toast here. Second, they sell the famous Dole Whip. Third, you'll find a great variety of delicious and creative cupcakes here. The restaurant opens early for breakfast. If you don't want the Tonga Toast, you can also order eggs, breakfast sandwiches, Mickey Waffles, and other breakfast items. Lunch and dinner selections include burgers, sandwiches, sushi, fish, and vegetarian chili. Brownies and apple pie are sold for dessert, in addition to the cupcakes. Specialty cocktails such as the Jose Cuervo Margarita and the Kahlua Mudslide are available, as are beer and wine. Non-alcoholic beverages are sold as well. Capt. Cook's is open daily for breakfast, lunch, dinner, and snacks.

Kona Island
Quick Service - $

Located next to Kona Cafe, Kona Island serves two purposes. In the morning it is a coffee bar. There is a good selection that includes Kona coffee, cappuccino, and espresso in various sizes. You can also grab a pastry to accompany your morning caffeine. For dinner, Kona Island turns into a Sushi Bar. All of your favorites are served. There is also a nice selection of sake and wines. Beer and cocktails are available, as well as non-alcoholic beverages. Kona Island is open daily for breakfast and dinner.

Barefoot Pool Bar
Pool Bar - $

What could be better than sipping a cold exotic beverage on a white sandy beach? Sipping that drink near a volcano with views of the Magic Kingdom would be nice! You can do just that at Barefoot Pool Bar. There is a full bar, and specialties include creations such as Captain's Mai Tai and Banana Cabana. Non-alcoholic drinks are available as well. Barefoot Pool Bar is open daily for beverages.

Tambu Lounge
Lounge - $

The exotic feel of the resort continues at Tambu Lounge. Located in the Great Ceremonial House, you can enjoy appetizers such as chicken wings or pulled pork nachos. Some of the specialty drinks include the Backscratcher, the Tropical Macaw, and the Island Sunset. There's a full bar so you don't have to order something tropical if you'd rather enjoy a personal favorite. Non-alcoholic drinks are also sold. Tambu Lounge is open daily for snacks and beverages.

SIXTY-THREE

DISNEY'S POP CENTURY RESORT

Value

Take a trip through history at Disney's Pop Century Resort. Larger than life icons that represent the 1950's through the 1990's are featured at this Value resort. You'll find items such as 45rpm records to showcase the 1950's and a Rubik's Cube staircase for the 1990's. The main pool, representing the 1960's, is called the Hippy Dippy Pool. The closest theme park is Disney's Hollywood Studios. Disney's Pop Century Resort is located in the ESPN Wide World of Sports Resort Area. In-room pizza delivery is available until midnight.

Everything POP Shopping and Dining
Quick Service - $

One of the nice things about the Disney food courts is that the atmosphere is different at each one. Everything POP Shopping and Dining is no exception. You'll find classic video games, bright lights, and even a gift shop. The restaurant opens early for breakfast. Choices include omelets, eggs, potatoes, breakfast meats, pancakes, Mickey Waffles, and other breakfast offerings. You can order coffee and other beverages including the iced coffee creation Popaccino. Lunch and dinner have a large selection to choose from, including burgers, sandwiches, pizza, pasta, and subs. The Create-Your-Own stations include salads, tacos, and burritos. There are plenty of bakery items for dessert, including the signature Tie-dyed Cheesecake. There is also plenty of ice cream available. Milkshakes and other hot and cold beverages are sold as well. The restaurant remains open until midnight, making it a great place for a late night snack. Everything POP Shopping and Dining is open daily for breakfast, lunch, dinner, and snacks.

Petals Pool Bar
Pool Bar - $

Located by the Hippy Dippy Pool, the Petals Pool Bar offers some great beverage choices. You can hydrate with the Ultimate Long Island Iced Tea or a Grand Margarita. Other specialty cocktails, beer, wine, and sangria are also sold. Non-alcoholic creations include the Orange Freeze and the Lava Smoothie. Petals Pool Bar is open daily for beverages.

SIXTY-FOUR

DISNEY'S PORT ORLEANS RESORT - FRENCH QUARTER

Moderate

Celebrate Mardi Gras and the spirit of New Orleans everyday at Disney's Port Orleans Resort - French Quarter. This Moderate resort features lots of jazz and colorful creations which will make you feel like it's Fat Tuesday, no matter what time of year you visit. You can ride in a horse-drawn carriage or take a stroll by the Sassagoula River. You can also easily walk to Disney's Port Orleans Resort - Riverside and enjoy what is offered there. The streets of Disney's Port Orleans Resort - French Quarter are lined with iron fences, just like you'd find in the real French Quarter. Relaxing fountains and bright colors add to the feel of the resort. Downtown Disney is a boat ride away. The closest theme park is Epcot. Disney's Port Orleans Resort - French Quarter is located in the Downtown Disney Resort Area. In-room pizza delivery is available until midnight.

Sassagoula Floatworks and Food Factory Food Court
Quick Service - $

Who says that you can't celebrate Mardi Gras all year long? At Sassagoula Floatworks and Food Factory Food Court, you can do just that. You'll see giant masks, trombones, ice cream cones, and other things that will put you in the mood to party. The food court opens early for breakfast. You'll find beignets (in addition to other bakery items), omelets, eggs, breakfast meats, Mickey Waffles, and of course, French toast. There are other choices as well and you can also get your morning coffee here. For lunch and dinner you might want a Po' Boy or a Bayou Chicken Sandwich. There are plenty of other sandwich choices, or order a burger or a pizza. Beignets and bakery items are sold at both lunch and dinner. Hand-scooped ice cream will keep the party going at the end of your meal. The food court is open until midnight so you can have something to eat once you've returned from the parks. Sassagoula Floatworks and Food Factory Food Court is open daily for breakfast, lunch, dinner, and snacks.

Mardi Grogs
Pool Bar - $

Located near the Doubloon Lagoon pool, Mardi Grogs is a great place to grab a drink when you need to relax. There is some covered seating, but you can also take your drink and watch the boats headed to Downtown Disney along the Sassagoula River. Specialty beverages include Captain's Mai Tai and Banana Cabana. Beers include TurboDog and Abita Amber, which are brewed in Louisiana. Other beers, wine, and sangria are also sold, as are non-alcoholic choices. Mardi Grogs is open daily for beverages.

Scat Cat's Club
Lounge - $

This lounge is a great place to stop by in the evening. On select nights you can enjoy the music of jazz musician Tom Casey. There's a full bar and specialty drinks include Sassagoula Swamp Water and Southern Hurricane. Scat Cat's Club is open evenings for beverages.

SIXTY-FIVE

DISNEY'S PORT ORLEANS RESORT – RIVERSIDE

Moderate

Feel like you're down on the bayou at Disney's Port Orleans Resort - Riverside. The relaxed pace of this Moderate resort will make you forget that you're at one of the most popular tourist destinations in the world. You can take a horse-drawn carriage ride along the Sassagoula River or head to Downtown Disney in a water taxi. Kids ages 4-12 can take part in a pirate cruise and the whole family can sing along during the Campfire on de' Bayou. One of the highlights of Disney's Port Orleans Resort - Riverside is Ol' Man Island. Take a dip in the pool there or relax in a hammock. The closest park is Epcot. Disney's Port Orleans Resort - Riverside is located in the Downtown Disney Resort Area. In-room pizza delivery is available until midnight.

Boatwright's Dining Hall
Full Service - $$

The ship building industry is clearly represented at this eatery. You'll see the wooden hull of a fishing boat, ship building tools, pictures of different vessels, and more. The restaurant is an easy walk from Port Orleans - French Quarter and you can take a water taxi there from Downtown Disney. Book your dinner so that you'll be able to enjoy YeHaa Bob Jackson when you're finished. He performs on select nights at the River Roost Lounge next door.

You'll find all of your favorites from New Orleans at Boatwright's Dining Hall. Start with Shrimp & Grits or Cajun-seasoned Crawfish Bites. Andouille-crusted Catfish, Crawfish Etouffee, and Voodoo Chicken are just a few of the entrees. You can get Jambalaya; a vegetarian version is available as well as traditional. You can also order prime rib, pork chops, or pasta. You won't want to skip dessert. Try the Pecan Pie, the Seasonal Bread Pudding, or the Bananas Foster Angel Food Cake. Specialty drinks include Ramos Fizz and Southern Hurricane. There is a selection of Abita draft beers (they're brewed in Louisiana), and other alcoholic and non-alcoholic beverages are available as well. Boatwright's Dining Hall is open daily for dinner.

Riverside Mill Food Court
Quick Service - $

You can't miss the water wheel (it powers a working cotton press) at Disney's Port Orleans - Riverside. Once you've found that, you've also found Riverside Mill Food Court. Bright colors and mismatched chairs make the dining area feel like home. You can watch the gears turn for the cotton press, powered by the water wheel outside. The food court opens early for breakfast, where you'll find standard items like eggs, breakfast meats, Mickey Waffles, bakery items, omelets, and pancakes. You can also order a Breakfast Power Wrap, a Breakfast Flatbread, or French Toast with fresh fruit topping. For lunch and dinner you can enjoy burgers, pizza, or sandwiches, or you can create your own pasta or salad. There are plenty of bakery items on hand for dessert, including fruit cobbler. Hand scooped ice cream is also served. Cappuccino, espresso, iced coffee, and other hot and cold beverages are available at all meals. The food court remains open until midnight to take care of those late night hunger pains. Riverside Mill Food Court is open daily for breakfast, lunch, dinner, and snacks.

Muddy Rivers Pool Bar
Pool Bar - $

What better name for a pool bar at Ol' Man Island than Muddy Rivers? Here you'll find specialty drinks such as Moscato Colada and Island Moon-shine. Draft and bottled beer, wine, and sangria are also sold, as are non-alcoholic beverages. If you're hungry, you can call from the phone next to the bar to order a pizza and have it delivered to you poolside. Muddy Rivers Pool Bar is open daily for beverages.

River Roost
Lounge - $
FAN PICK

At first glance this lounge might look like a relaxing place to grab a snack and have a drink. Sometimes it is relaxing, but everything changes Wednesday through Saturday evenings when YeHaa Bob Jackson arrives. He performs three shows each of those evenings and he'll have your entire party laughing. The show is appropriate for children, in fact they'll have a great time. You might want to take them to an early show because the last show of the evening can be slightly more adult. Appetizers at River Roost include nachos, crawfish tails, and chicken nuggets. There's a full bar, featuring Sazerac and Ramos Fizz. You can order an Abita draft; if you can't decide which one to try, choose the Abita Flight. While River Roost is a lounge, it's also family friendly. River Roost is open evenings for snacks and beverages.

SIXTY-SIX

DISNEY'S SARATOGA SPRINGS RESORT & SPA

Deluxe

Saratoga Springs, New York, is known for horse racing and mineral springs. Disney has recreated the feel at Disney's Saratoga Springs Resort & Spa. These are Deluxe villas where you'll find very unique places to stay. You can even book your vacation in a three bedroom tree house. While it is a Disney Vacation Club property, rooms are available to the general public as well. The spa is named Senses and it will allow you to relax and rejuvenate. There are two pools with slides, as well as three smaller pools. There are jogging trails, a fitness center, and bikes for rent. You can also play games such as foosball and ping pong in the Community Hall. Downtown Disney is a quick boat ride or walk away. The closest theme parks are Epcot and Disney's Typhoon Lagoon. Disney's Saratoga Springs Resort & Spa is located in the Downtown Disney Resort Area. In-room pizza delivery is available until midnight.

The Turf Club Bar and Grill
Full Service - $$

If you've ever been to Saratoga Springs, you know how important horse racing is. The Turf Club Bar and Grill is designed to be the type of place where you might head after a day at the races. You'll see items such as a wine rack made of horseshoes, a Disney themed racing jacket, and plenty of pictures of horses. The decor is a bit on the dark side, but there are large windows to let the light in. There is both indoor and covered outdoor seating. You can shoot a game of pool while you wait.

The menu at The Turf Club Bar and Grill features the chef's take on American classics. You can start your meal with a bowl of tomato bisque soup or an order of steamed mussels. Entrees include grilled salmon, prime rib, range-free chicken, and lamb chops. The Turf Club Pasta comes in three varieties: shrimp, chicken, and vegetarian. Some of the dessert selections are Seasonal Fruit Crisp, Chocolate Espresso Torte, and Buttered Toffee de Creme. Specialty drinks include The Preakness Cosmo, Saratoga Cocktail, and Three Minutes to Post Time. Other alcoholic and non-alcoholic drinks are also available. The Turf Club Bar and Grill is open daily for dinner.

The Artist's Palette
Quick Service - $

You'll feel like you're dining in an artist's loft at this eatery. Eclectic lighting fixtures, bright colors, and the works of artist Laura Fayer help to create an upbeat mood. There is a market at the location in addition to the restaurant. Open early for breakfast, you can grab something from the bakery, or enjoy a more leisurely meal. The Egg Florentine Breakfast Wrap might be a great way to start the day, or try the French Toast Strata instead. You can get eggs, omelets, breakfast meats, Mickey Waffles, and other items. Your morning coffee is available as well. There is a great selection of entrees served for lunch or dinner. In keeping with the resort's theme, you might want to order the Saratoga Salad with

Chicken. There are other salad options, flatbreads, sandwiches, wraps, and various panini creations available. You will also find some comfort food, with Meatloaf, Chicken Parmesan, and Apple BBQ Pork Loin all on the menu. For dessert grab a cookie, brownie, or another bakery item. Coffee and other beverages are sold. The restaurant remains open until 11:00pm for late night snacks. The Artist's Palette is open daily for breakfast, lunch, dinner, and snacks.

The Paddock Grill
Quick Service - $

At first glance The Paddock Grill might look like just another pool bar, but it is much more than that. It is really a quick service dining option, open for all three meals. While you can order a beer or a Strawberry Daiquiri, you can also get a full breakfast in a hurry. Open at 7:30am, breakfast offerings include a Country Breakfast Burrito, a Croissant Sandwich, bagels, muffins, danish, and other pastries. Lunch and dinner include Spice-crusted Fish Sandwich and Chicken Chop Salad. You won't find those items at a regular pool bar! Burgers, salads, and other sandwiches are also available, as are House-made Saratoga Chips. You can also get cake or ice cream here. If you're in the mood for a drink, there are both alcoholic and non-alcoholic options. The Paddock Grill is open daily for breakfast, lunch, dinner, and beverages.

Backstretch Pool Bar
Pool Bar - $

This pool bar also carries some food. You can munch on pretzels, nachos, or chips. If you're really hungry, they also serve sandwiches, hot dogs, and pizza. You can cool off with a Mickey Ice Cream Bar or Sandwich. If you're over 21, satisfy your thirst with a Long Island Iced Tea or a Pina Colada. There is also a Pina Colada that's made without alcohol. Other alcoholic and non-alcoholic beverages are also sold. Backstretch Pool Bar is open daily for snacks and beverages.

On the Rocks
Pool Bar - $

On the Rocks only serves beverages, and yes, many of them are served "on the rocks". There's a great view of the High Rock Spring Pool from the location. You can order a Saratoga Lager to keep with the theme of the resort. Or you might want to try the Citrus Blast or the Banana Cabana. Wine, sangria, and other cocktails and beers are also served. There are plenty of non-alcoholic choices as well. On the Rocks is open daily for beverages.

The Turf Club Lounge
Lounge - $

This lounge is located inside of The Turf Club Bar and Grill restaurant. You can order appetizers such as Crab Cakes or Onion Rings with Dips. Shoot a game of pool while you enjoy a Mint Julep or a Millionaire's Margarita. Saratoga Lager is served, as well as other brands of beer, wine, and specialties. The Turf Club Lounge is open evenings for snacks and beverages.

Sixty Seven

DISNEY'S WILDERNESS LODGE

Deluxe

Step into the Pacific Northwest at Disney's Wilderness Lodge. This Deluxe resort features the beauty and charm of the National Park Lodges from over 100 years ago. You'll find a waterfall, hot springs, and even a geyser. The Native American community is represented with totem poles, headdresses, and other special touches. There is a rustic beauty to the resort that will make you feel as if you've been transported to the American Northwest. The lobby of the lodge features a three-story stone fireplace. The closest theme park is the Magic Kingdom, it is just a boat ride away. Disney's Wilderness Lodge is part of the Magic Kingdom Resort area. Room service is available until midnight.

Artist Point
Fine Dining - $$$

This rustic, yet elegant restaurant is a signature dining experience. Lanterns are hung from the ceiling for the lighting. Large wooden beams add to the feel of the Pacific Northwest. Take a look at the murals; they depict the American frontier. The menu can change seasonally, depending on what is fresh. There is a dress code.

Dinner at Artist Point can start with the Artisanal Cheese Selection or the Yukon Territory Salad. The fresh entrees could include dishes such as Wild Caught Prawn and Crab "Bordetto", Cedar Plank-roasted King Salmon, or Korean Barbecue-inspired Berkshire Pork Loin. If you've never tried venison, you can order it here. For many, the Artist Point Cobbler is a "must try" dessert. Other sweet options include White Chocolate-dipped Pistachio Pound Cake and Gianduja Chocolate and Hazelnut Ganache. There is an extensive wine list, featuring over 130 selections from the Pacific Northwest. There are also several different tea options. Other alcoholic and non-alcoholic beverages are available as well. Artist Point is open daily for dinner.

Whispering Canyon Cafe
Full Service - $$

FAN PICK

If you think that you're in for a quiet meal at Whispering Canyon Cafe, you'll be surprised. Don't let the name fool you. The staff at the restaurant loves to have a good time, and they want to make sure that you do as well. They'll hold pony races, lead you in songs, and just plain have fun. The Old West theme is evident, with logs for ceiling beams and chairs based on the days of cowboys and Indians. There are lighting fixtures that look like teepees, and bandanas are used instead of traditional napkins. One word of warning, don't ask for ketchup unless you *really* want it.

What is unique about the meals at Whispering Canyon Cafe is that you can choose between an all-you-can-eat platter or order off the menu. At breakfast, the platter includes eggs, Mickey Waffles, potatoes, breakfast meats, and biscuits with sausage gravy. The a la carte menu features Eggs Benedict, omelets, hash, banana bread French toast, and other items. You can order a breakfast cocktail if you're of age, or juice, coffee, or another beverage. One treat that is available at all three meals is the all-you-can-drink milkshake. They come in chocolate, vanilla, and strawberry. For lunch, the all-you-can-eat platter is offered seasonally. A la carte items at lunch include Chuck Wagon Angus "Bacon & Egg" Burger, Smoked Chicken Quesadilla and Tuna Melt on Sourdough Bread. For dinner, you can build your own platter. You will order your choice of three different meats like pulled pork, ribs, chicken, beef strip loin, fish, or sausage. The platter comes with cornbread, salad, and sides. If you don't want the platter, you can order meatloaf, trout, steak, or even quinoa cakes. Whether you're there for lunch or dinner, you'll want to have dessert. Selections at either meal include Whispering Canyon Chocolate Cake, Apple-Caramel Pie, and Whispering Canyon S'mores. There are featured beers on the menu such as Sierra Nevada Pale Ale and Full Sail Session Black Lager. If you'd prefer a specialty cocktail, there are several to choose from, including the Moonshine Margarita and Pa's Maple Shake. There are Pacific Coast wines sold as well. There are also non-alcoholic beverages available, including those bottomless milkshakes. Whispering Canyon Cafe is open daily for breakfast, lunch, and dinner.

Roaring Fork
Quick Service - $

Another rustic themed restaurant at Disney's Wilderness Lodge is Roaring Fork. There is some indoor seating, but you're also welcome to take your food outside and enjoy the beauty of the property while you dine. The restaurant opens early, so you'll have plenty of time to eat and still make it to a theme park before it opens. This is where you'll find specialty Mickey Waffles. You can order Bananas Foster Waffles, Strawberry Waffles, or Chocolate Lovers Waffles; all in the shape of your favorite mouse. If you don't want waffles you can get eggs, a croissant sandwich, a breakfast flatbread, or pancakes. Lunch and dinner feature sandwiches (some grilled), pasta, flatbreads, and salads. Some items are available until midnight. There are baked goods sold all day as well. Roaring Fork is open daily for breakfast, lunch, dinner, and snacks.

Trout Pass Pool Bar
Pool Bar - $

This pool bar only serves drinks; you'll have to head inside to Roaring Fork if you're hungry. You'll find Moscato Colada, Captain's Mai Tai, and Black Cherry Lemonade here. Beer, wine, sangria, and other alcoholic beverages are sold. There are also non-alcoholic specialties such as the Orange Freeze and the Lava Smoothie. Trout Pass Pool Bar is open daily for beverages.

Territory Lounge
Lounge - $

This is a great place to relax after a long day. Territory Lounge has low lighting, a rugged theme, comfortable chairs, and a giant carved wooden bear. There is an appetizer menu that features Territory Lounge Crispy Chicken, Northwest Charcuterie, Oregon Pinot Grigio Fondue, and Steamed Edamame in Pod. A full bar is available and you'll find both beers and wines from the Pacific Northwest. Specialty creations include the Olive Truffle Martini and the Pear Blossom Cosmo. Non-alcoholic drinks are also sold and the lounge is family friendly. Territory Lounge is open evenings for snacks and beverages.

SIXTY-EIGHT

DISNEY'S YACHT CLUB RESORT

Deluxe

Disney's Yacht Club Resort is like taking a trip to coastal New England without having to leave sunny Florida. This Deluxe accommodation has a relaxed feel. There is a globe in the lobby, as well as models of old-fashioned yachts. Outdoors you'll see a windmill, a pirate ship, and a lighthouse. You can walk or jog around Crescent Lake, rent a boat or a bike, or play volleyball on the beach. Disney's Beach Club and all that it has to offer is right next door, and Disney's BoardWalk Inn (with the fun nightlife that it promises) is a short walk away. You can also walk to the International Gateway entrance to Epcot, or if you don't feel like walking, you can take a boat. A different boat or a walking path will get you to Disney's Hollywood Studios. Disney's Yacht Club Resort is located in the Epcot Resort Area. Room service is available 24 hours a day.

Yachtsman Steakhouse
Fine Dining - $$$

FAN PICK

This signature restaurant features a laid back atmosphere. It may not have as many elaborate touches as some of the other Walt Disney World restaurants, but that is part of its charm. The pine beams and the relaxed lighting add to the atmosphere. The meat served at Yachtsman Steakhouse is aged in-house and you'll have a chance to walk by the dry-aging room. The menu changes seasonally, bringing you the freshest dishes possible. There is a dress code.

You can start your dinner with a selection of Artisanal Cheeses, Shrimp Cocktail, or "The Land" Garden Greens. Entrees may include prime rib, filet mignon, buffalo, chicken breast, or the Catch of the Day. Even the sides change seasonally, but may include Truffle Macaroni & Cheese and Zuckerman's Farm Asparagus. The signature dessert is the Yachtsman's Sundae, but you might want the Seasonal Sorbet Trio or the Creme Brulee instead. After dessert, enjoy a coffee creation, with or without an added kick. There is an extensive wine list, or you might want a Cognac Flight instead. There are plenty of other alcoholic and non-alcoholic beverages available as well. Yachtsman Steakhouse is open daily for dinner.

Captain's Grille
Full Service or Buffet - $$

Captain's Grille continues the nautical theme of the resort. There are more model boats, windows that remind you of portholes, and even a sign overhead that says "Welcome Aboard". Since the resort is close to Epcot, you can easily get away from the theme park and enjoy a quiet meal without taking a lot of time out of your day.

Breakfast at Captain's Grille is served either buffet style or a la carte. The buffet includes pastries, pancakes, eggs, breakfast meats, smoked salmon, and other items. Coffee, tea, juice, and soft drinks are included in the price. If you want to order from the menu, the choices include Lobster Omelet, Citrus-scented French Toast, and Dark Chocolate Waffles. The lunch and dinner menus are quite different, although some items are available on both. For lunch, you might want to start with Lump Crab Cake. A must-try item is the Hand-cut Salt and Vinegar Fries. Lunch also features burgers, salads, and sandwiches such as the New England-style Lobster Roll and the Tomato and Mozzarella Sandwich. Once it's time for dinner, order Pot-braised Mussels and Clams or New England Clam Chowder to start your meal. For your main course try Market Fish, Rosemary-brined Pork Tenderloin, Chef's Pasta Creation, or New York Strip Steak. For a meatless entrée, there is the Chef's Vegetarian Inspiration. End lunch or dinner with Bananas Foster Cheesecake or House-made Gelato. Specialty cocktails like the Captain's Rum Runner, and specialty coffees such as Keoki Coffee are served. Keeping with the New England theme, you can order different types of Samuel Adams beer or a New England wine. Other alcoholic and non-alcoholic beverages are also served. Captain's Grille is open daily for breakfast, lunch, and dinner.

Ale & Compass Lounge
Lounge - $

If you're hungry and in a hurry in the morning, you might want to stop by Ale & Compass Lounge. You can grab a pastry, granola bar, fruit, and coffee here. There are a few more breakfast choices as well. In the evenings it turns back into a lounge. Appetizers such as Chilled Lobster Sliders and Buttermilk-fried Rock Shrimp are available. There is a large selection of wine, and high end spirits are available. You can also order specialty cocktails and other alcoholic and non-alcoholic beverages. Ale & Compass Lounge is open daily for breakfast and evenings for snacks and beverages.

Crew's Cup Lounge
Lounge - $

Crew's Cup Lounge is located right next to the entrance to Yachtsman's Steakhouse. If you're looking for a place to relax and grab a bite to eat or a drink, you'll find what you're searching for here. While it is considered a lounge, you can order a full lunch or dinner at Crew's Cup. There are sandwiches available, such as the Shaved Beef Sandwich and the Grilled Chicken Sandwich. You can also get the Cape May Clam Linguini, burgers, and lobster sliders. Wash your food down with a Strawberry Julep, a Jameson Irish Whiskey Sour, or another cocktail. You can order a Samuel Adams Beer Flight or another draft or bottled beer. Other alcoholic and non-alcoholic beverages are also served. Crew's Cup Lounge is open daily for lunch, dinner, and beverages.

SIXTY-NINE

SHADES OF GREEN AT WALT DISNEY WORLD RESORT

Shades of Green is owned by the United States Department of Defense. The resort (including the restaurants) is for active and retired US military members and their families. Since it is not owned by Disney, it does not have the classification that the other resorts have. The rooms are large and the price is reasonable. Guests receive many of the same benefits that other Disney resort guests receive, such as Extra Magic Hours. Shades of Green guests need to take buses to other parts of Walt Disney World, there is no monorail or boat service from the resort. It is part of the Magic Kingdom Resort Area. Room service is available 24 hours a day.

Mangino's Bistro
Full Service - $, $$

This Italian restaurant is a great place to enjoy a leisurely meal in the evening, or lunch if you're taking a day away from the parks. The atmosphere is laid back and comfortable. It's a place where you'll want to stay for a while. There is an open kitchen, so you can see the food being prepared.

For lunch you can order a soup and sandwich combo, there's a different choice each day of the week. Other lunch items include burgers, sandwiches, omelets, and pizza. Start your dinner with calamari or bruschetta, or sample a few different items with the Combinazione Mangino's. Entrees include steak, seafood, veal, chicken, pizza, and pasta. Chocolate cake, Key Lime Pie, cheesecake, and a dessert sampler are on the menu to end your meal. There is an extensive wine list, and other beverages are also available. Mangino's Bistro is open daily for lunch and dinner.

Garden Gallery
Buffet - $

If you're looking to fill up before a day at the parks, or you need to recharge at the end of your day, you'll want to check out Garden Gallery. The atmosphere is comfortable without being flashy, and the food is priced reasonably.

For breakfast, the buffet features fresh fruit, eggs, breakfast meats, potatoes, pastries, and other traditional breakfast items. You can also order a la carte. Menu items include omelets, pancakes, and breakfast hash. The dinner buffet changes, depending on the day of the week. You'll find items like soup, salad, pasta, meats, breads, and desserts. Garden Gallery is open daily for breakfast and dinner.

Evergreens
Quick Service - $

Is anyone up for a game of pool? There is a relaxed feel to this eatery and kids of all ages will love playing the arcade and other games. You can order sandwiches, burgers, and wraps here. Most are made in advance, so you won't have to wait long. You can also order pizza.

Beer, wine, and other alcoholic and non-alcoholic beverages are served. Evergreens is open daily for dinner, and weekends for lunch as well.

Express Cafe
Quick Service - $

If you don't want to leave for the day without eating, but you also don't want to take a lot of time for breakfast, Express Cafe is your solution. You can grab something quick and then catch the bus right out front. Breakfast items include breakfast sandwiches, pancakes, pastries, and fruit. You can also get your morning coffee here. Lunch and dinner are served as well. There are several sandwich options to choose from. Beer, wine, and other alcoholic and non-alcoholic beverages are sold. Express Cafe is open daily for breakfast, lunch, and dinner.

On the Greens
Quick Service - $

Swimming can make you hungry, as can golf. On the Greens is located near both the Magnolia Pool and the putting course, so you can easily satisfy your hunger and thirst. You'll find burgers, hot dogs, pizza, and sandwiches on the menu. You can grab ice cream for dessert. Beer, wine, mixed drinks, and non-alcoholic beverages are also sold. On the Greens is open daily for lunch, snacks, and beverages.

Java Cafe
Quick Service - $

If you can't get through your day without your Starbucks coffee fix, you'll want to stop by Java Cafe. All of your favorites are served. You'll also find the Starbucks food menu, so you can enjoy a biscotti with your Caramel Macchiato. You can order hand-scooped or soft serve ice cream here as well. Java Cafe is open daily for snacks and beverages.

Lucky's Snack Bar
Pool Bar - $

You want to spend part of your vacation relaxing, and Lucky's Snack Bar allows you the opportunity to do just that. You can munch on pizza or a hot dog, order a wrap, or maybe you'd prefer a fruit plate. There are plenty of snacks to choose from as well. You can also order a margarita or strawberry daiquiri, or maybe you'd prefer a glass of wine. Other alcoholic and non-alcoholic beverages are sold, including frozen drinks. Lucky's Snack Bar is open seasonally on weekdays only for lunch, snacks, and beverages.

SEVENTY

WALT DISNEY WORLD DOLPHIN HOTEL

Deluxe

The Walt Disney World Dolphin Hotel is hard to miss. The water-colored triangular main building is visible from several places on Disney property. You'll want to have your camera ready when you first see the fountain in the lobby! While the Deluxe resort is located in the middle of the magic, it is operated by Starwood Hotels and Resorts. Guests still enjoy many of the benefits of staying at a Walt Disney World resort hotel, but there are some differences such as a fee to park. The Dolphin is the home of Mandara Spa. Camp Dolphin is a safe place for the little ones if Mom and Dad want to spend some time alone. There are jogging trails, playgrounds, and other recreational opportunities. The hotel is a short walk to Disney's BoardWalk. You can take a boat or walk to either Epcot or Disney's Hollywood Studios. The Walt Disney World Dolphin Hotel is located in the Epcot Resort Area. Room service is available 24 hours a day.

Shula's Steak House
Fine Dining - $$$

The Shula in this case is Don Shula, legendary former coach of the Miami Dolphins. He and his son Dave run a chain of restaurants that are known for their top quality beef. This signature restaurant has a football theme that celebrates the Miami Dolphins and their perfect 1972 season, but that doesn't mean that non-football fans won't love it. Continuing with the theme, the menu is printed on a football. The atmosphere is relaxed. You're expected to stay for a while and enjoy what is, according to Don and Dave Shula, "The best beef that money can buy". You can even join Shula's 48oz. Club by finishing off a 48 ounce porterhouse.

When you dine at Shula's Steak House, expect to leave full. You can start your meal with Jumbo Lump Crab Cake, Colossal Shrimp Cocktail, or Premium Black Angus Steak Tartare. If you'd prefer a lighter start to your meal, you could order soup or a salad. Most of the entrees are steak, but chicken and seafood are available as well. New York strip, filet mignon, prime rib, and other cuts are served in different portions. The staff will show you the different cuts before you order so that you will get an idea of how much food you'll be receiving. Sides include baked potato, roasted corn, and Crab Macaroni and Cheese. If you still have room for dessert, you can choose from items such as Chocolate Soufflé, Apple Crisp, and Key Lime Pie. There is an award winning wine list. Specialty cocktails and other beverages are available. Shula's Steak House is open daily for dinner.

Todd English's bluezoo
Fine Dining - $$$

Atmosphere plays a large role at Todd English's bluezoo. Famed architect Jeffrey Beers created a space that is a work of art. The lighting effects and the coloring give the restaurant an underwater feel. It is sophisticated and unique. There is an open kitchen so you can see where the food (including the Dancing Fish) is prepared. If you're looking for a romantic meal, drop the kids off at Club Dolphin. They can stay there for free for two hours while you dine (certain restrictions apply).

The food at this signature restaurant is the creation of celebrity chef Todd English. The menu changes seasonally and is based on what is fresh. Appetizers might include dishes such as bluezoo's New England Style Clam Chowder and Heritage Pork Belly. The entrees are heavy on the seafood, but chicken, lamb, and beef are available as well. Choices might include Miso Glazed Mero, Two-pound Maine "Cantonese" Lobster, English Pea Ravioli, and This Evening's Dancing Fish. For dessert, you might want to try the Mai Tai Banana Cream Tart or the Warm Molten Chocolate Cake. Another thing that Todd English's bluezoo is known for is the cocktail menu. There are plenty of specialty creations with names like Smoking White Sangria, Zooberry, and One Night in Mexico. The wine menu has won awards, and there are also "suds to sip" and "suds to slam". There are also non-alcoholic specialty creations. Todd English's bluezoo is open daily for dinner.

Fresh Mediterranean Market
Full Service and buffet - $$

You'll need a hearty breakfast to spend a day in a theme park. That is exactly what you can find at Fresh Mediterranean Market. The atmosphere is casual with bright colors and plenty of lighting. Since the Dolphin is close to both Epcot and Disney's Hollywood Studios, you can leave the park of choice for a relaxing lunch without using up too much of your day.

There is a plentiful breakfast buffet at Fresh Mediterranean Market, or you can order a la carte. The buffet has the normal items like eggs, breakfast meats, and pancakes, but there are also some unexpected choices such as Wheatgrass juice extract. A la carte offerings include eggs, Belgium Waffles, and turkey hash. You can order coffee, tea, juice, or something with a kick for breakfast as well. Lunch is served a la carte. Start your meal with soup or a salad. Fresh Mediterranean

Market has lots of sandwiches to choose from for lunch. Ham, lobster, and pulled pork are some of the options, as well as the Grilled Chicken Panini. At lunchtime the buffet area features dessert, which is included with your meal. You'll find bite-sized cakes, tarts, creme brulee, and other sweet offerings. With your lunch you can also enjoy a specialty beverage such as Istanbul Coffee or Egyptian Honey Bourbon Tea, or order wine or beer. Other alcoholic and non-alcoholic beverages are also sold. Fresh Mediterranean Market is open daily for breakfast and lunch.

The Fountain
Full Service - $

The Fountain is a new take on the old-fashioned soda fountain and diner from years gone by. It has the same feel as you would have expected at such a place, but it is a more contemporary version. There's even a neon sign with the restaurant's name behind the counter. There are pictures on the walls of comfort foods, and you'll want to take a peek at the ice cream freezer before you order.

Start your meal at The Fountain with a cup of Chicken Noodle Soup and a Seared Salmon Salad. The entrees include hot dogs, burgers, and sandwiches such as the Classic BLT. Gluten-free buns or bread are available, just ask. While you're at The Fountain, you'll want to try a milkshake. They have traditional flavors, but there are also some creative choices such as PB&J or Coco Loco. An added kick is available for some of the shakes for adults. You'll also want to take a look at the ice cream menu. Hand-scooped and soft serve are available. The ice cream creations include the Caramel Apple Sundae and The Fountain Funnel. Cookies and pie are also sold for dessert. In addition to the milkshakes, you'll find beer, wine, Stewart's sodas, and other beverages. Open late, this is a great stop for a late night snack after IllumiNations. The Fountain is open daily for lunch, dinner, and snacks.

Picabu
Quick Service - $

Walt Disney World refers to Picabu as a "Buffeteria". It is not a buffet, but the restaurant serves items that you might expect to find on a buffet. It is not all-you-can-eat. The restaurant has a fun theme with statues on the walls of boats, palm trees, butterflies, and a fun character who is peaking around the corners. There is a store that sells snacks and sundries at the location. The best part of all is that the eatery is open 24 hours, although not all items are sold all day long. Some of the things that you can order for breakfast are omelets, waffles with your choice of topping, and the Picabu Breakfast. For lunch or dinner you can order burgers, hot dogs, lasagna, chicken, tacos, burritos, and even falafel. Pizza, sandwiches, soup, fresh fruit, collard greens, creamed spinach, and mac & cheese are also available. If you're not sure what to get, order the Picabu Family Meal. Cookies, muffins, brownies, and Key Lime Pie are among the sweeter offerings. Available beverages include bottled beer, wine, fountain drinks, hot beverages, juice, and other selections. Since the restaurant never closes, it's the perfect place for a late night snack. Picabu is open daily for breakfast, lunch, dinner, and snacks. Picabu is open 24 hours a day!

Cabana Bar and Beach Club
Pool Bar - $

Calling Cabana Bar and Beach Club a pool bar is almost like calling the Mona Lisa a painting. It's that, but so much more. Located near the Dolphin Lap Pool, there's plenty to eat if you're hungry. You can order egg rolls, peel and eat shrimp, or a Tostada Your Way, and that's just from the appetizer list! Entrees include wraps, sandwiches, and burgers. After dark, Cabana Bar and Beach Club comes alive. The bar is illuminated and the area has more of a nightclub feel. Specialty drinks include Cabana Berry, Banana Split, and Gator Rita. You can also order beer, wine, and other alcoholic or non-alcoholic beverages. Cabana Bar and Beach Club is open daily for lunch, dinner, snacks, and beverages.

Lobby Lounge
Lounge - $

Located next to the entrance to Mandara Spa, you'll find Lobby Lounge. In the morning you can get coffee and a pastry before you head out for the day. In the evening the location becomes a lounge that serves specialty drinks, beer, wine, and high end liquors. Other beverages are also sold. Lobby Lounge is open daily for breakfast and evenings for beverages.

Shula's Lounge
Lounge - $ FAN PICK

Do you want to try arguably the best steak at Walt Disney World, but you forgot to make a reservation at Shula's Steak House? Head next door to Shula's Lounge! It shares the same theme as the restaurant, as well as the entire menu. You can also order beer, wine, and other beverages. Cigars are sold as well. Shula's Lounge is open evenings for dinner and beverages.

Todd English's bluezoo Lounge
Lounge - $

Located inside Todd English's bluezoo, reservations are not required for the lounge. Soak up the unique atmosphere as you enjoy an appetizer. The menu includes Crab Nachos, Prosciutto Flatbread, and Crispy Calamari. You can also order off of the restaurant's dinner menu. Todd English's bluezoo is known for creative specialty cocktails, and you can order those as well. Champagne, wine, cordials, beer, and other beverages are also served. Todd English's bluezoo Lounge is open late afternoons and evenings for dinner and beverages.

Seventy-One

WALT DISNEY WORLD SWAN HOTEL

Deluxe

The sister of the Dolphin is the Walt Disney World Swan Hotel. Statues of the birds sit majestically on top of the main building. Like the Dolphin, the Swan is a Deluxe hotel that is operated by Starwood Hotels and Resorts. Guests receive many of the same privileges as other Walt Disney World guests, including Extra Magic Hours. There is no complimentary parking at the Swan. The hotel has a white sand beach, a health club, and more. Fantasia Gardens and Fairways Miniature Golf is a short walk away. You can also walk or take a boat to Disney's BoardWalk, Epcot, or Disney's Hollywood Studios. Walt Disney World Swan is part of the Epcot resort area. Room service is available 24 hours a day.

Il Mulino New York Trattoria
Fine Dining - $$$ **FAN PICK**

A world class restaurant from The Big Apple also calls the Swan home. Il Mulino New York Trattoria is the creation of chefs Fernando and Gino Masci. The New York restaurant has been pleasing guests for over two decades and it fits in perfectly with the luxury at the Swan. This signature restaurant's dining area is located behind the lounge and there is sometimes live music on the weekends. The kitchen can be seen behind glass. With the crisp lines of the architecture, you'll feel more like you're in a high end city restaurant than at a theme park hotel in Florida.

The food served at Il Mulino New York Trattoria is Italian. You'll start with a complimentary appetizer of an eggplant dish with salami on the side. The menu is extensive. You can order appetizers such as Portobello Funghi, Insaccati Misti, or Gamberi Al Mulino. The entree choices include pasta, pizza, steak, chicken, veal, seafood, and risotto. The pasta is made fresh daily. If you have any questions, just ask. The staff knows the menu inside and out. Desserts, or "dolci" as they're referred to on the menu, include Gelato, Cheesecake Italiano, and Tiramisu. Wine is available by the bottle or the glass, and the wine list features the wines of Italy's Gaja Winery. Other wines are also available. Specialty cocktails include Peach Bellini, Margarita Italiana, and Testarossa - Red Head. Beer, high end liquors, and other alcoholic choices are also available. Non-alcoholic beverages are sold as well. Il Mulino New York Trattoria is open daily for dinner.

Kimonos
Fine Dining - $$

If you're looking for incredible sushi, you'll want to try Kimonos. This award winning signature restaurant has a Far East feel to it, without being overdone. There are Japanese kimonos hanging from the ceiling as part of the decor. The sushi is created in the dining area, so you can watch the chefs and even ask questions. The nearby lounge features karaoke later in the evening.

The sushi creations change from time to time, depending on what is fresh. You can start your meal with a Seaweed Salad or a bowl of Tempura Udon Soup. If you're in the mood for an appetizer, try the Szechuan Spare Ribs or the Tempura Platter. The sushi is the star; the food looks as great as it tastes. The menu may include the cooked creations Coconut Shrimp Roll, Spider Roll, Vegetarian Summer Roll, and Shrimp Tempura Roll. If you'd prefer raw, the choices might include Tuna Roll, California Roll, Banzai Roll, or Spicy Rainbow Roll. Specialty cocktails include The Kimonos Dragon, Black Warrior Martini, and Snow. Beer, plum wine, sake, and other alcoholic and non-alcoholic beverages are also available. Kimonos is open daily for dinner.

Garden Grove
Table service, Buffet, and Character Dining - $$, $$$

Enjoy a picnic in Central Park without leaving Florida. At the center of Garden Grove is a 25 foot oak tree. During the day, sunlight floods the restaurant, while in the evenings the streetlights give it a more tranquil feel. Breakfast is served both buffet style and a la carte. Lunch is only a la carte. At dinner, the buffet is included with your entree purchase. On Friday nights, the buffet is known as "Seafood Sensation". Dinner is a character meal daily, and there are characters at breakfast on Saturdays and Sundays. The characters change from time to time, but might include Pluto, Goofy, Timon, or Rafiki. Garden Grove is often one of the less crowded character meals, so if you don't have a reservation elsewhere, you might want to see if something is available.

For breakfast the buffet includes eggs, omelets, cereal, breakfast meats, and pastries. On the a la carte menu there are several types of omelets including lobster. Other eggs, quiche, cereal, Raisin Bread French Toast, pancakes and Apple Crepes are also served. Coffee, juice, and other beverages are sold. Lunch includes soup, salads, lo mein, pepperoni flatbread pizza, and sautéed mussels. The entrees for dinner include prime rib, organic chicken, salmon, and the Chef's Vegetarian Creation. After you order you can visit the buffet, which includes the "Chop It or Toss It" salad station, soup, and desserts created by pastry chef Laurent Branlard. On Friday evenings the entire meal is a buffet, which is heavy on the seafood; (if you want lobster, the cost will be higher). Garden Grove is open daily for breakfast, lunch, and dinner.

Java Bar
Quick Service - $

You don't want to start the day before you've had your coffee and something to eat; so stop by Java Bar. You can grab a bagel or a pastry, and also get your morning coffee and juice. If you want something to help you recharge in the afternoon or early evening, you can get that here as well. Java Bar is open daily for breakfast, snacks, and beverages.

Splash
Pool Bar - $

Located near the Swan Lap Pool, Splash is a great place for a relaxing outdoor lunch or a cool drink. The restaurant features specialty subs such as Big Bird (chicken salad) and Rocky Balboa (prime rib). Tuna, turkey, vegetarian, and other subs are also served. You can order a whole pizza or just a slice and salads are also available. Ice cream is sold as well. You can also buy alcoholic and non-alcoholic beverages. Splash is open seasonally for lunch, snacks, and beverages.

Il Mulino Lounge
Lounge - $

In order to get to the Il Mulino New York Trattoria dining room, you'll have to pass through the Il Mulino Lounge. This hip lounge location features a light appetizer menu and a full bar. Some evenings there is live music as well. The signature cocktails include Pineapple Bellini, Infusion, and Margarita Italiana. Italian and other wines, beer, and high end liquors are also sold. Il Mulino Lounge is open evenings for snacks and beverages.

Kimonos Lounge
Lounge - $

Are you in the mood for karaoke? If so, then you'll definitely want to stop by Kimonos Lounge. Sample some sushi, sip on a specialty cocktail, and sit back and enjoy the show. If you're trying to get up the nerve to perform, you can order creations such as Oriental Grape, Kimonos Soda, or Pears and Brown Sugar. Sake, Asian beer, Japanese whiskey, and other alcoholic and non-alcoholic beverages are also available. Although it's a lounge, it is still family friendly. Kimonos Lounge is open evenings for snacks and beverages.

SEVENTY-TWO

101 MUST READ DINING TIPS

Here's a quick list of suggestions that might make dining easier on your Walt Disney World vacation. Not all tips will work for everyone, so pick the ones that make sense for your situation. Some subjects are covered in more detail elsewhere in this publication. These tips are in no particular order.

101) Make reservations as early as you can, up to 180 days in advance.

100) Keep checking back for hard to get reservations.

99) Drink plenty of water.

98) Make a budget and stick to it.

97) Keep your voices down inside the restaurants.

96) Keep your kids under control while dining.

95) Ask your Disney-loving friends for restaurant recommendations.

94) Ask cast members what their favorite restaurants are.

93) Check menus ahead of time.

92) Buy a Refillable Mug, but only if you'll use it.

91) Clean up after you're finished, don't leave a mess.

90) Plan for an occasional splurge.

89) Keep in mind that menus change.

88) If you're not sure, ask.

87) Order Mickey Check Meals for the kids.

86) Arrive a little bit early for your reservation.

85) Ask for window or other special seating.

84) Stop by a lounge instead of the full service restaurant if you don't have a reservation.

83) Remember that several of the signature restaurants have dress codes.

82) Eat breakfast; you'll need the energy.

81) Make your reservation online and save time.

80) Call 407-WDW-DINE (407-939-3463) and talk to an operator for hard to obtain reservations.

79) Take pictures of your meals and the restaurants.

78) Reserve a dinner show.

77) Reserve a character meal.

76) Finish your alcoholic beverage before you leave the park.

75) Dine during a parade for a less crowded quick service meal.

74) Wash your hands or use hand sanitizer before eating.

73) Read restaurant reviews before making your choices.

72) If there's a restaurant that interests you, try it - even if it received bad reviews.

71) Buy an insulated lunchbox and keep cold drinks in it.

70) Try at least one resort restaurant.

69) If you're an Annual Passholder or Disney Vacation Club member, always ask if there is a discount.

68) Book the Fantasmic! Dinner Package and enjoy VIP seating for the show.

67) Look for healthy options.

66) Snack on fresh fruit, available in all four parks.

65) Don't forget that some restaurants require two table service credits on the Disney Dining Plan.

64) Enjoy a Mickey Ice Cream Bar at least once on your trip.

63) Don't let dietary restrictions stop you, but make sure you inform the restaurant of your needs ahead of time.

62) Kosher meals are available in all four parks and in some resort restaurants.

61) Try the chef's specialty or a signature dish.

60) Receive a free chocolate sample at Downtown Disney's Ghirardelli Ice Cream & Chocolate Shop.

59) Stop by Club Cool at Epcot and try free international Coca Cola products.

58) Pick up a map and use it if you're unfamiliar with the park.

57) Book your vacation when the Quick Service Disney Dining Plan is offered for free.

56) Upgrade the Disney Dining Plan for more restaurant options.

55) Don't buy the Disney Dining Plan if you don't think you will use it.

54) Be polite to the cast members; they work hard to make your vacation special.

53) The gratuity isn't included at most table service restaurants; so please tip generously.

52) Keep track of how many different Mickey shaped food items you come across on your vacation and don't feel guilty about eating that cute face.

51) Snack your way around the world at the Epcot International Food & Wine Festival.

50) Expect long lines for lunch at Be Our Guest Restaurant.

49) Save time by eating at non-traditional meal hours.

48) Decide which quick service restaurants interest you the most before you leave home.

47) If it's your birthday, wear a free birthday button (available at Guest Relations) while you dine.

46) Leave a compliment at Guest Relations if a cast member made your meal even more memorable.

45) If you loved a dish, send your compliments to the chef.

44) On a hot, humid day, find a restaurant that has indoor seating and take a break while you eat.

43) Try something different that you can't get back home.

42) Save a special meal for the end of your trip so that you can leave with a bang.

41) Plan your meal at a Magic Kingdom Resort Area restaurant close to the fireworks and enjoy the show once you're finished.

40) If you drink, try a specialty cocktail that you won't find elsewhere.

39) If you don't drink, there are plenty of non-alcoholic specialty drinks that you might want to try.

38) Make a plan before you leave home, but be willing to stray from it if necessary.

37) Check the restaurant hours to make sure that the place where you want to dine will be open when you're there.

36) If the item that you wanted is no longer on the menu, ask if it's still possible to order it.

35) The Warm Cinnamon Rolls that used to be served at Main Street Bakery are now available at Gaston's Tavern in New Fantasyland.

34) Save time by eating all of your meals on Walt Disney World property.

33) Order Dole Whip at least once while you're at the Magic Kingdom.

32) Ask for a free cup of ice water at any quick service restaurant.

31) Order a cake for a birthday or other special occasion by calling 407-827-2253 at least 48 hours in advance.

30) Learn how the magic is made by booking a reservation for Dining With an Imagineer.

29) Dining should give you a chance to relax for a little while, so don't rush through your meals.

28) If you're not sure what to order, ask your server what his or her favorites are.

27) Don't forget to cancel your reservation if you're not going to use it, or you will be charged.

26) Know what you're going to order before you reach the cashier at a quick service restaurant.

25) Have your payment ready to keep the line moving.

24) Stop by Gardens Kiosk at Disney's Animal Kingdom if you have food allergies.

23) Don't overdo the alcohol.

22) Don't overdo the food, because you don't want to feel bloated.

21) Save money by having two kids split an adult meal instead of ordering two things from the kids' menu.

20) Book the Behind the Seeds Tour at Epcot and see where some of the food comes from.

19) Save some fun-sounding restaurants for your next trip.

18) Don't eat before hitting the thrill rides or the teacups.

17) Look for broiled or grilled dishes instead of eating a lot of fried foods.

16) Substitute apple slices or grapes for the French fries in most combos.

15) Save a little bit of money by asking for the burger or sandwich without the side.

14) Splitting an entree will save money and calories.

13) Sharing a dessert will allow you to splurge, but won't add as many calories as eating the whole thing by yourself.

12) If you forgot to make a reservation, ask the hostess at the check-in desk if anything is available.

11) Make your breakfast reservation before the park opens for a chance to see it without a crowd.

10) Don't skip your morning coffee.

9) Get away from the craziness and leave the Magic Kingdom or Epcot and dine at one of the close-by resort hotels.

8) Download the My Disney Experience App and make last minute reservations while waiting in line.

7) Keep your dining reservations in mind when making your FastPass+ choices.

6) Visit the Earl of Sandwich website to receive a coupon for a free birthday sandwich.

5) Check your email often while on vacation so that you won't miss a dining time by mistake.

4) If you're arriving in Central Florida too late to hit the parks, book a character dinner.

3) Lunch costs less than dinner at some table service restaurants.

2) You can bring snacks into the parks with you.

1) Remember that calories still count while on vacation.

About Rick Killingsworth

Rick visited the Magic Kingdom in 1971 for the first Christmas parade in their history. At nine years old, he was bitten by the Disney Bug. He can still remember the sights, the smells, and the sounds. It truly was magical. It would be twenty years before he could afford to take his young family back to "The World." It was the vacation of a lifetime, and they have been fortunate to go hundreds of times since. His daughters, now grown, still tear up when they see the castle (as does he).

About Paula Brown

Paula is a travel writer who grew up in Western Massachusetts. She is a graduate of New England College in Henniker, New Hampshire. She now lives in Orlando, Florida with her husband and daughter. They can be found at Walt Disney World several times a week. Paula is also a science fiction fan who is obsessed with *Star Wars*. She is the author of *Dream Wanderers*; the second book in the series is due to be released soon.